S0-DXD-679

The Collected Writings of Walt Whitman

WALT WHITMAN

Notebooks and Unpublished Prose Manuscripts

VOLUME V: NOTES

Edited by Edward F. Grier

NEW YORK UNIVERSITY PRESS 1984

Library of Congress Cataloging in Publication Data
Whitman, Walt, 1819–1892.
Notebooks and unpublished prose manuscripts.

(The Collected Writings of Walt Whitman)
Bibliography: p.
Includes index.
1. Whitman, Walt, 1819–1892—Diaries. 2. Poets, American—19th century—Biography. I. Grier, Edward F. II. Title. III. Series: Whitman, Walt, 1819–1892. Works. 1961.
PS3231.A36 1984 818'.303 [B] 83-24415
ISBN 0-8147-2991-6 vol. I.
ISBN 0-8147-2992-4 vol. II.
ISBN 0-8147-2993-2 vol. III
ISBN 0-8147-2994-0 vol. IV
ISBN 0-8147-2995-9 vol. V
ISBN 0-8147-2996-7 vol. VI
ISBN 0-8147-2989-4 (set)

MANUFACTURED IN THE UNITED STATES OF AMERICA

CLOTHBOUND EDITIONS OF NEW YORK UNIVERSITY PRESS BOOKS
ARE SMYTH-SEWN AND PRINTED ON PERMANENT AND DURABLE ACID-FREE PAPER.

The Collected Writings of Walt Whitman

THE PREPARATION OF THIS VOLUME,
AND COSTS ASSOCIATED WITH ITS PUBLICATION,
WERE SUPPORTED THROUGH GRANT NO. RP-*1726–80 FROM THE
Editing and Publication Programs
of the National Endowment for the Humanities,
AN INDEPENDENT FEDERAL AGENCY.

CENTER FOR
SCHOLARLY EDITIONS
AN APPROVED EDITION
MODERN LANGUAGE
ASSOCIATION OF AMERICA

CONTENTS

The Collected Writings of Walt Whitman

V. Study Projects.

A New Way & The True Way.

Manuscript in NYPL (Berg). Inscribed in black ink on verso of blue Williamsburgh tax bill form, 8½" x 4½". Bucke prints it with "The History," although the two are physically separate MS. WW owned and used as a scrapbook pp. 17–40 and 83–86 of Lorenzo D. Johnson's *Memoria Technica* (2d ed., 1847?), now in Duke, a method of learning dates which answers the requirements stated in these two MS. On the wrapper of the second set of pages is a newspaper clipping, endorsed by WW April 21, 1857. Both MS are probably of this year. First printed in *N&F,* 75 (Pt. III, #3; *CW,* IX, 48–49).

A New Way & The True Way of Treating in Books [:][1] History Geography Ethnology Astronomy &c &c &c/

by long lists, of dates, terms,[2] summary paragraphic statements, &c—/
Because all those things to be carried out, and studied in full in any particular department,[3] need to have recourse to so many books,—it is impossible to put them, or think of putting them, in any history—so that brief *Data,* all-comprehensive, and to be pursued as far,[4] and to as full information as any one will, afford the best way of inditing history for the common reader.—

1. Succeeding words in column on a brace.
2. Deleted: "short"
3. Deleted: "require" ; inserted above: "need"
4. Deleted: "into details details"

The History.

Manuscript not found. Text from *N&F,* 76 (Pt. III, #3; *CW,* IX, 49). Bucke prints this as the last part of "A New Way & The True Way," of which it possibly once was part. The date is probably 1857.

The History of the World,—viz.: An immense digested collection of lists of dates, names of representative persons and events, maps and census returns.

Language.

Manuscript in Ohio Wesleyan University Library. Inscribed in black pencil and black ink on inside front cover and inserted printed pages in a scrapbook described as made up of S. G. Goodrich, *Geographical and Historical View of the World* (ca. 1854), and Smith's *Atlas of Modern and Ancient Geography* (1855), interleaved with many sheets of yellow paper like the lining of *LG* (1855) and clippings, newspapers and pamphlets. Bound in half-sheet with homemade ties. I have not examined the scrapbook myself. Most of the entries seem to be marginalia. Manuscripts and clippings which were once probably part of this scrapbook were separated from it by Jacob Schwarz (judging from the bindings in which they are now cased) for his sale of Bucke material in 1936. See clippings in Rutgers and Duke, MS in NYPL (Berg), and *"Mathematics"* and "Ethnology." Bucke prints these in this order after the present MS.

The first part is a sort of index or table of contents with a few memoranda. The second, a printed list, beginning "names of the arts and sciences," is a series of marginal notes to printed terms, here in brackets, which are too closely related to the preceding to be excluded. A proper index, which would necessarily be of considerable length, would shed much light on WW's efforts to educate himself. I am much indebted to Professors R. F. Bauerle and John Reed of Ohio Wesleyan University for their assistance. See Richard F. Bauerle, "Whitman's Index to His Scrapbook: A 'Map' of His 'Language World,'" *WWR,* 26 (December, 1980), 158–162, 165–166. The dates are between 1855 and 1860. First printed in *N&F,* 151–152 (Pt. IV, #1; *CW,* IX, 207–209).

Language look in Census Reports[1]./

Religion Numismatics, (coins and medals) Topography (description of a city, town or place.) Geography Government, (politics, parties) Marriage Physiology Phrenology Literature Education (schools, teachers, leading philosophs)[2] Commerce Manufactures Products, agriculture, mines &c. Rivers, bays, ports, Climate Laws,[3] Jurisprudence; the Medical art. The fine arts pictures, statues labor saving machinery Architecture—both city and country[4] Crime, criminals &c. Prisons Legislation Newspapers Tariffs, Farming Ancestry [:][5]

1. In upper right corner on two lines with straight lines at left and below.
2. Parenthetical statement in black ink.
3. Inserted in left margin.
4. End of scrap 1.
5. Following two questions at right of a brace which includes the preceding five words.

Who are the most eminent men? Also women? Trades, mechanics, &c Servants and Masters Slavery death Cheapness & dearth luxury wages domestic animals artificial drinks Soirees[6] licentiousness Markets: Amusements, (festivals, games, holidays) War Iron Police [:][7] Architecture Fortifications ?Individual freedom Insurance, Condition of women Furniture Manners,[8] Social usages, customs, Diet,[9] Food, (Cooking) Costumes Public meetings [10]Travel, (roads, railroads, ships, steamers, canals) Holidays Post offices, (mail) (expresses)[11] Aqueducts Music, sculpture, painting,[12] fisheries. What heroes?— Most[13]eminent persons? poetry—poets?[14] Erpetology (from Gr.) Of reptiles—by Cuvier into four orders [:], 1st Chelonians tortoises, turtles, &c; 2d Saurians—lizards, crocodiles, &c.; 3d Ophidians—slow-worms, serpents, &c.; 4th Batrachians—frogs, toads, newts &c./[15] Visits (health longevity & Cleanliness Marine, both of peace & war War[16] Philosophy (look at phrenological list) weights and measures Express *Persons*[17] In "History & Geography of the World," introduce every where lists of *persons*—the great *persons* of every age and land[18]

[*1 Acoustics*.] hearing or sound [*2 Aeronautics*.] navigating the air [*5 Algebra*.] computing abstract quantities, by help of signs or symbols [*14 Casuistry*.] affairs of conscience [*16 Chirography*.] hand writing [*19 Dialectics*.]—reasoning (used by Plato for metaphysics [20 Dialling.] from "daeg," an instrument used to show the time of day [*21 Dynamics*.] matter in motion, moving powers [*24 Entomology*.] insects [*25 Ethics*.] right or wrong, Morals [*31 Geoponics*.] agriculture [*35 Horology*.] measuring time [*41 Logic*.] reasoning, connection of ideas

6. End of scrap 2.

7. Following two words in ink at right of a straight line opposite preceding three words.

8. Inserted in left margin.

9. Inserted in left margin.

10. Deleted: "Rail"

11. Word and parentheses in black ink. Deleted: "Name" following "Post offices"

12. Preceding two words in black ink. End of scrap 3.

13. Inserted above "emi" in "eminent"

14. End of scrap 4.

15. Entire entry on "Erpetology" in black ink.

16. Preceding two entries in black ink at right of straight line opposite "Visits . . . Cleanliness."

17. Black ink. First word on scrap 5.

18. The following material is inscribed on a printed list, pasted on what appears to be the table of contents of one of the two geography books. The bracketed numbered entries are inserted from a printed list of "Names of the Arts and Sciences," which, according to a headnote, was intended as a mnemonic device for the student. I have not examined the scrapbook nor in recent years WW's annotated copy of Lorenzo D. Johnson's *Memoria Technica: or The Art of Abbreviating Those Studies Which Give the Greatest Labor to the Memory,* 2d ed. (Boston, 1847) (Duke), but it may be that this list is part of the latter. The numbers are not explained in the list, but may refer to some of the associative keys which are used in *Memoria Technica*. Other material from *Memoria Technica* was used in the scrapbook. WW wrote the definitions (which the student was urged to look up) after the terms or in the margins on arrows. Only those written on a *separate* scrap are indicated in the footnotes.

47 *Meteorology.*] weather air [54 *Orthoepy.*] pronunciation [56 *Osteology.*] science of all that relates to the bones [57 *Pathology.*][19] 57 Pathology the causes, effects differences, &c of diseases [59 *Philology.*][20] 59—Words—Languages—Etymology, grammar, rhetoric poet & criticism—phonology and ideology [64 *Pneumatics.*][21] Weight pressure elastic fluids, especially the atmosphere [66 *Rhetoric.*] elocution Ethnology—the science of the different races of men, and their origins.— ?Sociology[22] Theosophy—divine wisdom and illumination Phonology, sounds, writing where each sound has a specific character. Philanthropy. Ideology, Science of the mind—history, elucidation and illustration of human ideas. Biology, Science of the mystery of life, term introduced by Treviranus of Bremen instead of physiology. Psychology, science of man's spiritual nature or of the soul. Etiology, an account of the causes of anything—particularly diseases.

19. See *n*21.

20. See *n*21.

21. The definition of "Pneumatics" was written at top of a scrap of paper pasted at right, opposite the term in the printed list. It was followed by the definition of "Pathology" as "Pathology—the causes, effects, differences &c of diseases" and of "Philology" as given above.

22. "Ethnology" and "Sociology" are also on the scrap, but not on the printed list. On another printed fragment headed "Numerical Key. Capitals of America and Europe," WW has corrected Kingston, Canada, to Ottawa. Ottawa had been designated capital in 1844. Terms and definitions from "Phonology" through "Etiology" are from *N&F*.

Mathematics.

Manuscript in NYPL (Berg). Inscribed in black ink on blue laid scrap (not a Williamsburgh tax blank), 3¼″ x 5¾″. Paragraph written with hanging indentation, but spaces at ends of lines after "numbered, &c.," "matter," and "bodies" indicate subdivisions of the thought between sentences and the paragraph. First printed as part of "Language," in *N&F,* 152 (Pt. IV, #1; *CW,* IX, 209). The date is probably the late 1850s.

Mathematics—The science that treats of quantity, whatever can be measured, numbered, &c. *Pure* or *Speculative* M. considers quantity abstractly, without relation to matter. *Mixed* M. treats of magnitude, &c. as existing in material bodies Arithmetic, geometry, algebra, trigonometry, &c. are branches of Mathematics.—

Ethnology.

Manuscript in NYPL (Berg). Inscribed sideways on verso of blue Williamsburgh tax form, approx. 4″ x 7½″, in two columns, further divided into subcolumns. Cf. "Language." First printed in *N&F,* 152 (Pt. IV, #1; *CW, IX,* 209). The date is 1857 or later.

Ethnology [*:*] The tracing of the divisions, parentage, and localities of races,—as whence they sprang, and what are their typical marks

Language [*:*]

Politics under this come all of what are called governments, laws, human rights, and the like.—[1]

Religions [*:*]

Literature [*:*] Iliad, Bible, Nibelungen[2] (Books of Egypt, Persia and Assyria are lost.)[3] Nibelungen Shakespeare Ramanaya Dante[4] Emerson[5] Voltaire Rousseau[6]
Histories Novels Essays[7] Newspapers[8]

Zoology [*:*] lists of names of all animals

1. End of first column. Line drawn down the middle of the leaf.
2. "Nibelungen" written above "Bible" , the brace and "Books" . See *"Neibelungen-leid* Song."
3. Preceding eleven words written across right half of leaf.
4. Deleted: [*illeg.*]. Preceding four names or titles in column. See "Spring of '59."
5. See "Emerson Essays—1st series."
6. See "J. J. Rousseau."
7. Preceding six words in column to right of preceding column. Line down leaf at left.
8. To right of "Emerson" in preceding column. Line down leaf at left.

VI. Words.

Truly the Things Commonest.

Manuscript in LC (#63, sheets # 287–288). Inscribed: [*288*] in black ink on white wove scrap, approx. 4⅞″ x 4⅞″. Blue rules recto and verso ⅜″ apart. [*287*] in black ink on white laid paper, approx. 8″ x 5⅛″. Blue rules on verso ½″ apart. For [*287V*] see "1st [:] Democracy." A slightly variant version of [*288*] is in LC (#73, sheet #456, 456A), which is not printed. The echo of "S of M," sec. 14, l. 259, and the high-falutin' Carlyle-ism of the style suggest (one would like to think) an early date. The writing and the use of small scraps support the speculation.

[*288*][1] truly[2] the[3] things commonest & cheapest,[4] nearest to us of[5] all our[6] daily lives,[7] are often the profoundest, the most curious[8] things—have their beginnings the farthest back, & carry the most with them[9] & are worthiest of thought,[10] notice, science. So reader dear[11] if I can catch thy attention, have at thee![12]

?for conclusion. Hast thou never thought (if not true absolutely it is least worth suggesting)[13] how [*illeg.*] there are [*287*] certain[14] studies[15] & researches[16] (not

1. Original opening deleted: "This indeed"
2. Deleted: "think"
3. Deleted: "what is" ; inserted: "things" above "is"
4. Deleted: "nearest a plenteous" ; inserted and deleted: [*illeg.*]. above "[*del.*] nearest a"
5. Inserted above "a" in "all"
6. Inserted and deleted: "whole" "daily" above "our lives" ; inserted: "daily" above "ves" in "lives"
7. Deleted: "—" "is" ; inserted: "are often" above "[*del.*] is" and "the"
8. Deleted: "in date" ; inserted: "things—have their beginnings" above "rious" in "curious" and the deletion and "the"
9. Preceding five words inserted above "farthest back" and the deleted: " & is" ; inserted: "are" above deleted "is"
10. Deleted: "notice" ; inserted and deleted above: "study" ; inserted: "notice" following the deletion and above "sci" in "science"
11. Preceding two words inserted above "if I"
12. Sentence written down the right side of the page, after following deletion. Deleted: "And [*ins.*] then the satisfaction, the fitness, the pleasure, the sanity, the growth [*del.*] and [*illeg. ins.*] mellowing and vigor & expansion of such"
13. Preceding nine words and parentheses inserted above "never thought [*del.*] that" and "now there are" ; deleted: "that" ; inserted above: "how [*illeg.*]"
14. Inserted above deleted "names" ; inserted and deleted: "nutriments" above "of studies" ; not deleted, not printed here: "of"
15. Emended to plural.
16. Emended to plural.

college courses, or technisms)[17] almost[18] as necessary for thee, for thy body & soul,[19] as[20] food, as good air, as human association and friendship? and that this very one of Names (*Language*),[21] is of them?

Then[22] the satisfaction the ease, the pleasure, the sanity, the growth upward, and the mellowing vigor, expansion, (I say the[23] *democracy*) of such study!

Nor to be taken up as an ungracious duty for school hours, or conned by rote from[24] text books, or,[25] reported from the lectures of the professors—[26] not to be got through with in the crude seasons of youth or early manhood or womanhood, & then laid aside. But taken leisurely—no haste—always eligible—fed by all[27] times, all occasions—truly a sane & exhilarating pursuit that can be made active

17. Preceding five words and parenthesis inserted on three lines above "researches" and "[*ins.*] almost" and "as"

18. "almost" inserted above "as"

19. Preceding five words inserted above "for thee as"

20. Deleted: "thy"

21. Preceding three words inserted above "one is of them"

22. First word deleted: "And" ; "then" not capitalized in MS. Inserted and deleted: "too" above wordspace between "then" and "the"

23. Preceding three words and both parentheses inserted above *"demo"* in *"democracy"*

24. Deleted: "boo"

25. Deleted: "learned" ; inserted and deleted: [*illeg.*] above "or" ; inserted: "reported" above "[*del.*] learned"

26. Deleted: "or" ; inserted: "—not to be" above the deletion and "got" . Redundant dash not printed.

27. Deleted: "days" ; inserted above: "times"

Rambles Among Words.

Manuscript not found. Text from William Swinton, *Rambles Among Words,* 2nd ed. (NY, 1864). According to Professor C. Carroll Hollis, "Whitman and William Swinton: A Co-operative Friendship," *AL,* 30, (1959) 438*n,* all American editions of *Rambles* (1859, 1864, 1871) are identical save for "prefatory material, table of contents page, and titles of the different pages."

William Lewis Swinton (1833–1892), journalist and textbook writer, and his brother John (1829–1901), journalist and reformer, emigrated with their parents from Scotland to Canada in 1843 and thence to the US. John, a printer, was in Kansas in 1856 and 1857, whereas William remained in the East, where he became professor of languages at Mount Washington Collegiate Institution in NYC. According to the record in WW's notebooks he met both brothers in 1856. See "[*illeg.*] Dick Hunt" and "George Walker". Hollis, however, on good grounds suggests (428*n*) that he met William in 1855 in connection with the performances of the great French tragedienne, Rachel. William introduced WW to Rousseau's *Confessions* and the *Social Contract* and evidently encouraged his interest in philology, Swinton became a daring and indiscreet war correspondent for the NY *Times* and after the war moved to California where he became professor of English in the new University at Berkeley from 1869 to 1874. He resigned this position and became a successful writer of schoolbooks.

When and how WW became interested in words is not clear, but his interest appears in his earliest notes. Regardless of any probable influence of Swinton, the notes in this volume and in *DN,* III for the posthumously edited *An American Primer* indicate that it was vigorous. The details of his collaboration with Swinton on *Rambles Among Words* are even more obscure, for neither man ever mentioned it. Swinton had published two "Rambles" in *Putnam's Magazine* in November and December, 1854, and Hollis suggests that the collaboration on *Rambles Among Words* occurred because

> Swinton had made arrangements to have an enlargement of his original articles printed as a book. Faced with dead-line pressure, he appealed to Whitman for help and got it via the notes made in the *Primer* and *Words* enterprises. Whether in deference to Whitman or because there was no time to do otherwise, he used these notes pretty much as he got them for introductory and concluding sections to the assorted lists of etymologies. It may have been that Whitman himself saw to the printing, for the use of "Programme" instead of "Table Contents" and of "Premonitory" instead of "Introduction" are certainly Whitman's (446).

To explain why WW's name does not appear in the book, Hollis suggests that his notoriety might have scandalized Charles Scribner, the publisher, or that its use would have endangered Swinton's position with the *Times* or with his school, or that WW refused out of gratitude for the "valuable education, guidance, and encouragement he had received from

Swinton," or that he felt that his name on a popular work of learning would damage his image as one of the roughs. Any or all of these factors may have operated, but one can hardly imagine that WW remained silent from diffidence, for he was concurrently planning a book on words and, as his notes show, was ready to lecture on any subject in heaven and on earth.

Although Hollis does not offer evidence to support his identification of WW's contributions, he cites the concurrence of Charles E. Feinberg, Harry Warfel and Gay Wilson Allen in his selection (44on). Stovall, however, has expressed considerable doubt as to WW's part (*Foreground,* 213). He finds words in the text of *Rambles* not listed in Eby's *Concordance,* thus apparently not in WW's active vocabulary. He also points out that although Swinton implied that the whole book was written in about 1854, apparently only two chapters were actually published then.

A more scientific approach to the problem appears in Lynne Stokes, "Some Statistical Techniques for Disputed Authorship," Institute of Statistics Mimeo Series, No. 932 (Chapel Hill: Department of Statistics, University of North Carolina, 1974), which was called to my attention by Professor Hollis. Stokes's analysis is too technical for this layman to follow, but I will attempt a brief description of her technique and findings. Her control texts for analysis were Swinton's two 1854 "Rambles" and an essay on novels, also from *Putnam*'s in 1854. For WW she chose Traubel's edition of *An American Primer* (Boston, 1904). Her first test was the Yule sentence-length test. The second was devised to quantify the appearance of Swinton's characteristic use of "long, complex sentences which are often begun with a connecting word or phrase" (14). The third test was designed to quantify "Whitman's unusual tendency to use many nouns, often strung together in series" (14). The fourth test was designed to compare quantitatively Whitman's smooth simple style with Swinton's complex style, i.e. the latter's "heavy use of parenthetical expressions and phrases" (15). It is best to present Stokes's findings in her own words.

> The results seem to contradict Hollis' supposition that the *Rambles* passages were lifted, with no changes, from Whitman's notes. The passages are too different from "An American Primer" in certain characteristics, as indicated by tests 2 and 4, to simply be two parts of a whole piece. The differences which showed up between *Rambles* and the Swinton essays on tests 2 and 4 should be more expected since they weren't claimed to be part of the same article. [She appears to me to overstate Hollis' claim.]
>
> However, the results of tests 1 and 3 do support the theory that there is a similarity in style between *Rambles* and Whitman's writing. This support is strengthened by the observation that the characteristics appear to be consistent within one writer's style, as indicated by the tests of "Novels" against the other Swinton *Putnam* articles.
>
> So the similarities of *Rambles* to Whitman appear to be more than coincidental, yet the two are not identical. There are several possible explanations. One is that Swinton used Whitman's notes heavily, but rewrote certain parts of them, producing a blend of their two styles. Another explanation is that Hollis' list of Whitman passages in *Rambles Among Words,* which was used for the *Rambles* sample, includes some mistakes, producing results falling halfway between the styles of the two men on some statistical tests.
>
> A statistical procedure cannot, of course, produce an unquestionable answer to a problem such as this one. Since results of the four tests in this case are not unani-

mously supportive of one or the other side, the interpretation is even more difficult and subject to individual judgement. However, the statistical procedures used do provide useful evidence, which considerably assists our assessment of the situation (23–24).

Unfortunately this analysis sheds relatively little light on individual passages, but I think it supports the general theory that the book is in some degree a collaboration. One can indeed feel the presence of WW very strongly in Rambles 11 and 12: "The Growth of Words" and "The Philosophy of Language." As Hollis points out, the list of French contributions to English in Ramble 11 is very like that in WW's "America's Mightiest Inheritance," *Life Illustrated* (April 12, 1856), 440–441. (There is, of course, the distinct possibility that WW got the list from Swinton in the first place.) The ideas and diction are characteristic. It would seem, however, that however eagerly WW collected bits of linguistic history and scattered etymologies, he was, as Hollis puts it, "an eager freshman sitting in on a graduate language seminar" (438). Although he had ideas about the origins and what the book calls the "philosophy of language," I think it would have been beyond him to marshal the evidence as the body of the book does. On the other hand, one can have ideas and intuitions, especially if one is a poet, considerably beyond those of the eager freshman.

It is the meaning of language to WW rather than his knowledge of philology which is important. Although he was unaware of language study beyond lexicography and etymology, language study for him was part of science and the modern. Philology was, indeed, one of the great 19th Century sciences. The lexicographer is, to WW, one of the lawgivers of poets. Beyond this, as a poet, he would have agreed with Emerson that words are signs of natural facts and that natural facts are signs of spiritual facts. For him the poet was indeed the namer. The creation of a new poetry demanded a new language.

The chapter headings in the following selections are not to be attributed to WW. They are included only to locate the passages in relation to the argument of the book. Running heads are not included.

[7] RAMBLE FIRST. PREMONITORY.

* * *

[8] The copiousness of meaning which Words enwrap is indeed more than all that was said or thought. Children of the mind, they reflect the manifold richness of man's faculties and affections. In language is incarnated man's unconscious passionate creative energy. There is an endless, indefinable, tantalizing charm in Words. They bring the eternal provocations of personality. They come back to us with that alienated majesty which a great writer ascribes to our own thoughts. They are the sanctuary of the intuitions. They paint humanity, its thoughts, longings, aspirations, struggles, failures—paint them on a canvas or breath, in the colors of life.

[9] To the illustration of the opulences of Words I design these pages: with Runic spells to evoke the pagan wanderers from their homes in the visionary eld—to read some of the strange lessons they teach, to catch of the wit and the wisdom, the puns and the poetries, the philosophies, the fancies and the follies that lurk in

and flash out from them, and to seize, flaming down, as it were, from the "firmament of bards and sages," some of the deep analogies, the spiritual significance, the poetic beauty and the rich humor that sport and dwell in even our common, every-day words and phrases.

* * *

[10] Medals of the mind we may call words. And as the medals of creation from the Geologic world reveal the workings of creative energy and the successive developments of the divine idea, so Words present a humanitary Geology where histories, philosophies and ethics lie embodied and embalmed. But this is a spiritual Geology, its strata built up of the rich deposits of mind. With passionate fervor man pours himself on nature. An irrepressible longing to express his secret sense of his unity with nature possesses him: and from the consciousness, all plastic and aglow, rush Words, infinitely free, rich and varied, laden with pathos and power, with passion, poetry, humor, thought.

Of course Language is a living Original. It is not made but grows. The growth of language repeats the growth of the plant. At first it is only root: next it puts forth a stem, then leaves, and finally blossoms. "One must not," writes William Von Humboldt, "consider a language as a product dead and formed but once: it is an animate being and ever creative. Human thought elaborates itself with the progress of intelligence; and of this thought language is a manifestation. An idiom cannot therefore remain stationary: it walks, it develops, it grows up, it fortifies itself, it becomes old and it reaches decrepitude."[1]

[11] Language must move with the movements of mind, as the ocean obeys siderial influences. A petrified and mechanical national mind will certainly appear in a petrified and mechanical language. But the provisions are perfect. The renovation of language is provided for, as the renovation of the races is provided for, by a subtle chemistry. The sublime democracy of speech! When a tongue has become dead and effete, the mind walks out of it. With an advance in the national mind—with the influx of a nobler spirit, comes a renovation of its language: by a passionate propulsive movement it ejects its old dead speech, and rises to larger and freer expression. Like the waters in spring, the rising spirit sweeps away the frozen surface of an effete society, literature, language and thought.

The great tidal movements in a nation's life are repeated in great tidal movements in its language. With new creations, thoughts and hopes emerge new demands on the horizon of its speech. The English language shows in its growth crises that mark real upsurgings from the spontaneous depths of human nature. In Chaucer is embalmed that rich primitive sensuous perception of English life, when the language became so opulent in expressions of sensible objects and simple feelings. The flood-tide in the national mind that came with the Sixteenth Century finds expression [12] in the Elizabethan literature, especially in Shakespeare in whom English reached its truly modern mould. And the vast billowy tendencies of modern life, too—the new political, social, scientific births—are making new

1. Wilhelm von Humboldt (1767–1835), polymath.

demands on the English idiom. It is for America especially to evoke new realizations from the English speech. Always waiting in a language are untold possibilities. On the lips of the people, in the free rich unconscious utterance of the popular heart are the grand eternal leadings and suggestions.

Of all the heritages which America receives the English language is beyond all comparison the mightiest. Language of the grand stocks, language of reception, of hospitality, it is above all fitted to be the speech for America. There is nothing fortuitous in language. It is for reasons the English idiom is here. In the English, more than all others, was concentrated the spirit of the modern, breaking up the old crystalline classic mould. It is for America grandly to use this grand inheritance. No language has, no language ever had, such immense assimilation as the English. Freely it absorbs whatever is of use to it, absorbs and assimilates it to its own fluid and flexible substance. This rich copious hospitable flow is to be encouraged.

In the growth of Words all the activities of the [13] mind conspire. Language is the mirror of the living inward consciousness. Language is concrete metaphysics. What rays does it let in on the mind's subtle workings! There is more of what there is of essential in metaphysics—more of the structural action of the human mind, in Words, than in the concerted introspection of all the psychologists. "In language," observes Frederick Schlegel[2] in a profoundly suggestive passage, "all the principal powers have a nearly equal part and share. The grammatical structure is furnished by the reason. From the fancy, on the other hand, is derived whatever is figurative; and how far does not this reach, extending into the primary and natural signification of words, which often no longer exists, or at least is rarely traceable? And so also that deep spiritual significance, that characteristic meaning, which in the original stem-syllable and radical words of some rich old language, invariably is regarded as a beauty, must be ascribed to the understanding, which so profoundly seizes and precisely designates whatever is peculiar, unless perhaps it is preferred to assign it to an immediate feeling which wonderfully harmonizes with or responds to it."

* * *

[14] A law that runs through the warp and woof of language is the familiar principle of a translation of sensible perceptions into the realm of ideas, into metaphysics and morals.

[20] RAMBLE SECOND.
THE WORK OF THE SENSES.

* * *

[21] All words are primarily sympathetic. Words are born of a passionate yearning. And it is through [22] the Senses that the mind goes out to nature: these the filaments and outreachings—these the subtle threads that link phenomena and the mind. I find an impressive testimony to this primary law of language

2. Frederich Schlegel (1772–1829), poet, critic, scholar.

in the word 'THOUGHT.' Evidently enough it is an abstraction from the verb to think (Saxon, thencan, past part. thoht), which Horne Tooke[3] deduces from *thing*—I am *thing*-ed, Me thinketh, that is Me *thingeth*—precisely analogous to the Latin 'REOR' from *res*—derivations that may intimate the extent to which *things* color *thoughts*.

* * *

[29] Sight is the most spiritual of the senses. Through Sight the structure of the world is revealed. Through it the perception of identity, growths, processes, vistas. Hence the breadth of the significance of this sense in [30] in the nomenclature of Science. If sight carries with it the architecture of the world, Sound brings the universal solvent which whirls matter back to the primal æther. In melody Nature whispers to man the secret confessions of her plan. Oken[4] asserts that melody is the voice of the universe whereby it proclaims its scheme or its innermost essence. They at least know this who have felt the mystical o'ermastering of Music. Music is the passionate yearning after more primeval natures.

The contributions of the Senses to Words are by no means exhausted. But the principle does not lead far. It is when the creative Reason, the idealizing Imagination begin their work, loading words with new burdens of meaning, that the master-workings of the mind in speech appear. And for a theory of speech somewhat progressive is required.

[31] RAMBLE THIRD. THE IDEALISM OF WORDS.

* * *

[32] This idealism of language rests on no whim, but is a primary and necessary fact. Up from the core of nature comes this wondrous symbolism. Words are emblematic because things are emblematic. And as Nature stands the splendid fable of spirit, so the informing Imagination converts the language of outward phenomena into types of the mind. There is no term applied to a metaphysical or moral fact but which, when opened up, is found to be the translation of some fact in nature. 'FERVOR' simply means heat; 'TRACTABLE,' that may be drawn along; 'ABUNDANCE' images an overflowing cup and 'TRANSGRESSION' is the crossing of the line that divides right [33] from wrong. In like manner, when we speak of one's taking 'UMBRAGE' we simply idealize a *shadow,* umbra—the dark *shade* that passes over one's mind. 'SUPERCILIOUS' is a picturesque translation of the act of raising the eyebrows or *supercilium*—the natural expression of hauteur. And a 'SCRUPLE' (of conscience) is a vivid rendering of the *scrupulus* or little bits of gravel that used to get into the very open shoes of the Romans, and produce trouble and hesitancy.

This allegory runs through the warp and woof of language. It is a primary act of the word-forming faculties, which take up a natural symbol and enshrine

3. "Diversions of Purley, p. 608 [Author]." Horne Tooke (1736–1812), radical and philologist. *Diversions* published 1786, 1798.

4. Lorenz Oken (1779–1851), naturalist, "nature philosopher."

for ever within it a thought. Let us trace some of the workings of this wondrous law.

* * *

[37] The law on which this idealism of Words rests has its roots deep in man's mental structure. For as material forms are the revelation of spiritual natures, so the vivid imagination is constantly bringing provocations to ampler translations of our everyday perceptions and experiences. From insight from a large perception of Analogy, from a longing and passionate heart comes the power of thus translating the presentings of nature into the expressive symbols of moral and metaphysical existences. To a sincere and tender nature words lend themselves plastic and willing to the formative laws of tte word-forming faculties. Illustrations of the working of these laws run through our and every language. When we speak of a 'cordial' man or manner, is it not plain that we are simply ascribing to the man or manner the quality of being *hearty* (cor, cordis, the *heart*)? 'EGREGIOUS' too is lifted out of its special, definite meaning of the animal chosen—e grege—*out of the flock,* and idealized in a vigorous image to represent any property so remarkable as to remove it from the ordinary rule and mark it as unique and unapproachable. The Latin term *prævaricator,* which originally implied a straddler with distorted legs has given us our verb to 'PREVARICATE,' which we readily perceive has been abstracted to imply a mental or moral *shuffling*. In like manner when Prince Hal addresses Falstaff in the words "how now my sweet creature of *bombast,"* he is using the noun 'BOMBAST' in its literal sense of soft padding used to swell garments: this primary acceptation, however, the word has now entirely lost, and we have transferred it to idealize a swelling, inflated style of talking, fustian—vox et preterea nihil. I see I have used the word 'FUSTIAN' in illustration of 'bombast': it is curious that this term has undergone precisely the same curious metamorphosis.

[38] These changes in the meaning of Words—this ebb and flow of significance—is constantly going on in a live language: and it is no extravagance to say that the moral and mental vitality of a people may be gauged in the quantity and quality of these transformations. For over these transformations the genius of the nation unconsciously presides, and the issues of Words represent issues in the national life and thought. This metaphor and metamorphosis of [39] Words is exceedingly curious. There is probably nothing in which psychologic laws and the organic workings of the human mind more vividly and vitally reveal themselves than here. For though, to the superficial eye, seemingly lawless and capricious, Words yet bristle with rational thought, while even the most startling metaphor and the wildest poetic image has a law and logic of its own.

* * *

[54] How sublime is the allusion in 'NATURE' (*natus, natura,* to be born), *the being born,* or indeed the reference in Latin is to the future, as though it would indicate that she is no dead mass, but a living and ever-evolving Whole. And indeed she is our mother, too—nourishing us tenderly on her breast, shedding

around us her balmy, balsamic influences, and gently at last rocking us to sleep with sphere-music and old eternal melodies. Shelley, her loveliest and lornest child, shall sing her pæan.

"Mother of this unfathomable world!
Favour my solemn song, for I have loved
Thee ever, and thee only; I have watched
Thy shadow, and the darkness of thy steps,
And my heart ever gazes on the depth
Of thy deep mysteries. I have made my bed
In charnels and on coffins, where black death
Keeps record of the trophies won from thee,
[55] Hoping to still these obstinate questionings
Of thee and thine, by forcing some lone ghost,
Thy messenger, to render up the tale
Of what we are. In lone and silent hours,
When night makes a weird sound of its own stillness,
Like an inspired and desperate alchymist
Staking his very life on some dark hope,
Have I mixed awful talk and asking looks
With my most innocent love, until strange tears,
Uniting with those breathless kisses, made
Such magic as compels the charmed night
To render up thy charge: and though ne'er yet
Thou hast unveiled thy inmost sanctuary;
Enough from incommunicable dream,
And twilight phantasms, and deep noon-day thought,
Has shone within me, that serenely now
And moveless, as a long-forgotten lyre
Suspended in the solitary dome
Of some mysterious and deserted fane
I wait thy breath, Great Parent, that my strain
May modulate with murmurs of the air,
And motions of the forests and the sea,
And voice of living beings, and woven hymns
Of night and day, and the deep heart of man!"

ALASTOR.[5]

[56] RAMBLE FOURTH.
FOSSIL POETRIES.

* * *

[56] ALL words are, more or less, poetry. For word-making is an organic creation of the mind and runs parallel with the processes of nature and is the

5. Shelley, ll. 18–49.

crown and consummation of the world. The Hindus, in their free and fluent mythology, conceived the second act of Brahma to have been the Naming: and it is reported of Pythagoras that he thought that of all wise men he was not only the most rational but also the most ancient who gave the names to things. The poet is by divine right the proper Namer. Through sym[57]pathy with the grand substantial Words of the world he imports into human speech the utterance of orphic Nature. Material forms—ocean, air, soil, fire, stars, life, growths—these are sublime primeval Words. These the Expressive passion dissolves into plastic symbols. And the poet gives voice to mankind.

* * *

[72] Thus profound are the suggestions of Words. And [73] even those we toss about with the most plethoric profusion and the most sacrilegious indifference are often found, when we catch the play of allusion, to be the most marvelous speaking pictures. For coming as they do from the informing mind, even the most startling metaphor and the wildest poetic image has a law and logic of its own. The Imagination bodies forth the forms of things, visionary, swift, shadowy; but the living Word—the strain or the statue or the picture, seizes the fleeting idols, and lo! they stand perennial and imperishable. Thence the Kinship of the Arts. The Arts are one in that all are outlets to the Spiritual. Beneath their finite guises gleam down glimpses of the Infinite that brightens over and embellishes all. High, clear and far up sounds their silvery voice, awaking in the vasty deeps of consciousness thrilling trembling echoes, faint and far away, of the old eternal melodies and making even

> "Our noisy years seem moments in the being
> Of the Eternal Silence!"

[74] RAMBLE FIFTH.
FOSSIL HISTORY.

* * *

[74] What vast historical results have come from the modern studies on Language! Comparative Philology studying languages as living organisms—subject to organic laws of growth and decay—has shown that we possess in speech a grand recorded History of Humanity, where in colossal outlines man, his affiliations, migrations, workings, growths, are drawn. [75] Primordial creation and manifestation of the human mind, the development of language runs parallel with the development of humanity. Language is a perfect Geology, with its strata, formations and developments, and these infinitely more intelligible than those of nature, because intellectual, and—in the sublime thought of Bunsen[6]—carrying within themselves their order of succession in their own law of development. And what a divining-rod has language proved in the hands of the mighty modern masters!

6. Christian Charles Josias Bunsen (1791–1860). WW read his *Egypt's Place in Universal History* (London, 1848).

This is the true Rosetta-stone with which a Champollion[7] and a Niebuhr[8] and a Rawlinson[9] have been able to set the antique nations on their feet and restore the lost threads of the genealogy of mankind. There is something sublime, and which opens up new spaces in man, in that constructive Criticism by which from slight linguistic fragments the great Niebuhr was enabled to restore the life and history of the ancient populations of Italy. And equally significant other great circles of induction. By Philologic Science the European nations have all been tracked back to Oriental fountains of wisdom and thought; Egypt has flashed up from the deeps of fifty centuries with her antique and august civilization, and now from the deciphering of the cuneiform inscriptions of West Asia are emerging those old Assyrian and Babylonian [76] worlds, venerable with years, coevals of primeval man.

But with these colossal results of Comparative Philology it is not our present purpose to deal. What I would show is that in Words themselves we have pregnant histories embalmed—that in these medals of the mind we have the record of "ancient and modern intellectual dynasties," of vast moral and social revolutions, of the unfolding spirit of man. Words are the amber that enwraps and retains these marvelous stories, the wit and the wisdom, the fancies, the follies and the failings of humanity incarnated for ever.

* * *

[103] This, indeed, is one of the most important functions of words: that they report and describe themselves, and in their simple composition, ofttimes tell us more than do the Encyclopædias. Words thus become a complete *catalogue raisonnée* of all thoughts and things; and while they are crystalized poetries and philosophies, they are at the same time important scientific organs and instruments.

* * *

[106] The historical significance of Words springs from the fact of their being born of spontaneity. Words thus formed unwittingly, and on which the national mind, making and moulding, has wrought, must be the very expression of the national life. They are the sanctuary of the intuitions. Here we should find a people daguerreotyped in the very lineaments of life.[10] Nay even our common, every-day words and phrases will many a time furnish keen hints of ethnic peculiarities. Thus what is 'on the *carpet*' (*sur le tapis*) to the Frenchman, for the Englishman gets 'on the *anvil;*' nor are the 'ESPRIT' and 'CAUSERIES' of the one any more characteristic than the 'SPLEEN' and 'HUMOR' of the other; and yet the Englishman possesses a 'HOME,' while the Frenchman has only a 'CHEZ NOUS' (*at our*

7. Jean François Champollion (1790–1832), Egyptologist. WW quotes Champollion's deathbed witticism in "A Backward Glance," *Prose 92,* II, 712–713.

8. Barthold Georg Niebuhr (1776–1831), historian, *Römische Geschichte* (1812), etc.

9. Sir Henry Creswicke Rawlinson (1810–1893), orientalist. Read by WW.

10. "Il est certain que la langue d'un peuple contient, s'il m'est permis de m'exprimer de la sorte, les véritables dimensions de son esprit. Il est la mesure de l'étendue de sa logique et de ses connaissances.—*M. le President de Brosses. Traité de la Formation Méchanique de Langues, etc.* Tome I. 74 [Author's quotation]."

place). And so the Parisian's *joli* (*pretty*), to the Cockney—who is apt to cluster most of his ideas of a '*pretty* fellow' around mirth and enjoyment—becomes [107] quite 'JOLLY.' And this disposition leaks out through his very amusements, so that even with his 'cards' in his hand, he will brawl and babble of 'clubs' and 'spades' (*pique et trêfle*). There is said to be no equivalent for the Italian 'CONCETTI;' while nothing could prove more mournfully the degeneracy of that once heroic people than the fact that a villain or an assassin is to them a 'BRAVO' (a *brave* man).

* * *

[109] RAMBLE SIXTH.
WORDS OF ABUSE

Falstaff. Away, you starveling, you elf-skin, you dried neat's tongue, you stock-fish,—O for breath to utter what is like thee!—you tailor's yard, you bow-case, you vile standing tuck:

Prince Henry. Well, breathe awhile, and then to it again; and when thou hast tired thyself in base comparisons, hear me speak but this.

First Part of Henry IV. ii. 4.

YOU remember that the disclosure which Prince Hal makes of the merry prank played on "lean Jack" and his companions effectually closed the crater of that volcano which could vomit forth naught save wit and braggardism: otherwise we might have had a perfect exhaustion of Billingsgate from that "trunk of humors, that bolting-hutch of beastliness, that swoln parcel of dropsies, that huge bombard of sack, that stuffed cloak bag of guts, that roasted Manning-tree ox with the pudding in his belly, that reve[110]rend vice, that grey iniquity, that father ruffian, that vanity in years!"

As it is, however, we will find no lack of material wherewith to supply the hiatus. For here, at least, language is full to overflowing. It is a current which frets and foams—rushing on dashing and impetuous; which o'erleaps the barriers of custom and convention, and sweeps into its resistless torrent history and metaphor and allusion and truth and falsehood and poetry and passion and prejudice and fact and fable.

Rousseau conceived language to be the natural product of the Passions. And really the thought receives no small degree of warranty when one marks the prodigious word-fecundity of Love and Hatred—how they have ransacked heaven and earth for symbols, exhausting nature and piling hyperbole on hyperbole. Take away from any speech what these have done for it, and how small a remnant will be left! As the skeleton forms the frame-work on which the splendid drapery of the human form is placed, so the most highly elaborated speech has its roots in homely and hearty idioms and instincts—elemental utterances of human nature.

Among the most instructive of this class of words are the terms which the speech-forming faculties have loaded with burdens of abuse. A representative, that [111] has grown familiar to us all, of this widespread family of words is the genus

Billingsgate. Billingsgate pushes to enormous proportions a principle that is vital in speech. Billingsgate is the burlesque of word-building.

The metaphysics of the Abusive is exceedingly curious. The very anatomy of Passion is here exposed. Here, too, we may study elemental human nature—may read the primary thinkings and feelings of men in their first rude efforts towards expression. There are Words that remind me of the monster organisms of a primitive Geologic world. And there are workings of elemental fires visible in Language, as volcanic rocks come mounting and molten through the rib-walls of the planet.

What a subtle Analogist is Passion! It harries Nature for emblems and reads the types of humanity in bestial structures and instincts. Of the workings of this law in Words we have already met with traces. We have seen how that 'rascal' bears the primary meaning of a *mean worthless deer*—how 'fanatic' implies a *temple-devotee,* and how 'clown' has its genesis in a tiller of the ground.

And more of these Abusive symbols.

In merrie England when the sovereign made his 'progresses' throughout the kingdom, the train of [112] courtiers, nobles, etc., was generally followed by the attendants, and the rear brought up by the lowest class of menials—by the scullery-servants, the turnspits, the coal-carriers and others of that ilk—rather a *black* guard, we should say: and, in fact, they were jocularly designated by this very term—an appellation which, in the shape of our 'BLACKGUARD' remains even to the present day; though why those poor devils came to be the exclusive representatives of scurrility and meanness, it might be difficult to determine—unless, indeed, as we may well suppose, they were by no means ignorant, and as little sparing in their employment, of those peculiar elegancies of diction which are playfully ascribed to that classic region where they sell the best fish and speak the best English. Burton, by the way, speaking of the various ranks and gradations of devils, alludes to this "guard:"

> "Though some of them are inferior to those of their own ranke, as the *Blacke* guard in a prince's court."
>
> *Anatomy of Melancholy,* p. 42.

From 'blackguard' we ascend to the formuling of a principle which we find exercising quite an important influence over the Abusive Element in speech, namely, that particular trades or professions or ranks [113] in life which involve something effeminate, or mean or opprobrious—or which are supposed to do so—are taken as the types of these qualities. Thus what vile sarcasm on tailors which wickedly declares them to be but a vulgar fraction of a man is of quite dateless antiquity, while *shoemakers* are proverbially 'SNOBS.' However, we find some compensation and consolation in the fact that on this subject, too, the standards of judgment vary. In France, for instance, they do not typify this class by a shoemaker, but by a *grocer*—an 'épicier' being the very beau ideal of twopenny flash and beggarly magnificence. Another word that will conveniently come under this same category is 'FLUNKEY'—a term which, in these latter days of *flunkey-ism,* has become significant of so much, but which primarily imports merely a livery servant, a sense in which the Scotch still use it.

Of similar significance is the word 'KNAVE'—a term which has sadly lost caste—sinking down from an innocent *boy* or *youth* (as the German for boy is still *knabe*) to the very depth of rascality. The intermediate step, however, throws a ray of light on the terminus at which the word arrives. For this middle meaning is that of a *servant*—often enough, we know, apt to be *knavish*.[11] The course it has taken is, there-[114] fore, this: Primary meaning, a *youth;* secondary, a *servant;* tertiary, a *'knave.'* I shall simply exemplify under its secondary signification. Thus in the Duke of Lauderdale's (apocryphal?) translation of the Bible, the reading for, "Paul, a servant of Jesus Christ" is said to have been, "Paul, a *Knave* of Jesus Christ." And in the following quaintly-curious passage from Chaucer, we have the most unequivocal proof of this employment:

"Ne tak no wif, quod he, for husbandrie,
As for to spare in houshold they dispence:
A *trwe servant* doth more diligence
Thy good to keep, than doth thin owen wif,
For she wol claimen half part al hire lif.
And if that thou be sicke, so God me save,
Thy veray frendes or a *trwe knave*
Wol kepe thee bet than she that waiteth ay
After thy good, and hath don many a day."

The Merchantes Tale.

Deep, too, are the traces in Words of the working of the spirit of caste. 'VULGAR' properly implies what has relation to the *vulgus* or common people, as 'VULGATE' means the translation of the Scriptures made for this same *vulgus*. And it is an interesting conformation of this thwarting of meaning that 'LEWD' which carries with it the meaning of vile, [115] profligate, is also from a Saxon root signifying the common people—the *lay* people. So, 'MEAN' has an analogous origin with the *many*—Saxon *mœneg;* and 'CHURL' is just the Saxon for a man, a fellow—*ceorl:*[12] a sense which the Scotch *carle* still retains as 'cantie carle,' that is, a *merry fellow*. Again, 'BOOR' is Dutch for *farmer;* 'RUSTIC' is having relation to the *country;* 'PAGAN' is primarily a dweller in a *paganus* or hamlet; 'SAVAGE,' or *salvage* as the truer orthography would write it (Spanish *salvage,* Italian *selvaggio*), is a dweller in the *woods* (*sylva*) a *backwoodsman:* and 'VILLAIN' is primitively the serf or peasant (*villanus*) attached to the *villa* or farm. Nor does it originally bear with it any opprobrious meaning. Thus, in Chaucer:

11. "'Valet' and 'varlet' were, it is surmised, originally one word [Author]."
12. "Whence Carl, Carolus, Charles, etc. [Author]."

"But firste I praie you of your curtesie
That ye ne asette it not my *vilanie,*
Though that I plainly speke in this matere,
To tellen you hir wordes and hir chere
Ne though I speek hir wordes proprely."

Prologue to the Canterbury Tales.

'VAGABOND,' too, is well worth exploring, being, etymologically, merely one who is given to *wandering* [116] *about*—vagabundus—or, as we also say, 'vagrant'[13]—and primarily carries nothing opprobrious with it. The Prince Gonzaga di Castiglione, at least, intended to employ it in an altogether complimentary manner when, being at table with Dr. Johnson and a host of learned pundits, he called out to Johson: "At your good health *Mr. Vagabond!*" imagining *that* to be assuredly an appropriate epithet for the author of the *Rambler!* It is curious, and not uninstructive to note in connection with this, how the *staidness* of our ancestors has stamped respectability on every thing that is *settled;* while it has cast a slight on every thing that approaches to *roving.* Thus Swift uses 'stroller' as precisely synonymous with 'vagabond;' while one given to roving is proverbially a 'ne'er-do-weel' (a *never-do-well*) as the Scotch say. Furthermore, a 'CORSAIR' (French, *corsaire;* Italian, *corsare;* Spanish, *corsario*—all from Latin curro—*cursus,* to run), is just [117] one who, with his vessel *runs over,* or scours the sea. 'WANTON,' too, is said to be merely one who is given to *wandering;* and there is a derivation of 'WRETCH'—in Saxon *wroecca*—which would make it out to be simply one who is *wrecked*—who is driven about and who has no certain dwelling-place!

Let me take an additional instance illustrative of this class of abusive words. It shall be 'IDIOT'—a word that has undergone some strange vicissitudes and forcibly illustrates how in Words secondary strata of signification frequently overlap the primary. The original meaning of *idiotes* is a *private person,* in contradistinction to one engaged in public affairs. Its secondary signification was one *who had no professional knowledge of any subject whatever:* and Plato makes such a collocation as this, ποιητὴς ἢ ἰδιώτης—a poet or an . . . *idiot,* by which term we are to understand a *prose-writer.* Its tertiary signification, and springing naturally out of its secondary, was that of an *ignorant, ill-informed man.*

Thus far and no farther, in Greek; thus far and no farther, in Latin. But *it never meant an 'idiot:'* that stretch of application was reserved for our modern imaginations. For even as late as the days of Wickliff, I find it employed in its legitimate signification. Thus: [118]

13. "Both of these words spring from one root—vagor, to *rove,* to ramble; vagabond being a corruption of *vagabundus;* and 'VAGRANT' a corruption, through the French, of the present participle. The story that these words and their analogues enwrap is curious enough. The very fact of being a wanderer would seem to presuppose some sinister design; and express provision is made, at least in all *civilized* countries, for the punishment of this very class. In England, for instance, the ancient punishment was, I believe, boring the ear, whipping, etc. [Author]."

"For if thou blessist in spyrit, who filleth the place of an *idyot* [qui supplet locum *idiotae*] how schal he seie amen on thi blessyng?"

I. Cor. chap. 14.

Here 'idiot' is, we know, rendered, by subsequent translations, 'he that occupieth the room of the unlearned.'

The reason of this unwarranted application of 'idiot' might be difficult to determine, unless it be that he who has not been able to get beyond the condition of a private person (ἰδιώτης) and attain to some office or honor, presents thereby prima facie evidence of not having the wit to do so and is, therefore, to be regarded as witless and imbecile!

But the Abusive faculty, not content with ransacking human nature for appellations black and bitter, is fain to go and beg or borrow from the lower animals epithets fitted to its ends. "Divers words expressive of contempt beeing," as an old English Archaeologist has it, "properly the names of some vile things, and in contempt and disgrace, full often, *and with great breach of charitie,* injuriously applyed unto men and women." It is no respecter either of persons or things. Willing or unwilling, it presses universal nature into its service.

[119] 'CRONE' (whence our 'crony'), for instance, is said to be properly the appellation for a *toothless old ewe,* and then applied, in passion and sarcasm, to an old woman—an old 'hag,' which, by the way, meant primarily an enchantress or fury. 'SHREW,' also, is asserted by Lye to have been taken from the *schreawa,* or *shrew-mouse*—a little creature whose spitefulness was proverbial and whose bite and venom are even said to have been fatal.[14] The variations in the [120] orthography of 'VIXEN' will lead us, by the nearest road, up to its source: the steps are as follows: Vixen, fixen or fixin, *fox*-en = *she-fox:* from which point of view our readers will readily perceive its peculiar applicability. And one can imagine some old hag, white and foaming with rage, endeavoring to conjure up something overwhelming wherewith to stigmatize some of her fellows—and at last screaming out, "You . . . you . . . you 'QUEAN!' "—that is, *you barren old cow—cwean* being the Saxon designation therefor.

As for 'CAT' and 'BITCH' and 'CUR' and 'HORSE' and 'ASS' and others such

14. "In regard to this word Webster says: 'I know not the original sense of this word . . . but *beshrew,* in Chaucer is interpreted to *curse.*' Most assuredly it is and quite properly, too! The fact is Webster was led astray by Todd (see Todd's Johnson's Dict.: *in loco*) who makes the *noun* (a shrew-mouse) a derivative from the *verb* (to shrew, *to curse*). Whereas the reverse is undoubtedly the case. This arrangement, too, exhibits, and accounts for, the natural development of the derivatives. Thus:

A 'SHREW' is a woman possessed with the contentious spitefulness and venom of a shrew-mouse.

To 'SHREW' is to wish one to be struck as with the mortal venom of a shrew-mouse, and, in general, to *curse.*

'SHREWD' is just *shrew-ed,* curst, malicious—in this sense used a thousand times by Shakespeare and his contemporaries; and then softened down to what is merely *sly, sagacious.*

To 'BESHREW' is simply another (strengthened) form of 'TO SHREW'; and hence Chaucer's interpretation thereof [Author]."

like, (of which we have a numerous enough tribe), they require no particularization. But it might puzzle one's wits to say what special stigmatic force there lies in 'MANDRAKE,' unless one receive all the wild fables that cluster around that strange plant.

In the following, for example, it is undoubtedly used in an abusive sense—where Falstaff, addressing his *page* says: "If the prince put thee into my service for any other reason than to set me off, why then I have no judgment. Thou whoreson *mandrake,* thou art fitter to be worn in my cap, than to wait at my heels," etc.—*Second Part of Henry IV*. I. 2.

Here, we perceive, the applicability hangs on the [121] old notion of the mandrake's bearing a certain resemblance to the human figure, especially to a *diminutive* person. On this quaint fancy, Nares[15] quotes the following curious passage from Lyte: "The roote is great and white, not muche unlyke a radishe roote, divided into two or three partes, and sometimes one upon another, *almost lyke the thighes and legges of a man.*"

It was, moreover, supposed that this plant, when torn up from the ground, uttered groans so horrible as to drive any one mad who chanced to hear it.

By the way, 'MANDRAKE' is a corruption from *mandregora*—the peculiar soporific effects of which a familiar passage in Othello have imprinted on the reader's memory:

> Not poppy, nor *mandragora*
> Nor all the drowsy syrops of the world,
> Shall ever medecine thee to that sweet sleep
> Which thou ow'dst yesterday!"

Thus we often times find embalmed, even in words expressive of contempt, quite an important fact or fable. From the unpromising 'TAWDRY,' for example, we evolve quite a piece of history. For it is asserted to be a contraction from *St. Aubrey* (or Saint *Ethelrida*)—a name commonly applied to an annual fair held at *St. Audrey's* day, and at which all kinds [122] of frippery and trinkets were bought and sold: but as these articles generally possessed more *glitter* than *gold* and their splendors were too often sadly faded, it soon came to acquire the meaning which we now attach to the word 'tawdry:' *'That was bought at St. Audrey-fair!'* and so 'tawdry.' By the way, the fair saint herself is said to have been rather attached to finery—so much so, indeed, as to have died of a swelling in the throat, sent as a special visitation on account of an ardent youthful fondness for fine *necklaces!* Many of my readers may remember the very strange story which Horne Tooke compels from 'POLTROON.' He takes it from *pollice truncus*—one that has *deprived himself of his thumb,* a derivation in which he is supported by the elder Etymologists, as Vossius, Skinner and Menage.[16] "Multi enim illo tempore, quia necessitate

15. Probably Robert Nares (1753–1829), author of *A Glossary . . . of Words, Phrases, Names and Allusions . . .* (London, 1822, 1825, 1859, etc.).

16. Possibly Gerhard Johann Vossius (1577–1649), historian and philologist, or his son Isaak (1618–1689); Stephen Skinner, M.D. (1623–1667), author of *Etymologicon Linguae Anglicanae* (London, 1671); Gilles Menage (1613–1692), scholar, author of *Les Origines de la Langue Françoise* (Paris, 1672 etc.).

ad bellum cogebantur prae ignavia sibi *pollices truncabant,* ne militarent!"[17] Some doubt has indeed been cast on this etymology and yet here is a passage giving so perfect a realization of the primary idea of 'poltroon' that one can scarcely resist accepting it:

> "In October 1795, one Samuel Caradise, who had been committed to the house of correction in Kendal, and there confined as a vagabond until put on board a King's ship, agreeable to the late Act, sent for his wife the evening before his intended de[123]parture. He was in a cell and she spoke to him through the iron door. After which he put his hand underneath, and she with a mallet and chissel, concealed for the purpose, *struck off a finger and thumb,* to render him unfit for his Majesty's service."

And similar in origin, is 'SCOUNDREL'—said to be the Italian *scondaruole,* that is, a soldier who ab*sconds* or skulks at muster-*role:*

> "Go, if your ancient, but ignoble blood
> Has crept through *scoundrels* ever since the flood!"
>
> *Pope*

And similar, too, are 'DASTARD,' 'COWARD,' and 'CRAVEN.' A 'CRAVEN' is one who has craved or *craven* his life at his enemy's hands. 'DASTARD,' is from the Saxon verb *Dastrigan,* to be scared, frightened. And 'COWARD' is from a verb that is now obsolete in English, though it is still a living vocable in the Scotch idiom—to *cower,* to shake, to shiver. Of its use I find such examples as this:

> "Winter with his rough winds and blasts causeth a lusty man and woman to *cowre* and sit by the fire."

Or this:

> "And she was put, that I of talke
> Ferre fro these other, up in a halke;
> There lurked, and there *cowred* she."
>
> *Romaunt of the Rose.*

[124] Our slightly contemptuous term 'STICKLER' has rather an unexpected derivation. A citation from Shakespeare will let us into the secret. In *Troilus and Cressida* after

> "Achilles hath the mighty Hector slain,"

17. "For at that time many people forced to war, out of cowardice *cut off their thumbs* rather than fight."

he exclaims:

> "The dragon wing of night o'erspreads the earth,
> And *stickler* like the armies separates," etc.

Like a 'stickler,' that is, like an *arbiter*. A 'stickler' in a duel was, therefore, what we now term a 'second;' and as their duty—namely that of seeing fair-play, equal advantages etc., between the combatants—would often lead them to chaffer and contend and 'stickle' in regard to special points or punctilios, we can readily conceive how it came to acquire the meaning in which it is now used. The reason of their being called '*stick*lers' is said by Stevens to have been from their carrying white *sticks* as emblems of their duty.

'HERETIC' gives us some keen hints respecting the causes of religious intolerance and the *odium theologicum*. For *Hairetikos* (Greek haireo, *to take or choose for oneself*) originally implies simply one who chooses an opinion for himself, without any reference to the [125] truth or falsity of that opinion. But as bigotry never can endure that any man *choose* a belief that *it* does not *choose* for him and is never half so much at home as when anathemizing all who cannot subscribe *credo* to its every dogma, we can readily conceive how this innocent word acquired the meaning of one who holds erroneous and, consequently, *bad* opinions! Hobbes, in the following passage well illustrates this word:

> "The word *heresy* is Greek, and signifies a *taking* of anything, particularly the taking of an opinion. After the study of Philosophy began in Greece, and the philosophers, disagreeing amongst themselves, had started many questions, not only about things natural, but also moral and civil, because every man *took* what opinion he pleased, each several opinion was called a *heresy;* which signified no more than a private opinion, without reference to truth or falsehood."
>
> *Hobbes' Historical Narration concerning Heresy.*

It should also be noticed that 'INFIDEL' literally but imports one who is *faithless* (infidelis) to our beliefs. In the wars of the crusades the epithet 'infidel' was applied to the Mohammedans, even as the Normans called them 'MISCREANTS'—mescreaunts—which is also *unbelievers*. And it is a curious fact that the Turks, resenting, stigmatized the Christians as 'gia ours,' which, I am told, signifies in their language *infidel* or *unbeliever,* also!

[126] We are all familiar with what infinite contempt the Greeks were wont to look down upon all foreign nations—branding them universally as 'BARBARIANS.' The word 'barbarian' itself, however, is by no means so easily traced. Gibbon makes it Syrian, while others declare it to be merely intended as a general imitation of a (to the Greeks) foreign tongue. Thus we see how entirely relative are all such terms, whether ethical or ethnical. But so do words acquire a factitious value. How are we under the sway of Words! They tyrannize over and terrify us—

"Assume the nod,
Affect the god,"

as though they really *had* some inherent virtue and valor of their own, and were not in themselves most poverty-stricken and impotent!

In thus converting words into epithets of slight, sad injustice is often done to innocent terms. Indeed it frequently happens that words that are now employed in a scornful or opprobrious sense, were once terms of honor. Of this process of degradation 'IMP' affords a striking illustration. In Shakespeare 'imp' constantly means a *son,* and, indeed, its primary signification is a shoot or scion. Thus

[127] "Save thy grace, king Hall, my royall Hall.
The heavens thee guard and keepe, most royall *impe* of fame."
First Part of Henry IV.

And Spenser employs it in addressing the Muses:

"Ye sacred *imps* that on Parnasso dwell,
And there the keeping have of learnings threasures."
Faerie Queene.

'BRIGAND' is most palpably formed with *malice prepense:* for originally it signified merely one who lives on a *brig,* or summit—a mountaineer. Surely the word deserves a better fate! So does 'IMPOSTER;' but, indeed, any species of *putting on* (*im-posing*) is so apt to be an *imposition* that there is no wonder the word has taken this course. But we cannot offer this excuse for a 'BELDAME'—which is every letter a *fine lady* (a *belle dame*); or, at least it is nothing worse than a *grandmother.*[18] Chaucer furnishes examples of its employment in the first sense, and Shakespeare in the last. In the First Part of Henry IV., for instance, we find Hotspur speaking as follows:

[128] "Oft the teeming Earth
Is with a kind of colic pinch'd and vex'd
By the imprisoning of unruly wind
Within her womb; which, for enlargement striving,
Shakes the old *beldame Earth,* and topples down
Steeples and moss-grown towers. At your birth
Our *grandam Earth,* having this distemprature,
In passion shook."

18. "*Beldame* was the word for grandmother; *belsire* for grandfather. Note that a French *lady* (dame) sobers down to an English 'dame' [Author]."

And why a *house-wife* or *huswife* (pronounced *huzzif* and hence the Scotch *'hizzie'*)—honest, thrifty soul—should degenerate into a mere 'HUSSY' seems quite inexplicable. There is surely *malice prepense* here; or else some sad degeneracy in housewives themselves! But, indeed, 'NINNY' has, if possible, received even worse usage. It is certainly so, at least, if we derive it from the Latin *nanus,* a dwarf. And as for 'NINCOMPOOP' he mournfully confesses that he is *non compos*—not of a sound mind! And yet surely 'CURMUDGEON' (*coeur mechant,* bad heart) has not so *bad a heart* as it would make us believe; while lubber, it is said, primarily implied just a tall, strapping fellow; 'JUNTO' *ought* to be nothing more than a body of men—junctus—*joined together;* a 'NATURAL' has been compelled to bear the burden of a *fool,* and 'SILLY' has its root in the German 'selig,' *blessed!*

'DOLT' is descriptive enough: it is simply one [129] who is *dulled.* So 'LOUT' which is connected with *low,* and 'MONSTER,' which is just a *sight.* 'RUFFIAN' is of the same root with *robber* and a 'ROUÉ' is a fellow so bad as to deserve to *be broken on the wheel!* A 'DRAB' all too truthfully declares herself to be the *drabbe*—the *lees,* or, as we say, the very *dregs* of society; while 'SCURRILITY' palpably declares that it is only fit for the mouth of a *scurra,* or buffoon. A 'CHARLATAN' (Spanish *charlar,* to prate) is quite as evidently merely a *prating* fool, and all that he says sheer 'RUBBISH' (originally something *rub*bed off, *refuse*); while a 'PETTIFOGGER' has *pettiness* or littleness written on his very face. 'CANT' is a *thing* of which unfortunately we have no lack; and yet the *word* itself is involved in considerable obscurity. However, a likely enough origin for it is the Latin *canto* (*cano*), to sing: and hence that peculiar whining, sing-song tone common to jugglers, sturdy vagabonds and other imposters religious and scientific. From the *manner* it was afterwards transferred to the *thing* itself.

Many a time, too, the Abusive reaches out to fantastic lengths. 'HAIR-BRAINED' is just *hare-brained,* a 'SCAPE-GRACE' is one who has *escaped* merely by *grace* or favor, and 'JACKANAPES' is jack and ape. So we have 'BORE,' 'BOOBY,' 'BLACKLEG,' 'BUMPKIN,' [130] 'LOOSE-FISH,' 'SMELL-FEAST,' 'TRENCHER-FRIEND.' 'SCAMP' is connected with *scamper;* 'CAITIFF' is one who is taken—literally, *captive.* And how often do we hear persons stigmatized as 'NUMSKULLS' and 'THICKSKULLS' and 'BLOCKHEADS'—though why they should be *block*-heads, I know not; unless it be that the head of such an one may be supposed to be possessed of all the stolidity and all the *woodenness* of a *block.* As for 'RAPSCALLION,' 'SLUBBERDEGULLION,' etc., language is here whirled away into the realms of the hopelessly grotesque.

Interesting, too, are the opprobrious names that have been applied in scorn, contempt or hatred to parties and sects. The terms 'WHIG' and 'TORY,' for example, have both their origin in the malignity of the opposition. Their derivations are, however, too familiar to induce us to delay over them. However *pure* the 'PURITANS' may have been, both in walk and conversation, it did by no means save the name from falling into sad contempt; and however *methodical* the 'METHODISTS' were, it did not prevent the derision, which Sidney Smith, from the Edinburgh Review so plentifully lavished upon them, from taking effect in the scornful associations which, for so long a time, attached to the name.

In like manner, we can easily conceive how the [131] 'QUAKERS' came to be designated by this appellation, and Dean Swift, in a passage of dubious character,[19] which I shall not quote, gives us the origin of the party called 'ROUNDHEADS.' In a note he says: "The fanatics, in the time of Charles I. ignorantly applying the text, 'Ye know that it is a shame for men to wear long hair,' cut theirs very short. It is said that the Queen once seeing Pym, a celebrated patriot thus cropped, enquired *who that roundhead man was,* and that from this incident, the distinction became general, and the party were called 'ROUNDHEADS.' "

Our own rich and free political life is constantly giving rise to numberless party-names of more or less interest and significance. 'HUNKER' and 'LOCO-FOCO' and 'FIRE-EATER' and 'DOUGHFACE' and *'Black*-republican' and the 'shells' 'HARD' and 'SOFT' and 'KNOW-NOTHING' and 'BARNBURNER' are samples, of which there are thousands, of this prodigious political activity. But as I find I shall have to devote a Ramble to the subject of Names I shall here abruptly stop.

'ROGUE' is an abusive with a double sense, being employed both in an offensive and an amiable applica[132]tion—as is also the case with 'roguish:' so I shall here take occasion to make a digression on *Amiably Abusive terms.*

And how does Love bend even the most refractory words to the purposes of endearment. Every thing it conquers, and compels into its service. Under its sweet sway 'BEAR' becomes an amiable sobriquet for a husband;[20] nor does 'MOUSE' seem contemptible—nay, altogether endearing, as in Hamlet,

"Pinch wanton on your cheek; call you, his *mouse.*"

But Love's veritable vocabulary finds not its way into dictionaries—learned academies take no cognizance of it. The soil in which it flourisheth is by the hearth-stone and around the ingle-side. And thus do the home and hearth exercise their own sweet yet potent influence over language. They preserve it from corruption—moulding it into their own beautiful forms.

[133] A very curious and very fruitful province under the dominion of the Abusive element is Oaths. Of cursing and swearing—that senseless and sinful practice—we speak not; but of those more innocent, yet characteristic *exclamations* and other popular and peculiar idoms and phrases by which we often contrive to communicate thoughts and fancies and feelings which it would be impossible otherwise to convey. Thus I know of no equivalent for the common exclamation 'The Deuce!' It bears with it a burden of significance not its own and which no other term can fitly represent. By the way, this word is said to be the Gallic name of a demon or evil spirit. Augustine, in his *City of God,* mentions the word:

19. "Tractate on 'The Mechanical Operation of the Spirit' [Author]."

20. " 'Tis said that since the publication of Miss Bremer's 'Neighbours' (wherein, it will be remembered, a 'bear' figures in this way) thousands of wives have adopted this amiably abusive term. It would, of course, be impossible here to attempt entering on the subject; the vocabulary of endearment is a private one. I would merely mention the French 'BICHE,' a *hind*—which is very popular as an appellation of this sort [Author]."

"Quosdam dæmones quos *dusios* Galli nuncupant."[21]

An emotion there is, which only *'whew!'* can perfectly symbolize: and so with a thousand lights and shades of meaning, which only such interjectional articulations can fully convey. Indeed we should say that some of the keenest instruments and organs of thought had not yet found their way into words. The 'DICKENS!' for instance, which is said to be just the 'deil!' and—but 'tis needless to enumerate.

[134] I shall not enter into the dark abyss of terms formed by that disgraceful practice of swearing: it is curious, however, to note the characteristic oaths of different nations. Thus the Frenchman swears 'Par bleu' and by his 'mille tonnères!' while the German growls out his 'Donner und Blitzen!' or 'Donner und Teufel!' as Jean Paul often has it.

So we see that oaths are not only national, but individual. Thus how famous is Socrates' 'By the dog!' And Charles' 'Odd's death!' Just as notorious, however, is the 'God's death!' of good Queen Bess. Swearing, indeed, Elizabeth affected as she did many other manly accomplishments. For if she could sing 'ditties,'

"———In a summer's bower,
With ravishing division to her lute;"

she was also quite as able, when occasion required, heartily to cuff her courtiers. It would seem, however, that ladies once enjoyed a much larger share of this peculiar prerogative than at present.

We should, at least, conclude so from Hotspur's exhortation to his wife:

"*Hotspur*. Come, Kate, I'll hear your song, too.

Lady Percy. Not mine, *in good sooth*.

[135] *Hotspur*. Not yours, *in good sooth!* 'Heart, you swear like a comfit-maker's wife! Not you, in *good sooth;* and, *As true as I live;* and, *As God shall mend me;* and, *As sure as day;*

And giv'st such sarcenet surety for thy oaths,
As if thou never walk'dst further than Finsbury.
Swear me, Kate, *like a lady* (!), as thou art,
A good mouth-filling oath; and leave *in sooth,*
And such protests of pepper-gingerbread,
To velvet guards and Sunday citizens!"

First Part of Henry IV. III. 2.

'ZOUNDS!' is a common enough exclamation, and is probably a contraction of *God's wounds*—a form which we find in Chaucer, who is overflowing with quaint asseverations of this kind. Thus we find,

"I make a vow by *Goddes digne bones*."

The Pardoneres Tale.

21. "Certain demons whom the Gauls call *dusii*." "See Webster [Author]."

'PERDY,' again, is just a corruption for *par dieu* (by God). So, 'GRAMERCY' returns—*grand merci*—great thanks. Of this primitive form Chaucer will afford us an example:

> *"Grand mercy,* lord, God thank it you (quod she)
> That ye have saved me my children dere."
>
> *The Clerkes Tale.*

'BY'R LADY,' that is *by our lady* (the Virgin Mary), [136] and 'BY'R LAKIN'—that is, *by our ladykin*—a diminutive of the preceding—were once (when 'our lady' received more veneration than she now does) very popular forms of asseveration. So Snout the tinker, exclaims:

> "By'r *lakin,* a parlous fear!"
>
> *Mid Summers Night's Dream,* III.1.

Falstaff, on the contrary, is constantly swearing 'BY THE LORD!' and declaring (what he certainly well merited) 'I'LL BE HANGED!' Whereas Justice Shallow prefers to point his declaration 'BY YEA AND NAY,' or 'BY COCK AND PYE' (a corruption for *God and Pye*—the latter being the name given to the Popish book of church offices—By God and the Book!) Another whimsical form of swearing was 'By these ten bones!' i. e. the *fingers* or 'by these pickers and stealers' (Hamlet). See Shakespeare, Jonson, etc.

We of the Saxon brood are perhaps as abusive in our language and as terrible in our oaths as any nation on the face of the earth. So much so, that we can scarcely tax Caliban with extravagance when he declares:

> "You taught me language, and my profit on't [137]
> Is, I know how to curse; the red plague rid ye
> For learning me your language."
>
> *Tempest.*[22]

It is averred, indeed, that the Italians outstrip us in this matter, as in many other arts—worthy and unworthy; but this is to be regarded as dubious!

We have seen how Shakespeare wields this class of words—conjuring up the most fantastic or ludicrous or scurrilous combinations—piling term on term and capping the climax of the ridiculous or the abusive. Like a Titan, he laughs and sports amid the spoils of language—playing with and tossing about words—or rattling them like a tempest of hail stones about the ears of some luckless wight.

22. "Caliban imprecates the 'red plague.' The names of frightful diseases are often used as imprecations. Thus, the old 'Pox on you!' was, previous to the introduction of vaccination, a fearful curse. Thank vaccination, then, for removing both the thing and the word!

So with a 'murrain!' etc., etc. [Author]."

"Ha, thou *mountain-foreigner!* Sir John, and master mine,
I combat challenge of this *latten bilbo;*
Word of denial, *froth and scum,* thou liest."

Merry Wives of Windsor, I.1.

"Out of my doors, you *witch,* you *hag,* you *baggage,* you *polecat,* you *ronyon.*"

Ibid, IV.2.

[138] "Get you gone, you *dwarf;*
You *minimus,* of *hind'ring knot-grass made;*
You *bead,* you *acorn.*"

Mid-Summer Night's Dream, II.2.

"*Falstaff.* Strike; down with them; cut the *villains' throats,* oh! *whoreson caterpillars! bacon-fed knaves!* they hate us youth; down with them; fleece them.

Hang ye *gorbellied knaves;* are ye undone? No, ye *fat chuffs;* I would your store were here! Oh, *bacons,* on! What, ye *knaves,* etc."

*First Part of Henry IV.*II.2.

However, Falstaff many a time gets paid back in his own coin:

"You will, *chops?*

Farewell, thou *latter-spring!* Farewell, *all-hallown summer!*

Peace, ye *fat-kidney'd rascal!* . . . Peace, ye *fat guts!*

Call in *ribs,* call in *tallow.*

Here comes *lean Jack,* here comes *bare-bone!*"

And so we leave off, even as we began:

"Why, thou clay-brained guts; thou knotty-pated fool; thou whoreson, obscene, greasy, tallow-keech———!"

[135] RAMBLE SEVENTH.
FRANCIES AND FANTASTICS.

* * *

[139] And Speech reflects this infinite richness and variety. For if language has run pliant and plastic into the mould of our every-day thoughts and feelings, lending itself to the uses of the Understanding and the Common Sense, and smacking of our workshop world, yet can it also

"Babble of green fields."

* * *

[157] Diminutives, indeed, are the natural language of love: a principle which could receive no more forcible illustration than the abbreviations of proper names. This is constantly done by familiarity and friendship. A monosyllable—which the popular instinct always struggles towards—is warm and cozy—hearty as the pressure of a friend's hand; a polysyllable is stiff and formal—suspicious as the obsequious bow of a courtier. 'Frank' and 'Ben' and 'Will' are seated at the heart's hearth-stone, while *Malachia, Obediah* or *Jeremiah* are knocking, unheeded at the door.

* * *

[167] Often times, too, these every-day, bandied words and phrases have an expressive power that more elegant substitutes would but lamely realize. How significant, for instance, are 'close-fisted,' 'mealy-mouthed,' to 'rule the roast,' to 'egg on' (to anything), 'hood-wink,' 'quiz,' the 'hypoes,' 'bamboozle,' 'balderdash,' 'ink-horn' terms, 'fast' boys, 'rich' stories. So we speak of one's having 'brass' or 'tin,' or of one's being in a 'pickle;' and we exclaim 'ginger!' and we speak of a person in a state of intoxication (which, by the way, is related in its very origin to [168] *poison*—toxicum) as being 'tight,' 'tipsey,' 'boosy,' 'potvaliant,' 'muddled,' 'fuddled,' 'fou,' 'corned,' 'half seas over,' 'the worse for liquor,' 'drunk as a piper,' or as having a 'brick in his hat!' And how far might we go before we would find such expressive symbols as 'blue-stocking' (*bas bleu*) or 'hail-fellow,' or 'all the go,' or 'catch-penny,' or 'fire-eater,' or 'dead-letter,' (a term which the Post Office has given us?) or 'chatter-box,' or 'crusty,' or 'inuendo,' (literally a *nodding* at) or 'leg-bail,' or 'cut a swell,' or 'hobby,' or to 'palm,' (anything on one), or 'luggage,' which is just something *lugged* about! Though what special applicability there is in the old phrase 'honest as the skin between the brows,' it might be difficult to tell; and equally hard to tell how the phrase to 'sow one's wild oats' arose, and why it was that *oats* should have been selected from among grains as emblematic of the dissipation and excess of youth; while to 'curry favor,' smacks quite of the stable; the once popular exclamation, 'Cry you mercy, I took you for a joint stool,' seems purely fantastic, and I suppose brandy is called the *water of life,* 'eau de vie,' 'aqua vitae,' 'usquebaugh,' (for they all have the same meaning) according to the law of *lucus a non*—precisely because it proves in so many cases the water of death!

[176] RAMBLE EIGHTH. VERBAL ETHICS.

* * *

[188] But here it is that the marvel and miracle of language begin. For the divine influx, working on the unfolding Conscience and the ascending Spirituality of man, is constantly operating to elevate and ennoble words. How often do Words, through the inspiration that is breathed into them, become virtuous and valorous beyond their native ability. They lend themselves plastic to the moulding power

of something higher than human Will. For man cannot free himself from God. The spell of divinity is on him.

"The hand that rounded Peter's dome,
And groined the aisles of Christian Rome,
Wrought in a sad sincerity:
Himself from God he could not free;
He builded better than he knew,
The conscious stone to beauty grow!"[23]

* * *

[193] Profoundly significant, too, is it to muster words with reference to the traces of the workings of the hot passion, the prejudice, the depravity, shall we say? of human nature.

[200] RAMBLE NINTH.
MEDALS IN NAMES.

* * *

[201] Names of home—the sacred names of mother and sister and wife—the sweet idyl of the names of children—the clustering associations of the names of the troop of amis! Names of bards, benefactors, martyrs, dear to the heart of the world—Names of the primeval supremes, of the founders of the antique Religions: Brama, Osiris, Zoroaster, Prometheus, Orpheus, Jove! The execrated names of tyrants and oppressors—names uttered with compressed lips—names of warriors and conquerors writing their fiery legends on man's mind as the lightning writes on rocks! Names of the dead—names embalmed—tombs in a battle-field, o'ergrown with grasses and flowers!

* * *

[228] The theory of nomenclature finally ascends into the aesthetical realm—vast and hitherto all but unexplored domain. The necessities of Literary Art—especially as expressed in the drama and novel—require the creation of ideal Names. And often high and highest art is displayed in the workings of creative Imagination on nominal emblems for these avatars of the mind. The masters of the modern Novel all work, consciously or unconsciously, on the problem of Names. I know books that suggest ideal pedigrees, a new heraldry of the mind, and carry farther out the boundaries of Metaphysics.

To Modern times and to America, too, the thought of Naming presents itself. Once, we know, every name was significant. There have been seasons, in the elder ages, of flood-tides in the creative faculties, when Nature disclosed her secret throught and gave it to man to name her—when to mountain and stream, field and flood were added names that are poems. Why should not we, too, come into this Orphic secret? Why should we masquerade in the old costume? Imperative is the demand for a fresh, free, appropriate nomenclature for American Geography,

23. Emerson, "The Problem," ll. 19–24.

[229] Inventions, Contributions, Personalities. Already the new needs make the old perfections meagre and inadequate. To you, Poets and Builders, sublime invitations! To quarry and to build in the new architectures of humanity.

[230] RAMBLE TENTH.
SYNONYMS AND THEIR SUGGESTIONS.

* * *

[230] An adequate treatment of English Synonyms is still a desideratum. Crabbe's work was written before Philology became a science, and the little volume edited by Archbishop Whately[24] clean skips etymology and all its seminal suggestions. Mr. Taylor ("English Synonyms Discriminated") commands the etymologic method, and has furnished an important contribution to Synonymy: but his work is not at all proportioned to the copiousness of our language. Of much profounder philosophic significance is the *The*[231]*saurus* of Mr. Roget,[25] who has given us a metaphysical classification of Thoughts and Things with their corresponding Verbal Symbols—"furnishing on every topic a copious store of words and phrases, adapted to express all the recognizable shades and modifications of the general idea under which those words and phrases are arranged." These various works are all useful auxiliaries; but I return to the assertion with which I set out, that an adequate treatment of this subject is still something to be desired. A great Synonymy, after the modern Philologic Methods, would be a most important contribution to the Philosophy of the English language. Much is in the subject; much grows out of it.

* * *

[232] The causes of the growth of Synonyms lie deep in the roots of a nation's life and language. Relations, external and internal, act—amalgamation of races, literary influence and action of other nations, the prominent elements of national civilization, with other and subtler causes. With a people of active imagination there is always a tendency to drape the crowning facts and factors of its life with a copious richness of expressive forms. And it is significant to notice the manner in which even individual elements in a nation's civilization have been affected with verbal powers. In the era of chivalry there was a host of expressions to render the idea of *horse*. In Sanscrit, the language of Hindostan, where the *elephant* plays a part as important as the horse among ourselves, words abound to designate this pachyderm. Sometimes it is denominated the 'twice-drinking animal,' sometimes as 'he who has two teeth,' sometimes as 'the animal with the proboscis.'[26] This is still more strikingly manifest in the Arabic, which is said to have the enormous multitude of several hundred words for the 'ship of the desert.'

24. Probably Richard Whatley (1787–1863), Archbishop of Dublin, *Elements of Rhetoric* (1828).

25. "Thesaurus of English Words and Phrases, Classified and Arranged so as to Facilitate the Expression of Ideas and Assist in Literary Composition. London, 1852 [Author]." Peter Mark Roget (1779–1869).

26. "Alfred Maury [Author]."

[233] These divers influences have all acted on the English Speech. Complex in its organism as no language is, it inherits all that antiquity conceived and freely augments and enriches itself with importations from the modern idioms. Born thus of the marriage of several stocks and tongues, a copious equivalence runs through the English language, and it frequently depends on a writer's choice whether his diction shall bear the features of this or that branch of his linguistic ancestry.

* * *

[262] And new vistas open upon the suggestions of Synonyms. How profoundly significant are these correlatives often of national characteristics! What subtle glimpses do they afford into national manners and morals! The distinction, for instance, which etymologic anatomy lays bare, between the Teutonic 'banish' and the Roman 'exile' gives us an insight into certain fundamental social characteristics. For 'banish' is evidently the being subjected to the *ban,*[27] or proclamation—whence we gather that the French and Teutonic mode of punishment was by *public proclamation;* whereas the Latin 'exile' as clearly points to *exsilere* as its root—suggesting Cicero's definition—"perfugium potius supplicii, non supplicum."[28]

[265] RAMBLE ELEVENTH.
THE GROWTH OF WORDS.

"An idiom is an organism subject, like every organism, to the laws of development. One must not consider a language as a product dead and formed but once: it is an animate being and ever creative."

Wilhelm von Humboldt.

The conception of language that has arisen prophetic on the thought of modern times is a high and great one. Speech is no more the dead mechanism it used to be conceived. Each language is a living organism; the totality of languages a grand series of organisms, all built after the same archetype, the same skeleton; but each presenting its special structural stamp, as fish, reptile, bird, mammal, are all modifications of one primitive Idea.

Yes! Language is indeed alive! Primordial creation and manifestation of the mind, Language throbs with the pulses of our life. This is the wondrous [266] babe, begotten of the blended love of spirit and of matter—physical, mystical, the Sphinx! Through speech man realizes and incarnates himself; and Oken has an oracular utterance that "without speech there is no world."

27. "This verbal root crops out through several compounds and derivatives. The '*bans* of marriage,' for example, are just the *proclamations* of marriage. So, our common phrase 'to be under *ban,*' is evidently to be under *sentence*. Furthermore, to 'abandon' is—*à* (*le*) *ban donner*—to *give* over to *the ban*. And a 'bandit' is quite as palpably one *ban-dit* ban-proclaimed, sentenced by the *ban*. Italian Bandito pl. *Banditti* [Author]."

28. "A place of refuge rather than punishment." "De Vere's Comparative Philology [Author]."

It is one of the current wranglings, How language originated: as though Language were not an innate energy and aspiration! Language is not a cunning conventionalism arbitrarily agreed upon: it is an internal necessity. Language is not a fiction, but a truth. Language is begotten of a lustful longing to express, through the plastic vocal energy, man's secret sense of his unity with nature.

This vitality of speech manifests itself in a two-fold manifestation: in the possession of a distinctive personality and identity—in material elements and formal laws that stamp it with the stamp of linguistic individuality; and, further, in that other characteristic of every living organism—in the exhibition of growth, progress, decay—in the ongoing of processes of absorption, assimilation and elimination—in the inworking and outworking of the creative energy.

And it is in this sense that the English language is alive—as displaying successive processes of growth and development within the limits of its linguistic individuality.

[267] The causes of that marvelous identity we call the English Language lie deep in the manifold influences that have made the English Nation. The History of a Language is measurable only in the terms of all the factors that have shaped a people's life. A nation's history is the result of the double action of internal impulses and external events. And Language expresses the infusions from all these—subtily absorbing the ethnology of a nation, its geography, government, traditions, culture, faith. Shooting its deep tap-root into eldest antiquity, drawing from the pith and sap of that grandest of all families of races and tongues—the Indo-European stock; receiving living grafts from France and Italy and Scandinavia, this divine tree of the English Speech has grown up into its sublime proportions nurtured by the history of a thousand years.

Of this superb Speech—the grandest in the world—we have no adequate treatment. There is no History of the English Language. Nor any Dictionary of the English Language. We have no such work on the English Language as the Germans possess in the "Teutonic Grammar" of Jacob Grimm,[29] who has with masterly method and largest appreciation of modern Philology, traced the formative influences of the German speech, as it has shaped itself into [268] conscious individuality. A History of the English Language, rising out of a full appreciation of the Philosophy of Speech (to which must go that large hospitality and impartiality that flows from the thought of the Ensemble), answering to the requirements of modern research, and after the broad, free methods America lets down, has yet to come. To the achievement of this epic work may well go the loftiest energies of both branches of the Anglican stock and speech!

How far would the philosophy of the English Language reach! What a retrospect of ages, growths, processes, accretions, events, forces, impulses! In the motions of man's creative energy how all is interwoven with the all! How celestial forces ascend and descend and hand each other the golden pails!

29. "Jacob Grimm [Author]." Grimm (1785–1863), philologist, folklorist, *Deutsche Grammatik* (1819 etc.).

An appreciation of the organic laws of the English Language in its historic unfolding is inseparable from considerations that embrace the ensemble of Languages. For ascending through the Anglo-Saxon idioms to the stock to which they belong—the Germanic or Teutonic group of tongues, we are here carried back into that grand radiation of race and speech which modern philologic criticism has formuled as the INDO-EUROPEAN line of peoples and tongues; nor do we stop till we have reached the [269] Persian and Indian fountains of wisdom and language. Thus it is that it is only by embracing causes, forces and impulses as old as the Japhetic man that we can rise to a full appreciation of the Philosophy of the English Language.

The Japhetites[30] embrace the noblest antique and later races—the Brahminic Indians, the Persians, Medians, Greeks, Romans and European peoples—theirs those noble and highly developed languages, the Sanskrit, Zend, Persian, Hellenic, Latin, Germanic, Keltic, Teutonic. In the Vedas of the Indians, especially the hymns of the Rig-Veda, and in the Zend-Avesta of the Persians—primeval documents of the Iranic world—we see the germs of all we call Europe. Here were the beginnings of the cultures of the occidental world. Science was born in that mind, the intuition of nature, the instinct for political organization and that direct practical normal conduct of life and affairs.

From this mind, too, flowered out the grandest and most spiritual of languages. The Japhetic or Iranic tongues are termed by the master-philologers the Organic Group, to distinguish them from the Agglutinative and Inorganic speech-floors that underlie them [270] in the Geology of Language. They alone have reached the altitude of free intellectual individuality and organism. To them belongs the splendid plasticity of Sanskrit, Greek, German, English! Such are the primeval lines in the genesis of the English language. And so it is that sounds and structures—words and forms—that were heard along the Ganges, five thousand years ago—words heard in Benares and Delhi, in Persia and Greece—are now scaling the Rocky Mountains of the Western world!

We descend. Crises present themselves in the growth of language, connected with mighty mental and social movements—crises that mark eras in History. The English—along with all the present idioms of Europe, French, Provençal, German, Italian, Spanish, Portuguese—refers itself back to that great period of ethnic flux, the few centuries succeeding the dissolution of the Roman Empire. This epoch introduces us to the birth of idioms: the laws that govern the development of language are here seen in vital play. The two elements were the German and Roman. The vigorous, individual, egotistic German, acting on the decaying Latin spoken by the remains of the Romans and by Keltic populations through France and Spain, "dissolved and as it were burst the compact structure of the Latin tongue." New forces and [271] affinities came into action. The Teutonic genius gave its own inflections, conjugations and forms, working on Latin roots, breaking

30. "Sometimes termed *IRANIANS* or *ARYANS* from *Iràn,* the native name of Persia [Author]."

up the crystalline structure of the classic mould, freeing the grammatical forms from their absorption in the terminations of nouns and verbs, and erecting them into independent prepositions and auxiliaries. This passage from synthesis to analysis is the career of all languages. How markedly is this visible in the English! The glory of the English is that it is essentially modern—essentially unclassical.

I have shown the admirable marriage of Germanic and Roman elements present at the birth of the historical English Speech. The subsequent history of this language shows the copious infusions of new elements and the unfolding of those prolific germs, under the guidance of the influences, internal and external, that went to shape the English nation and mind.

It is this indeed which especially characterizes our tongue—its eminently composite and complex structure. It is to the scheme of Language what the diluvial rocks of the Secondary formation are in Geology. And as these have been formed by floods and inundations—water-borne and crumbling debris of antique worlds: so is the English language built out [272] of the drift and detritus of other and elder tongues. This fact is in the line of the genius of the English race, which is unequaled in absorption and assimilation, in receptive and applicative power.

To exhibit in epic unfolding the harmonious blending of these formative elements into the grand organism of the English Language does not come within the scope of these pages. How have I longed to work on this great problem! May my aspirations some day be realized!

But within the brief limits that are left me I may have time to notice some of the most eminent contributions that have gone to the making of our language.

And first, it is needless for me to remark that the heart of our language is Anglo-Saxon. This is the spine on which the structure of our speech is hung. Drawing from the substance of the grand Germanic stock—a stock in which the instinct of personal and political independence has always been powerfully present—what infusions of passion and power and noble manly strength did our language thus receive! Saxon, too, is the whole body of grammatical forms and inflextions; Saxon are the articulations—the conjunctions, articles, pronouns; Saxon those powerful instruments, the Prepositions and Auxiliaries!

And yet, had the Saxon been left to itself, it never [273] could have grown into the English tongue. It needed a new element. This is found in the Norman French introduced with that great political and social revolution, the Norman Conquest—a conquest that has been made the theme of much sentimental twaddle, but which was no doubt precisely the best thing that could have happened. A double action forthwith began—on the grammar and on the vocabulary, the latter copiously enriching itself with numerous terms indicative of the new political and social relations—of war, of law—of the arts and elegancies of society, which, having had no existence in Saxon life, found no utterance in the Saxon language. In regard of Grammar—of structural forms and inflections—the French influence was powerful, but indirect. Indirect, I say; because the French gave few or any forms of its own. And yet one can scarcely exaggerate the power of that influence in freeing the nascent English speech from those useless and cumbersome forms with which the Anglo-Saxon was overloaded. "The Saxon forms soon dropped away, because they did not suit the new roots; and the genius of the language, from having to deal with newly imported words in a rude state, was induced to neglect the inflexions of the native ones."[31] Let a single illustra[274]tion suffice. A complex system of the formation of the plural of nouns obtained—some nouns making that number in *a,* others in *an,* others in *as,* others in *u;* the Norman infusion, however, led to the adoption of *s* as the universal termination of all plural nouns, that being the French method and at the same time the termination of the ancient Anglo-Saxon masculine.

I have said that with the French inoculation a vast enriching of the vocabulary took place. This enriching was of course progressive—was, indeed, the work of centuries. The value of this legacy cannot be overstated: it embraced thousands of our most expressive and most important words. Of the prodigious activity with which the French genius wrought on the English language, for the four or five centuries succeeding the Conquest, we have a significant record in Chaucer. Chaucer, indeed, perhaps exaggerates the French element; and it was no doubt on account of this penchant that he in his own day received the nickname of the "French brewer." But it cannot be that Chaucer did anything more than crystallize into literature verbal forms already in solution among the floating word-capital of the day. For never otherwise could he have been the popular poet he was. What a lusty leap the English Lan[275]guage had taken since the Norman Conquest the Canterbury Tales vividly mirror forth. 'Twas the flush of adolescence, rich and juicy and spendthrift: manhood, compact, equable, had yet to come. Let me quote a few passages from Chaucer showing the average proportion of French in his diction. To bring it home to the eye I shall italicise the chief Norman engraftings.

Whanne that April with his showers sote
The droughte of March hath *perced* to the rote
And bathed every *veine* in swiche *licour,*
Of which *vertue engendred* is the *flour:*
Whan Zephirus eke with his sote brethe
Enspired hath in every holt and hethe
The *tendre* croppes, and the yonge sonne
Hath in the Ram his halfe *cours* yronne,
And small foules maken *melodie,*
And slepen all night with open eye,
So priketh him *nature* in his *corages,*
Than longen folk to gon on *pilgrimages,* etc.

To Canterbury with *devoute courage,*
At night was com into that *hostelrie*
Wel nine-and-twenty in a *compagnie.*

31. Jacob Grimm [Author].

At *mortal batailles* hadde he been fiftene.

He was a *veray parfit gentil* knight.

[276] Therfore in stede of weping and *praiers*.

Men mote give silver to the poure *freres*.[32]

Th' *estat* th' *araie,* the *nombre* and eke the *cause,*

Were it by *aventure,* or *sort,* or *cas*.

In *prison*
Perpetuel, he n' olde no *raunsom*.

Of course amid these thousand-fold French importations many, many were not finally adopted into the vernacular. Put through the assay, they were not found fit to be stamped with the seal of popular acceptation. In Chaucer I find such Gallicisms as these—'gaillard' (gay), 'debonair' (good-natured), 'devoir' (duty), 'lointain' (the distance), 'jouissance' (enjoyment), 'misericorde' (tenderheartedness), 'pierrie' (precious stones), 'rondeur' (roundness—the 'Earth's rondeur'), with scores of suchlike, some of which will no doubt again make their appearance in our language, many of them expressing thoughts or things not so well expressed by any we have. But as I shall make the Unworked Mines of the English Language the theme of a future volume I shall not be tempted into farther illustration.

And now we must descend the stream of our lan[277]guage to that period when those copious tributaries from the classic fountains poured their grand affluents into the rich river of English Speech. And here we have to mention the deep debt we owe to that illustrious nation, Italy—which for so many centuries led the van of European civilization—in operating the renaissance of Greek and Latin language and thought. The breath of antique genius passed over the English mind like the air of Spring, bursting and blossoming in luxuriant growths of thought and speech. The period of this creative movement is that mighty Sixteenth century, from the reign of the Eighth Henry through the Elizabethan era. Not by hundreds merely, one may say, but by thousands, were Latin and Greek words then naturalized into the English speech.

Nor is the quality of these importations of less significance. It was theirs to satisfy the needs of the higher intellectual and spiritual expression which that new upsurging from the spontaneous depths of human nature brought. Philosophy, Science and Poetry put on that rich feuillage of verbal forms that gives such masterly expression to English literature. In a word, the classical contributions furnished the spiritual conceptions, and endowed the material body of the English

32. "What we now write 'friars': frères, brothers [Author]."

speech with a living soul. Under [278] the hands of the fine geniuses of the Sixteenth and Seventeenth centuries the English Language rounded into compact, kosmic mould.

Of those three grand factors—Saxon, French, and Classical—is our language made up. It is the mutual influence and action of these that form the warp and woof of our English speech. Not but that other elements are, in greater or smaller proportions, present, and weave their threads into the divine web; but these are the main sources whence our language has enriched itself—these the main sources whether of its terms or its powers, of its material elements or its formal laws.

Of these minor tributaries the Italian, German, Norse, Portuguese, Spanish, Dutch, deserve special mention. From Italian we have such accretions as 'virtuoso,' 'bravo,' 'bandit,' 'charlatan,' 'gazette,' 'con amore,' etc. The maritime and commercial activity of the Portuguese during the Sixteenth and Seventeenth centuries has left us some significant words. Thus 'fetishism,' a term applied by them to the low idolatry and sorcery of the African tribes, is simply the Portuguese *feitico,* sorcery, witchcraft. Their relations with the African coast have also given us 'palaver'—Portuguese *palavra,* talk, speech; and applied by them to a council of African chiefs. It is, [279] moreover, to the long monopoly by the Portuguese of the East Indian trade that we are indebted for the introduction of various oriental words, as 'taboo' from the Sandwich Islands, and the phrase 'run-*amuck*' from the Malays. The Dutch have left the impress of their maritime activity on our language. 'Sloop,' for instance, and 'yacht' and 'schooner' are all of Dutch etymology. To later German we owe the suggestions of many valuable metaphysical symbols, made after the antique—not the least significant of which are the much-used 'objective' and 'subjective.' Nor is this all, there being scarce a tongue on the planet which the all-absorbing Saxon genius has not laid under contribution to enrich the exchequer of its conquering speech. The aboriginal American dialects, for instance, have given us 'tobacco,' 'wigwam,' 'papouse,' 'moccasin,' 'Yankee,' 'potato,' 'chocolate,' and others. The Slaves have contributed 'plough,' word and thing. Arabia shows her powerful influence on the culture of the Middle Ages in such terms as 'algebra,' 'zero,' 'almanach,' 'alkali,' 'alembic,' 'elixir,' 'alcohol,' etc. Hebraisms, too, are not lacking—witness 'sabbath,' 'jubilee,' 'hallelujah,' 'amen,' 'cabala,' 'Messiah,' etc. Turkey sends us 'tulip,' 'turban,' 'dragoman;' Persia, 'bazaar,' 'caravan,' 'azure,' 'scarlet;' China, 'tea' and [280] 'Nankeen;' Hindostan, 'calico,' 'chintz,' 'curry,' 'lac;' the Malays 'batam,' 'gamboge,' 'rattan,' 'sago.'

The growth of words runs parallel with the unfolding of a nation's life. Every addition to practical civilization, every scientific generalization, commerce in all its branches, foreign literary influence, diplomacy, religion, philosophy, sociology are the perpetual agents of linguistic increase.

A curious law attaches to the origin of words by which they are forced to undergo a period of probationship before they receive the stamp of legal currency. Every new word passes through an embryonic stage previous to emerging as a normal member of the organism of speech, and perhaps for half a century or more finds a place in no dictionary. The advent of every neologism is met by a powerful conservatism opposing the innovation: and only after a severe ordeal does it raise itself to a place in the peerage of language. With its emergence in the Dictionary it has passed the grand climacteric, and may henceforth count on a longer or shorter lease of life. Thousands of words, too, make their debut as slang—gipseys and outlaws that are afterwards reclaimed by civilized society. And it is curious to [281] observe how many of our stateliest terms rest on some free popular idiom, some bandied catch-word—spontaneous creation of the hour.

In the Essays of Montaigne there is a vivid illustration of the subtle steps by which words often find their way into language. In order to facilitate his acquisition of Latin, then the common speech of the learned, he was, in his childhood, allowed no other medium of communication; and not only his teachers, but his parents, attendants, and even his nurse, were obliged to learn enough Latin to converse with him in it. The result was, as he tells us, that the peasants on his father's estate, and gradually the people of the neighboring villages, adopted many of the Latin words which they heard constantly used in the family of their feudal lord; and, writing fifty years later, he declares that these words had become permanently incorporated into the dialect of the province.

'Mob' is a word that made its appearance in the English language in the time of Charles II. as a piece of pure slang, and I have already quoted from the Spectator characterizing it as a ridiculous expression which might however finally make its way into our language! How long did 'bore' struggle to maintain its hold! It expressed, however, a positive idea, not otherwise conveyed, and has finally, in our own [282] time, won its way into the Dictionary. You look in vain in any vocabulary of the English language for 'sociology' (creation of Auguste Comte) 'solidarity,' 'placer:' they are all most valuable contributions, however, and will no doubt soon receive Dictionary endorsement. 'Telegram' again, which appears in the new editions of the English dictionaries, is an example of how an imperious necessity will force words into immediate acceptance and recognition.

The French contributions to our language, so copious and rich, were never more important than they have been within the present century. Let me enumerate some that we have received within that period, with others that look a little farther back. I shall give such as suggest themselves to my mind, without any attempt at completeness.

Accoucheur—Accouchement: Valuable contributions to our language, and now getting into popular use.

Attaché: A diplomatic term, implying one *attached* to the suite of an embassador, and now creeping into more general use. Thus we speak about the *attachés* of a reigning belle.

Au fait: "Posted up"—up to the mark, having an off-hand familiarity with the matter in hand.

[283] *Badinage:* Half-earnest jesting—a delicate modification of raillery.

Blasé: Past participle of the verb *blaser,* to surfeit, and popularized by the comedy of "Used Up."

Bon-mot or simply *Mot:* Literally a *good word*—a good thing.

Brochure: A pamphlet: from the verb *brocher,* to stitch.

Coup: A stroke or blow, and in compounds implies any sudden action. The compounds are very numerous, *coup-d'état, coup-de-grace, coup-demain, coup-de-soleil, coup-d'oeil, coup-de-théatre,* etc.

Debris: A symbolism from Geology, where it means masses of rock etc., detached by attrition or mechanical violence.

Debut: First public appearance. *Debutant, Debutante,* the person making it.

Elite: The flower—literally the *elect* or *chosen*.

Employé: A word of the greatest utility and coming into universal use: the meaning is any one *employed*.

Ennui: Weariness, sense of tedium.

Ensemble: The totality as distinguished from the details. A noble word with immense vista.

Façade: Chief *frontage* of a building—a term borrowed from the French architects.

Goût: Relish, aesthetic taste.

[284] *Naïve, Naïveté:* Most desirable words, with the French elisive charm, and implying a combination of the ingenuous, candid, winning.

Nonchalance: cool carelessness and indifference.

Outré: Etymology the same as *ultra* and carrying with it the sense of the extravagant and grotesque.

Passé: A term whose import is realized with tremendous force by ladies of a certain age. *En passant,* by the way.

Penchant: Inclination, proclivity.

Persiflage: Light, mocking banter.

Personnel: Originally, corps of *persons* employed in contradistinction to the *materiel;* but now coming to mean, also, the sum of characteristics constituting one's personality.

Précis: A summary or abridgment. A valuable word.

Prestige: A most useful word, supplying a positive want in our language. The original meaning was a piece of smuggling or imposture; but the word now bears with it the idea of *the presumption which past successes beget of future ones.*

Programme: A word of universal use in America in the sense of a printed synopsis: a desirable contribution, which the French has given us, taking it from the Greek.

[285] *Protegé:* One under the patronage or protection of another—Roman *clients.*

Rapport: Implies, in French, *relation; en rapport,* in relation with; and used in English to convey the idea of an affinity or sympathy of sensation. The word owes its currency to our modern mesmeric and "Spiritual" phenomena and philosophy.

Redacteur: An editor, compiler etc.; *redation,* the digesting or reducing to order literary or scientific material.

Renaissance: Regeneration, new birth: mainly applied to the revival of the fine arts, but susceptible of any breadth of application.

Séance: A sitting, applied mostly to sittings for scientific purposes.

Soirée: A word early adopted, and after the analogy of which we have more recently introduced *matinée*.

[286] RAMBLE TWELFTH. ENGLISH IN AMERICA.

By a combination of circumstances the English Language became the speech of America. There was nothing fortuitous in this. For English is eminently the speech of the Modern. The English Language expresses most typically those tendencies which all show more or less. Into the make of the English, more than any other idiom, has converged the spirit of the modern, breaking up the crystalline structure of the classic mould—the splendid newness, the aspirations of freedom, individualism, democracy.

Nurtured by the influences that have made the English nation, the English Language expresses the infusions from all these—expresses aristocracy and monarchy among the rest. Meanwhile do we not feel that a change has, these eras, passed over the private spirit of man? The genius of a new age broods, fiery and fecundating, over the nations. Authority, [287] tradition, caste go hopelessly. New tests, demands, verdicts come, disconcerting the old decorums in opinions, manners, literature. Audacious aspirations arise. A lofty augury beckons on to new cerebral and spiritual shores.

A speech to correspond! These oceanic movements in the age must make flood-tide in the Language, also. For speech moves with the movements of mind, as the ocean obeys celestial influences. Always Language is incubated by the mind of the ages. Transported to the new and vaster arena of America, the English language comes under the conditions, outer and inner, that are shaping the American mind. It is qualified by all that makes American life—by the geographic and climatic conditions, by the ethnology of America, by her politics, sociology, manners, mentality.

Of course the English Language must take on new powers in America. And here we are favored by the genius of this grand and noble language, which more than all others lends itself plastic and willing to the moulding power of new formative influences. Was it supposed that the English Language was finished? But there is no finality to a Language! The English has vast vista in it—vast vista in America.

[288] It is the sum of the uses of precedents, to a live nation, that it shall match the same with better from its own soul, and consume them before its audacious improvisations. A nation cannot live on reminiscences: it can only live on influx. The English Language, expressing the genius of the English race and its culture history, thought, is still inadequate to the utterance of America, and must

take on new proportions before it can become the living garment of this new life of humanity.

The future expansions of the English Language in America are already marked in the great lines of development this idiom shows. It is for us freely to follow the divine indications. And here a spinal fact is the composite character of our language: to what new realizations is it lifted in America! The immense diversity of race, temperament, character—the copious streams of humanity constantly flowing hither—must reappear in free, rich growths of speech. From no one ethnic source is America sprung: the electric reciprocations of many stocks conspired and conspire. This opulence of race-elements is in the theory of America. Land of the Ensemble, to her the consenting currents flow, and the ethnology of the States draws the grand outline of that hospitality and reception that must mark the new politics, sociology, literature and religion.

[289] Language, too, must feel this influence. And this is to appear not merely in the copious new verbal contributions the various idioms may bring, but in the entire spirit of the Language—moulded more and more to a large hospitality and impartiality. The theory of English scholars and literateurs, for hundreds of years, has been the theory of repression. They have discouraged and cramped the spontaneous expansions of the Language—discouraged inoculations from the French, from Latin, Greek, Italian. What pitiful cant, too, does one hear every day about Saxon! as though it were not the very theory of the English Language—the very genius and animus of it—to take its food from all sources! This ridiculous nonsense is to be utterly dismissed.

What starvation has this insane purism effected! What a poor, indigent, watery affair is our literary expression! Books cling to the old traditions and timidities—no full, free, utterance, untrammeled, mystical: no influx, no abandonment. Surely the time has come to dismiss this old impotence. And what means arise for enriching the arsenal of expression! What new creations surge and swell the ampler currents of our time! New thoughts, new things, all unnamed! Where is the theory of literary expression that stands for the new politics and soci[290]ology? that puts itself abreast the vast divine tendencies of Science, that absorbs the superb suggestions of the Grand Opera?

I can see but one limitation to the theory of Words—the theory of Things. Is it for us who are borne on the billowy tides of this new humanity to limit the unfolding opulence of God—to put a girdle round the widening future of our civilization and our speech? Freely, then, may the American literat proceed to quarry and build in the architecture of the English Language. Of course the conditions of this free expressive activity are high. To him who would mould our language must go many qualities—must go large knowledge of the philosophy of speech, must go rich aesthetic instincts, among the rest.

The sources of future enrichings of the Anglican speech, are the same old fountains. In our native roots, in the plastic forms of the antique, in the noble modern idioms are the magazines of word-wealth. How much has the French language been to English! How much has it yet to give! Nation of sublime destinies, noble, naïve, rich with humanity, bearers of freedom, upholding on her shoulders the history of Europe for a thousand years! The Italian gifts, too, direct and indirect, are not nothing to America. Spain is not nothing. How much they have to con[291]tribute—Italy with her rich and rosy nature, her grand style of music and consummate intuitions of art; Spain, so noble, so proud, so much to manners, to behavior! I would not underrate the German and Scandinavian influences—mighty race, spiritual, aspiring, individual, melancholy, prudent.

The flower and aroma of a Nation is its Language. The conditions of a grand language are a grand life. For words are metaphysical beings, and draw of the life of the mind. Not in these wondrous hieroglyphs of Words, not in these mystic runes, is the power: in the Mind which loads these airy messengers with burdens of meaning is the vis and vivification of speech. Over the transformations of a Language the genius of a nation unconsciously presides—the issues of Words represent issues in the national thought. And in the vernal seasons of a nation's life the formative energy puts forth verbal growths opulent as flowers in spring.

Names the Niam-Niams.

Manuscript in Yale. Inscribed in black pencil on leaf cut from pocket notebook, margin at the bottom, 5¾″ x 4″. Blue rules ¼″ apart. The names in pencil are in the writing of the 1850s; the address in ink in a later hand.

names
the Niam-Niams,[1] the Baltas[2] the[3] the[4] Tonga-Taboos, the Quichuas, ([5]ancient Peruvians)[6] or the Aleuts of our own[7] far north-west

John P. Soule[8] photographer & publisher 338 Washington/Boston

1. A Central African tribe.
2. Not identifiable.
3. Deleted: "and"
4. Deleted: "the"
5. Deleted: "or"
6. Deleted: "or"
7. Deleted: "N"
8. A John P. Soul is listed as a photographer at 130 Tremont St. in the Boston Directory of 1861. No Soul or Soule is mentioned in *Corr.* or *DN.*

Names or Terms.

Manuscript in LC (#73, sheet #478). Inscribed in black pencil on white wove scrap. Blue rules 5/16" apart. The writing suggests a date in the 1850s. WW also complains of this error in *DN,* III, 709.

Names or terms[1] get helplessly misapplied & wrench'd from their meanings—sometimes a great mistake is perpetuated in a word, (as the term calling the American aborigines *Indians*—the mistake is rectified but the word remains[2]

1. Original opening deleted: "Words" ; inserted above: "Names or terms"
2. Deleted in ink: " 'Wed'[?]"

Words the Origination.

Manuscript in Virginia (Barrett). Inscribed in black ink on blue Williamsburgh tax blank, 7⅛" x 4⅜". Possibly a note omitted from *Rambles among Words* or *An American Primer*. This was written between 1857 and 1860.

words[1]

The origination and continuance of[2] metre, and of rhyme afterward, are were[3] not only from their pleasantness to the barbaric ear, but more[4] from their infinite convenience[5] to the memory, in[6] arresting, & retaining tales & recitations & passing[7] along what they tell from person to person,[8] generation[9] after generation,—preserving[10] the epic song or[11] ballad[12] ages and ages, as was often done in old times,[13] without the aid of writing or print.—

1. In black pencil at upper right, set off by a loop from side to side below.
2. Deleted: "rhyme, or of"
3. Written above "are" in pencil.
4. Inserted above wordspace between "but" and "from"
5. Deleted: "in"
6. Deleted: "continuing" ; inserted in pencil: "arresting & [*del.*] holding returning" above "in" and "[*del.*] continuing" ; inserted on next line: "tales & recitations &" above "passing"
7. Deleted: "on" ; inserted above: "along"
8. Deleted: "and from"
9. Deleted: "to" ; inserted above: "after"
10. Deleted: "the" ; inserted and deleted: "as war after" above "preserving [*del.*] the"
11. Inserted and deleted: "ballad" above "and"
12. Preceding dash and six words inserted on a line above "ages . . . without" and line noted below.
13. Preceding seven words and comma inserted above "without"

The Western Boatmen.

Manuscript in LC (#73, sheet #462). Inscribed in black ink on white laid scrap. *OED* gives the term as an American colloquialism with earliest citation in 1879. The writing, which is quite firm, and the reference to boatmen in the present tense suggest a date possibly in the late 1850s or early 1860s.

The western boatmen have a slang phrase[1] He'll They'll It'll ? Will it Doubtfull if it'll [:][2] do to tie to.

1. Following terms in column. Deleted: "Hei"
2. Brace.

N Y World.

Manuscript in LC (#73, sheet #445). Inscribed in black ink on white laid scrap. Blue rules ½″ apart. The date is January 23, 1874.

N Y World Jan. 23 '74

In the British Islands the English language is spoken in[1] about sixty dialects & written in That of Hertforeshire is the best literary common English

1. Inserted and deleted: [*illeg.*] above "in"

Coffee from Kaffa.

Manuscript in LC (#73, sheet #518). Inscribed in black pencil on white wove scrap. The first two entries are placed irregularly one before the other. *"Words"* is scrawled at the foot of the page. With it is a clipping of an editorial from the Philadelphia *Public Ledger and Daily Transcript* of February 19, 1874, on "Dictionaries." *DAS* and *DA* give "moke" only as meaning "negro," with first citation in 1856. The date is February 1874 or after.

Coffee from *Kaffa* a region
of Abyssiynia
the coffee plant grows wild.

Mocha, the seaport town
of Yemen, arabia,
—"Moke"

Words —Right in the Midst.

Manuscript in LC (#63, sheet #305). Inscribed in pencil on white laid scrap. Blue rules ½″ apart. The date is 1874 or 1875.

Words

words[1]

—Right in the midst of 1874–5, in the midst of the whirling & current scenes of New York[2] life, a leading daily journal,[3] to give a desperate cut at some scheme proposed in Congress consigns it "to the tombs of the Capulets." In fact the names of the papers the Tribune, the Herald, the Mercury, &c &c

1. At upper right.
2. Deleted: "streets &"
3. Deleted: "and"

Deathsman.

Manuscript in LC (#73, sheet #449). Inscribed in columns in black ink and black pencil on gray wove scrap. Accompanied by a small clipping on Parisian slang (LC #449A). The date is after 1875 or 1876, the year in which WW wrote Sweeten's name in his address book ("D. W. Wilder").

deathsman[1] i.e. executioner, scatterling[2] (idle, improvident person—vagabond) moonling—(lunatic) yland, for island (words[3]
Andrew Sweeten, Expressman, 30, blonde, 3907 Haverford[4]

1. Word in ink partly torn off. Written in below in black pencil by WW.
2. Word in ink partly torn off. Written below in black pencil by WW.
3. Written with a heavier pen.
4. Black pencil. In column in black pencil: "168 [x] 3 [=] 504."

Names Jan 20 '78.

Manuscript in LC (#73, sheet #431). Inscribed in black ink on scrap of white note-paper. On verso is the beginning of an undated letter in another hand. The date is January 20, 1878.

Names

Jan 20 '78—(telegraphic)—H M Stanley, the African explorer, at a great banquet to him in Paris, proposes that the great river Congo should be called *Livingstone*—(Bad—bad)

Words Names.

Manuscript in LC (#73, sheet #476). Inscribed in black ink on white wove scrap, approx. 6″ x 3″. Blue rules ⅜″ apart.

words[1] *Names*

Some one should authoritatively re-name the mountains (? by act of Congress)/ The great[2] rivers & many of the smaller[3] are saved to us by—Majestic & musical names—Monongahela Alabama
"Dakota" is right "the proud & vengeful Dakota warriors")

1. Written at upper left.
2. Deleted: "& many of"
3. Preceding five words inserted above "are saved to"

Go into the Subject.

Manuscript in LC (#73, sheets #457, 457A). Inscribed in black ink and blue crayon on white wove scraps. [457] has blue rules ⅜″ apart. On same leaf as "this[?] has made." The somewhat ragged writing suggests a date after 1873.

go into the Subject at once.[1]

About Names?

Some gossip about Names [2]

Out of[3] such thoughts,[4] I am going to[5] gossip with thee, Reader, about[6] names—that is,[7] indeed, about LANGUAGE. [*457A*][8] In a[9] philosophic sense all words, all in the dictionary,[10] are names:[11]—but we will,[12] restrict the use of the term a good deal, in this gossip.

1. In blue crayon.
2. In blue crayon.
3. Deleted: "these" ; inserted above: "such"
4. Preceding four words inserted above "I am going"
5. Deleted: "write in a free strain" ; inserted above: "gossip with thee, Reader,"
6. Deleted: "Names" ; inserted above: "names" ; deleted: "—that is about Words"
7. Deleted: "in fact" ; inserted above: "indeed"
8. LC sheet number.
9. Deleted: "phil"
10. Preceding four words and comma inserted above "all words, are" and "na" in "names"
11. Deleted: "and"
12. Inserted and deleted: "in this gossip" above "restrict"

? Divide into Two.

Manuscript in LC (#73, sheet #436). Inscribed in red ink, black ink, purple crayon and black pencil on white wove scrap. Entries are written one after the other down the page. The repetition of titles from related MS, the placing of entries, and differences in writing and in writing materials suggest that this MS was perhaps a cover sheet for other similar scraps and that WW made entries at various dates in the early 1880s. See "Slang in America" (1885), *NB, Prose* 92, 572–577.

? divide into two articles / —"Words, words, words." & Names & Slang in America[1] / Words /[2] Two budgets [?] /[3] Words & Names & Slang[4] *Names and Slang in America* /[5] ? or reverse it *Slang and Names in America*[6]

1. Preceding thirteen words in red ink at top left in small writing.
2. Both slashes and "Words" in larger hand at angle midway across leaf.
3. In red ink at angle across leaf. The queried word is probably blotted rather than deleted.
4. In red ink at angle across leaf.
5. Large writing in black ink in two lines as a title. Probably the original entry.
6. Preceding eight words and question mark in purple crayon.

(Colorado.

Manuscript in LC (#73, sheet #459). Inscribed in black pencil on tan wove scrap. The last three words are in a smaller hand and may have been written later than what precedes. The date cannot be determined.

(Colorado[1]

"Long's Gray's & Pike's peak for three of the most beautiful & majestic mountains in the world" Letter from Colorado

1. Title at right with loop at left.

Laconic New Yorkers.

Manuscript in LC (#73, sheet #451). Inscribed in black ink on white wove scrap. The NYC "L" or "El" system was built between 1870 and 1878. *DA* gives 1879 for its earliest citation. The date must be in the late 1870s or before November, 1885.

laconic New Yorkers call the Elevated Railroad "the L"

Bonanza.

Manuscript in Texas (Hanley). Inscribed in pencil on white wove scrap. WW simply translates the Spanish *bonanza* and is apparently not familiar with the American Spanish or derived American English meanings. I am informed that he blends the Spanish noun, *borra,* which has the figurative meaning of "useless words," and the third person singular present of the verb *borrar,* "to rub out." The *DAE* cites "bonanza" as early as 1844, but most citations in all English senses are from the 1880s. No date can be assigned.

bonanza ie goodness *borra* i e (literally *useless words*) (or *rub out*) the reverse of bonanza

Words "Blizzard."

Manuscript in LC (#73, sheet #433R). Inscribed in black ink on white wove paper. With it is a clipping of an anecdote about a Bedouin. On verso is part of a letter to WW dated March 12, 1879. *OED* gives "quiz" as an Americanism, with the first citation dated 1886. Not in *DA*. No date can be assigned, other than before November, 1885.

words

"quizzed"—as soon as the[1] members-elect arrived they were taken to the candidates' head quarters,[2] consulted as to their wishes for committee-chairmen, & quizzed about their choice of Speaker (i.e. cross-questioned,[3] pumped, argued with)

1. Deleted: "new"
2. Deleted: "and"
3. Deleted: "and"

About Names.

Manuscript in LC (#73, sheet #461R). Inscribed in black ink on inside back of a white envelope. Date of postmark illegible. The MS probably was written between 1879 and 1885.

about Names/

The papers Andrews's *American Queen* a weekly N Y.[1] The Herald Tribune

1. A weekly magazine of "art, music, literature and society," which was founded in 1879, became simply *American Queen* in 1882 and in 1885 became the notorious *Town Topics*.

Then the New Word.

Manuscript in LC (#73, sheet #472). Inscribed in black ink on brown wove scrap. With the MS is an unidentified newspaper clipping (sheet #472A) giving a Dakota man's definition of a blizzard. The origin of the word is unknown (although it may not be American), but it seems to have come into general use in this sense in 1880 or 1881, as WW remarks. See also "Words 'blizzard.' " The date is spring or later in 1881 and before November, 1885.

Then the new word,[1] *blizzard,* quite settled by[2] the late furiously storming[3] winter of 1880–'81.

1. Deleted: "q"
2. Deleted: "this [*illeg.*]" ; inserted: "the late"
3. Deleted: "just past"

Words "Blizzard."

Manuscript in LC (#73, sheet #466R). Inscribed in black ink with hanging indentation on white wove scrap. On verso indecipherable fragment of WW's writing, possibly relating to a payment of $30 for a column. See "Then the new word." The date is probably after the winter of 1880 and before November, 1885.

Words

"blizzard" a furious, freezing, gale, perhaps snow,[1] hail, or half-[2]congeal'd rain, arctic[3] circumstances & materials[4] with the demoniac spirit of the tropics

1. Deleted: "and"
2. Deleted: "frozen" ; inserted above: "congeal'd"
3. Deleted: "[*illeg.*] surround"
4. Preceding two words inserted above "tances" in "circumstances"

?For Beginning.

Manuscript in LC (#73, sheet #475). Inscribed in black ink and black pencil on two pasted-up scraps: the top is written on the inside of a stamped envelope of a variety used between 1874 and 1886; the lower with a letter on verso dated January 22, 1881. The notion of language as America's mightiest inheritance is one which WW had expressed three times in something of the same language in the 1850s: "America's Mightiest Inheritance," *Life Illustrated* (April 12, 1856), *NYD*, 55–65, "Our Language, and Future & Literature," Notebook #12, *DN*, III, 809–811, and passages contributed to William Swinton's *Rambles Among Words* (NY, 1859), 12, 286ff. (See *"Rambles Among Words,"* p. 1628). The date is between 1881 and November, 1885.

? for beginning or ? for conclusion

By far the most precious inheritance of our[1] America is the English[2] tongue. I should[3] say that without it—certainly without a[4] uniform spoken and written dialect,[5] elastic, tough and eligible to all, and fluid and enfolding as air—,[6]—the Liberty and Union of these Thirty Eight or Forty States, representing so many diverse[7] origins and breeds[8] would not be practicable. (Conclusion[9]

For[10] the chief and indispensable condition a[11] political union such as ours[12] and (only to be firmly knit and [*illeg.*] preserved, by a general interpenetration and community of social and personal[13] standards, religious beliefs and[14] litera-

1. Inserted in black pencil above "of"

2. Deleted: "l"

3. End of line at right. In space which would normally be occupied by the next line is the deleted "the idea that over"

4. Deleted: "common" "do" ; inserted: "uniform" above "[*del.*] common" ; inserted in pencil, deleted in ink: [*illeg.*]

5. Inserted: "[*del.*] and tough and" above "and . . . eligible"

6. Preceding eleven words inserted above "and written . . . Liberty"

7. Inserted in black ink above "es" in "States"

8. Preceding seven words inserted in pencil (and ink, see *n*7 above) above "Forty . . . not"

9. Written at right end of line. End of first scrap.

10. Deleted: "if"

11. The left edge of the second scrap has been torn off irregularly, damaging the text. Inserted: "a" ; inserted and deleted: "the" before "political"

12. Deleted: "of the United States" ; inserted: "and" above "[*del.*] of"

13. Preceding two words inserted above "social" and "stan" in "standards"

14. Inserted above wordspace between "beliefs" and "literature"

ture, essentially the same,)[15] is a copious and [*illeg.*] uniform language,[16] embodying principles of growth, change, and sloughing [*illeg.*][17]

15. Deleted in black ink: "and accepted personal standards all[?] making the pedestal" "the" "a [*illeg.*] different" ; inserted in black ink: "essentially the same,)" "is" "copious and [*illeg.*] uniform"

16. Period probably emended to comma. Inserted and deleted in black ink: "with"

17. Preceding seven words inserted above "language"

With Arriere-Threads.

Manuscript in LC (#73, sheet #474). Inscribed in black ink and purple crayon on recto of letter dated March 27, possibly in the same handwriting as that on the envelope used for "(? Conclusion." This text is the final version of the last lines of that MS. This was written in 1881.

with arriere-threads to all pre-history;[1] and though[2] but breaths and vibrations of the invisible air more[3] freely[4] weld[5] the inhabitants of New York Chicago, San Franciso and New Orleans to[6] the vanished peoples[7] retrospects of the past—to a hundred unknown nations[8]—than could all the steel and iron of the globe

1. Preceding six words in black ink. Succeeding in purple crayon.
2. Deleted: "more" ; inserted above: "but"
3. "more" inserted in ink above "air"
4. Inserted in crayon above "we" in "weld"
5. Deleted: "ing"
6. Deleted in ink: "all the [*illeg.*]" ; inserted and deleted in ink above the illegible deletion: "all" ; inserted in ink: "the" above "va" in "vanished"
7. Deleted in ink: "of" ; inserted in ink and deleted: "all the" above "[*del.*] of" and "the" ; inserted in ink: "retrospects of" above "the past" . Period deleted in crayon.
8. Inserted and deleted in crayon: "—more" above "than"

(? Conclusion.

Manuscript in LC (#73, sheets #454 and 455). Inscribed in black ink with black pencil emendations on the inside of a split-open envelope [454], addressed to WW at 431 Stevens St., and white wove scrap [455] pasted together. The last half dozen lines, not printed here, are a heavily revised draft of "with arriere-threads," cancelled with a purple ink slash. The date is 1881.

(? Conclusion[1]

And what a pregnant & far-reaching fact that quite[2] every[3] sentence we articulate[4] with our voices, and every type-line[5] worked off from[6] the printing[7] presses[8], here, to-day, 1881 by the Hudson, the Arkansas, the Tennessee or the Rio Grande,[9] retains[10] subtle,[11] living, entirely unbroken chains of[12] succession back through the Middle Ages, the Gothic and Osmanlic incursions, the Roman sway, Greece,[13] Judah, India, Egypt the Aryan mists

1. In pencil at right. Deleted: "It is a profound consideration" ; "I" not deleted, not printed; inserted in ink: "And what a pregnant & far-reaching"

2. Inserted in pencil.

3. Deleted in pencil: "word" ; inserted in pencil above: "sentence"

4. Deleted in pencil: "by" ; inserted in pencil: "with" above "by"

5. Inserted in pencil and deleted: "turned off" above "line" and "fr" in "from" ; in black ink over pencil: "written" "worked off"

6. Deleted in ink: "the" ; inserted and deleted in ink above: "our" ; inserted in ink following: "the"

7. Inserted in ink above vacant space before "presses"

8. Added: "es"

9. Inserted in pencil and deleted: [*illeg.*] above "nde" in "Grande" and "holds"

10. Deleted in ink: "sure" ; inserted above in ink: "subtle"

11. Deleted in pencil: "and" ; inserted above in pencil: "living" . Deleted in ink: "[*illeg.*] threads" ; inserted above in ink: "unbroken chains" . Deleted in pencil: "& chains"

12. Half the line left empty. End of [454]. Deleted in ink: "of succession" ; inserted and deleted in ink: "and retrospect and trace," above "[*del.*] of succession" and "back" ; inserted in ink: "of succession" above "[*del.*] retrospect"

13. Deleted in ink: "& Judea, Egypt" ; inserted in ink: "Judah, India, Egypt [*del. in ink*] India the Aryan myth" . Purple-ink line across page separates text from cancelled portion, which is almost entirely illegible.

Words.

Manuscript in LC (#73, sheet #432). Inscribed in black ink with black pencil emendations. On verso fragment of letter from Frank H. Parsons which mentions quotations for producing a half-morocco, gilt-top *LG*. According to Carolyn Wells and Alfred F. Goldsmith, *A Concise Bibliography* . . . (Boston, 1922), *LG* was so issued in 1882 and 1891 and 1892. The date of the MS is probably after 1882 and before November, 1885.

Words

As a suggestion how words grow[1] & how far back, and how different, the original forms of those[2] we now use, there was the old[3] Saxon hlafdig, (female giver or distributor of bread,)[4] gradually evoluted into our present[5] word *lady*.

1. Deleted: "or develope,"
2. Deleted: "words we no" "terms is"
3. Deleted: "word"; inserted and deleted above: "name"; inserted in black pencil: "Saxon" above "hla" in "hlafdig"
4. Deleted: "now turned into"; inserted in pencil: "gradually" above "w" in "[*del.*] now" and "turned"
5. Inserted above "ur" in "our" and "wo" in "word"

How Much There Is.

Manuscript in LC (#73, sheet #458). Inscribed in black ink on scrap from inside of a blue envelope postmarked November 27, 1883.

How much there is in men's and women's common names—(See Dictionary)

(For Name?.

Manuscript in LC (#73, sheet #434). Inscribed in black ink on inside of scrap of envelope from Insane Asylum, London, Ont., postmarked May, 1883.

(for name?[1] ? "Words, Words, Words"

1. Above and at left margin. The following is indented.

Among French Convicts.

Manuscript in LC (#73, sheet #473R). Inscribed in black ink on white wove scrap, 5⅛″ x 3⅞″. Blue rules ⅜″ apart. Since the verso is a draft for "With Husky-Haughty Lips, O Sea!" (see "Viccissini Sav"), the date must be about 1884.

Among French convicts the name of the guillotine is always "the widow"

? Or Names.

Manuscript in LC (#73, sheet #435). Inscribed in purple crayon on inside of envelope postmarked May (?), 1884. The entries are in column down the page. See "Slang in America," *Prose 92,* II, 572–577.

? or *Names* simply or Names in America for 2d article Slang for 1st

(Slang Words).

Manuscript in LC (#73, sheet #430). Inscribed in purple crayon on white wove scrap. On verso letter dated March 7, 1884. *DAS* gives no date for its citation; *DA* does not list it. The date is March, 1884, or later.

(slang words)

Brevity is a leading[1] [*illeg.*] requisite[2]

In Salt Lake City the gigantic ware house formally named "Zion's Cooperative Mercantile Institution" is shorten'd into "the Co-op store."

1. Deleted: "The" ; inserted above: "Brevity is a" . Inserted below preceding and deleted: "great feature" ; inserted below: "leading [*illeg.*] requisite" ; lowercase "is" capitalized.

2. Entire sentence inserted at left of title.

Southern Gen. Bee.

Manuscript in LC (#73, sheet #469). Inscribed on faded white wove scrap in purple crayon, except for last entry, which is in black ink. On verso is the following deleted sentence in purple crayon: "The old issues are settled for good and an entirely new one now brought forward to be met." The anecdote is from P. G. T. Beauregard, "The Battle of Bull Run," *Century,* N.S. 8 (November, 1884), 96. The date is late 1884.

Southern Gen. Bee, in a critical moment at first Bull-Run said to Gen. Beauregard, *Look at Jacksons* brigade; it stands there like a[1] *stone wall* Century Nov. '84/ (how names come)

1. Deleted: "*stone*"

Names of Races.

Manuscript in LC (#73, sheet #467). Inscribed in pencil on white scrap of paper from commercially manufactured notebook. Upper left corner rounded. Blue rules ¼″ apart. No date can be assigned other than before November, 1885.

Names

Of[1] races, places,[2] countries much of the essence of their History, often the subtlest part,[3] is in their Names. Instance the classic[4] peoples, the Orientals, our own West

1. Deleted: "persons or" ; inserted: "races," above "sons" in "[*del.*] persons"
2. Inserted above "ces" in "places" . Deleted: "the" ; inserted: "much of the" above "essence"
3. Preceding four words and comma inserted above "History"
4. Deleted: "countries"

A Good New Word.

Manuscript in LC (#73, #468). Inscribed in black ink on white wove scrap. Blue rules ⅜" apart. *OED* gives citations from 1839, 1863, and 1883 in the religious sense. The secular sense of one who takes part in a celebration is not recognized by *OED, Century, OED Supplement* (1972) or *Webster's New International,* 2d ed. (1929). It is in the 3d edition (1966). The writing suggests a late date, before November, 1885.

a good new word, viz: *celebrant*

The Full History.

Manuscript in LC (#73, sheet #470). Inscribed in black ink on the lower of two pasted-up, white, wove scraps, the top scrap being the inside of an undateable envelope addressed to WW by Dr. Bucke. No date can be assigned other than before November, 1885.

The[1] full history of[2] Names[3] would be the total of human, and all other history.

1. Inserted above wordspace and deleted: "total" ; inserted above deletion: "full"
2. Deleted: "Words" ; inserted above: "Names"
3. Deleted: "is" ; inserted above and in right margin: "would be"

List of Serviceable.

Manuscript in LC (#73, sheet #471). Inscribed in black ink on white wove scrap. First sentence in hanging indentation; words in column below at left margin. *OED* gives fairly regular citations for "surveillance" from 1799 and for "prestige," in the sense of fame or authority, from 1815. The writing suggests a late date, probably before November, 1885.

List of serviceable[1] words from the French coming into more or less use, by modern years. Surveillance prestige

1. Inserted above "of words"

? Conclusion Sentence.

Manuscript in LC (#73, sheet #465). Inscribed in black ink on white wove scrap. No date can be assigned other than before November, 1885.

? conclusion sentence[1]

The whole[2] osseous[3] muscular and fleshy structure[4] of language is its Names, (nouns) and the Verbs are[5] its blood and[6] circulation.[7]

1. Blue crayon at upper left.
2. Inserted above "os" in "osseous"
3. Preceding three words inserted on an arrow.
4. Inserted and deleted: "muscles & flesh" above "structure of"
5. Preceding three words inserted above "and its" and "bl" in "blood"
6. Deleted: "dynamic be"
7. Deleted: "Struct[?]"

I Shall Treat.

Manuscript in LC (#73, sheet #464). Inscribed in black ink on scrap of ledger paper. On verso various single and double vertical red rules and printed words "Dear Sir:" Clipped-off words are visible at the bottom. No date can be assigned other than before November, 1885.

I shall treat[1] names as the essence and[2] last representive crystallization[3] perhaps *of civilization,* certainly of language. Briefly,[4] they *are* language; for every thing else both[5] concentrates there, and radiates thence again, [*illeg.*]

1. Deleted in black ink at beginning of paragraph: "It will be seen that I treat" ; inserted in purple crayon: "I shall treat" above "[*del.*] that I treat"
2. Deleted and reinserted above in black ink: "last"
3. Inserted: "perhaps [*illeg. del.*] *of civilization,* certainly" above "tallization" in "crystallization" and "of language" and "B" in "Briefly"
4. Deleted: "it is" ; inserted above: "they *are*"
5. Inserted above "else" . WW did not correct the singular form of the following verbs.

(For Words).

Manuscript in LC (#73, sheet #463). Inscribed in black ink and purple crayon on white wove paper, 8¼" x 5½". Blue rules ¼" apart. The writing and content indicate a date before November, 1885.

(for Words[1])

Every principal word ? name[2] in[3] our language is a condensed octavo volume, or many volumes[4] The word *Jehovah*[5] weaves the[6] meaning of the past, present and future tenses—personalizes[7] Time, as it was, is and ever shall be

The word[8] name[9] Buddha[10]—*Intelligence*

? the word Homer[11] i.e. compiler Editor

1. Loop at left.
2. "? name" inserted above as possible alternate.
3. Deleted: [*illeg.*]
4. Preceding sentence in blue crayon, small writing jammed between title and first line in black ink.
5. Deleted: "is woven of" ; inserted above: "weaves"
6. Deleted: "mean"
7. Deleted: underscore under "personalizes"
8. Inserted and deleted in black ink: "name" above "word"
9. Inserted in purple crayon above "[*del.*] name" as possible alternate.
10. Deleted: underscore under "Buddha" ; deleted: "Intell" . Preceding redundant dash not deleted, not noted.
11. Deleted: underscore under "compiler"

Then We Can Often.

Manuscript in LC (#73, sheet #460). Inscribed in black ink on faded scrap of white ledger paper, 3¾" x 5¾". "words" is deleted under the second line of the MS. *OED* cites examples of "to wire" from 1859 to 1891. The writing suggests a late date, before November, 1885.

Then we can often decide absolutely[1] the date of[2] an event (at least in what era, it did *not* occur) by some word used.[3]

In 1878 the officers of New Orleans, acknowledging a large sum of money received[4] for the relief of the Yellow Fever sufferers, briefly add that if farther aid is needed, "we will *wire* Philadelphia"—that is, they will send word over the telegraph wires.

1. Deleted: [*illeg.*]
2. Deleted: "since" ; inserted above: "an"
3. Sentence crammed in at top over deleted "(words" and "In 1878 . . . New Orleans,"
4. Deleted: "from"

Among Workers.

Manuscript in LC (#73, sheet #450). Inscribed in black ink on scrap of bill. First entry with hanging indentation. *DAS* does not record either italicized term. No date can be assigned other than before November, 1885.

among workers in glass-factories the the word is *di* for diamond/
among railroad men *loky* for locomotive

A Good Word.

Manuscript in LC (#73, sheet #477). Inscribed in black ink on white wove scrap. *OED* records "verve" as in general use after about 1870. Not in *DAE* or *DA*. Eby's *Concordance* does not list the word. No date can be assigned other than probably before November, 1885.

a good word—*use it*

VERVE—(pron. just like *verse*)

Fr. Excitement of imagination such as animates a poet, artist, or musician, in composing or performing—rapture, enthusiasm spirit, energy

Zeus.

Manuscript in LC (#73, sheet #448). Inscribed in black ink on white laid scrap. On verso, end of an unidentified fragment of a letter by WW which speaks of his being laid up. The writing indicates a late date, before November, 1885.

Zeus[1] is quite certainly from a Sanscrit word meaning the sky

1. False start deleted: "Deus or"

For Words.

Manuscript in LC (#73, sheet #447). Inscribed in black ink on notepaper, 9¼" x 6". Blue rules ⅜" apart. No date can be assigned other than before November, 1885.

for Words[1]

for the true lexicographer is not merely the "harmless drudge" Johnson defines him to be, as[2] any more than[3] general collection of words with their[4] definitions and pronunciations achieves the true Dictionary

1. Deleted paragraph: "for the true Dictionary is not merely a collection of words with the [*illeg.*]" . Space for four or five lines follows.

2. Deleted: "any more than the true Dictionary"

3. Deleted: "a full"

4. Deleted: "meanings"

Words. as of a Flute-Player.

Manuscript in LC (#73, sheet #446). Inscribed in black ink on white wove scrap. WW had listed *"embouchure"* among interesting French words in a notebook which must date before 1855 (Notebook 15, *DN,* III, 823), but the date of this MS is probably before November, 1885.

Words.

as of a flute-player "he has a good *embouchure*" (ang-boo-shúr) emeute (ā-mūte)

Names Jackaroo.

Manuscript in LC (#73, sheet #444). Inscribed in blue pencil on tan laid paper, approx. 4⅛" x 4⅞". Hanging indentation. *OED* gives a date of 1880 for its first citation for "jackaroo"; *DA* cites uses of "tenderfoot" in a Western context from 1849. The blue crayon suggests a late date, before November, 1885.

Names

Jackaroo—a (young) new comer in Australia

Tender-Foot—a new comer at Leadville, (or in the mines of Colorado any how)

Names "Chippewa."

Manuscript in LC (#73, sheet #443). Inscribed in black ink on scrap of white wove paper, 7" x 4 3/16". Blue rules 3/8" apart. The meaning of "new n.w. Territory" is not clear, for at no time in WW's maturity could the North West Territory have been called "new." The Chippewas, however, were native to that region, where they still live, and their name would have been inappropriate further west in the northern plains states. No date can be assigned other than before November, 1885.

Names
"Chippewa" is the best name for the new n.w. Territory/

"Wyoming" is an inappropriate name doesn't belong out there at all

"Idaho" (gem of the mountains) is not a very appropriate name.—would have been better, applied to Colorado./

The great western mountain peaks (Colorado) three or four of them, (as Pikes Peak) among the grandest in the world, are seriously injured by vulgar names

All These Are Supplied.

Manuscript in LC (#73, sheets #438, 439, 440). Inscribed in black ink on two scraps, [*438*] the inside of a blue envelope originally pasted close to [*439*] as a backing-sheet. Although it is incoherent, WW evidently meant it to be a sequence. The insert from [*439*] perhaps belongs elsewhere. The writing, however, is of his later years, probably before November, 1885.

[*438R*] All these are supplied by the mighty[1] English tongue.[2] It[3] would almost seem[4] to be some heaven-designed miracle, the slow process-[5]growth of[6] thousands of[7] years, in the Eastern Hemisphere,[8] brought slowly on[9] and wafted to these shores, for our special purposes[10] to-day & all coming days. And for our union it is all in all.[11]

[*440R*] More the[12] old Confederation, or[13] Constitution, with all its articles a[14] compulsorily[?] resistlessly averaging us,[15] Army and Navy, and all the[16] law courts. Swifter and vaster than[17] any electric[18] [*illeg.*] every square rod of[19] America's [*illeg.*][20] of her fifty million people [*439R*] or passive, quietly adapting itself to all opportunities, all phases & stages of Life.

1. Inserted after "the" in the right margin.
2. Inserted above "sh" in "English"
3. Deleted: "almost"
4. Inserted and deleted: [*illeg.*] ; deleted: "as a" ; inserted: "to be some" above "[*del.*] as a"
5. Inserted above "slow"
6. Deleted: "many"
7. Inserted: "of" above "y" in "years"
8. Preceding four words inserted above "ars" in "years" and "brought slowly"
9. Deleted: "to the"
10. Deleted: "in the United States"
11. Preceding sentence inserted above "coming days"
12. Deleted: "articles of" ; inserted: "old" above wordspace between the deleted words.
13. Right edge of leaf trimmed.
14. Right edge of leaf trimmed. Deleted: "Unifying and," ; inserted and deleted: [*illeg.*] above "Unif" in "[*del.*] Unifying" ; inserted above "ing" in "Unifying" and "and": "Compulsorily"
15. Inserted above "g" in "averaging"
16. Deleted: [*illeg.*]
17. Deleted: "electric" ; inserted: "any" above "ric" in "[*del.*] electric"
18. Right edge of leaf trimmed. Deleted: [*illeg.*]
19. Deleted: "N"
20. Right edge of leaf trimmed.

Names and Slang.

Manuscript in LC (#73, sheet #437). Inscribed in red ink, purple pencil, black ink, and black pencil on a white wove scrap. *DA* gives a citation for "old Hickory" as a nickname for Andrew Jackson as early as 1815. WW uses it in "Slang in America" (*Prose 92*, II, 575, l. 101). Since this is a trial title, it probably dates from a time close to November, 1885.

Names and[1] *Slang*[2] *in America*[3] Words[4] Language[5] "old Hickory"[6]

1. Preceding two words in red ink at left above *"Slang"*
2. Purple pencil deleted in red ink: *"and Names"*
3. Preceding three words in purple pencil.
4. Printed in black ink.
5. Printed in black ink.
6. Black pencil.

VII. American Writers.

Emerson Essays.

Manuscript in NYPL (Berg). Inscribed in black pencil with black ink additions on white wove paper, 10⅛″ x 8″. Blue rules on recto ¼″ apart. Writing does not follow rules.

Although we do not know when or how WW became acquainted with Emerson's writings or how close the acquaintance with his work was, it is obvious that an unorthodox young editor with literary ambitions, no matter how trite his work, would have been extremely dull not to have known a good deal about Emerson by the mid-1840s. As Stovall points out (*Foreground,* 285), although WW was teaching on Long Island when Emerson first lectured in New York in 1840, he was a journalist in New York when Emerson lectured there in 1841, 1842, and 1843. Horace Greeley, the famous editor of the *Tribune,* read the *Dial,* printed long reviews of Emerson's lectures and from 1844 to 1846 employed Margaret Fuller as a critic. WW himself wrote for the *Democratic Review,* which viewed the new trends with favor. Whether or not he reviewed Emerson's lecture of March 5, 1842, in the NY *Aurora,* he was writing for it. He was unquestionably familiar with and attracted to Emerson's ideas for some time before he wrote this MS or mentioned him in the *Eagle,* December 15, 1847. The clearest sign of his early enthusiasm is in "Pictures" (1854?): "and there, tall and slender, stands Ralph Waldo Emerson, of New England, at the lecturer's desk lecturing," and in 1857 he casually listed him along with Christ, Socrates, and the Bible in a note for a poem of "Wise Books" ("[*illeg.*] Dick Hunt"). In those early years he gladly hailed Emerson. His enthusiasm peaked, perhaps, when in 1864 he told J. T. Trowbridge that Emerson had brought his simmering to a boil.

By 1867, however, WW was willing to allow John Burroughs to state authoritatively in *Notes on Walt Whitman* that he had not read Emerson until 1856. The cooling is perhaps natural, if extreme. Emerson himself had become much more conventional in his thought, and WW had learned what he could from him. There also appear to have been troublemakers working on both men, and he bitterly resented Edward Emerson's derogatory footnote on his father's opinion of him in *Emerson in Concord* (1889). See Jerome Loving, *Emerson, Whitman, and the American Muse* (Chapel Hill, 1982). "Emerson's Books, (The Shadows of Them)" in 1880 was a genially destructive contribution to a festival issue of the *Boston Literary World,* but on his triumphant 1881 visit an invitation to visit the Emersons seems to have healed his wounds, real or imaginary. The present MS is enthusiastic, but it is worth noting that it expresses his persistent reservation: that Emerson was too bookish.

For references to Emerson, other than the MSS which follow, some significant only as indications of awareness, see "Ethnology," "George Walker," "[*illeg.*] Dick Hunt," "English runic," "American poets," "With the names," "Get Emerson's remarks," "His earliest printed plays," "Wealth of Poets," "The Bible Shakespere," "La Fayette," and "Dr. L. B. Russell." See also *Corr.,* I–IV, passim, *Prose 92,* passim, Traubel, passim. Critical and historical notes are in Shephard, *Walt Whitman's Prose* (NY, 1936) 199–106, 323–97, Moore John B., "The Master of Whitman, *SP,* 23 (January, 1926), 77–99, Gohdes, Clarence, "Whitman and Emerson" *SR,* 37 (January, 1929), 79–93. Stovall, *Foreground,* 282–305 and Loving, op. cit. First printed Stovall, ibid., 290.

Emerson

Essays—1st series—copyrighted 1847/

shrewd & wise reflections, tinged with the[1] library, smacking of Epictetus and[2] Marcus Antoninus and Montaigne and the[3] other old experts—largely[4] metaphysical, with[5] near or distant suspicions of[6] German Fichte and Schelling[7]—but Hegel[8] seems hardly to[9] appear[10] at all;[11] pentiful flowing rivulets of fine thought[12] epigrammatic expressions of the first water,[13] on Self-Reliance,[14] the Over-Soul Compensation, (these[15] are perhaps[16] the best,)[17] Spiritual laws, Heroism, Intellect, and Art. Those on Friendship and Love are[18] the least good[19] in the volume.[20] Indeed pure[21] gold, nay diamonds themselves, may be found in nuggets & first class gems[22] the Volume, and not stingily bestowed.[23]

What can be[24] superber than the portrait[25] of[26] that curious and baffling element of Character we may call *soul-greatness,* eligible[27] to almost every man & woman,[28] high or low.

p 263—& 4 Essays fist series[29]

1. Deleted: "books," ; inserted above: "library,"
2. Deleted: "Mon"
3. Inserted above "o" in "other"
4. Preceding six words inserted above "igne" in "Montaigne" and "metaphysical"
5. Deleted: "dis"
6. Deleted: "the"
7. Deleted: parenthesis; inserted: "but" above "He" in "Hegel"
8. Deleted: "does not" ; inserted: "seems" above "[*del.*] not"
9. Inserted.
10. Final "s" deleted.
11. Deleted: "running"
12. Deleted: "and"
13. Preceding four words and comma inserted above "expressions on"
14. Uppercase "S" written over lowercase.
15. Inserted and deleted: "last two" above "perhaps" ; inserted: "are" following the deletion.
16. Deleted: "is"
17. Deleted: "of all.)"
18. Deleted: "less" ; inserted above: "the least"
19. Deleted: "of" ; inserted above: "in"
20. Parentheses deleted before and after preceding sentence. Inserted in black ink: "[*del.*] But Indeed" above "Pure"
21. Capital not reduced in MS.
22. Preceding five words inserted in black ink on two lines in the right margin following "in". Deleted: "these Essays" on the following line.
23. Preceding seventeen words written in two lines with deep indentation.
24. Deleted: "finer" ; inserted above: "superber"
25. "ure" deleted from "portraiture"
26. Deleted: "what" ; inserted: "that curious and baffling element of character" above the deletion and "we may call"
27. Inserted and deleted: "if they only knew it" above "to almost"
28. Deleted: [*illeg.*]
29. The reference is to "The Over-Soul," a paragraph beginning "This energy does not descend into individual life. . . ." (*Essays,* I [1847], Centenary Edition, [Boston, 1903], 289–290.)

The Superiority of Emerson's.

Manuscript not found. Text from *N&F,* 128–129 (Pt. II, #163; *CW,* IX, 159–160). Bucke says that it is written as a note to a clipping, which Stovall identifies as "New Poetry in New England," *Democratic Review* (May, 1847) (*Foreground,* 286; see also "Bells and Pomegranates.") The manuscript is not now with the clipping in Duke. The date is probably 1847 or thereabouts, but just possibly as late as 1855.

The superiority of Emerson's writing is in their character—they mean something. He may be obscure, but he is certain. Any other of the best American writers has in general a clearer style, has more of the received grace and ease, is less questioned and forbidden than he, makes a handsomer appearance in the society of the books, sells better, passes his time more apparently in the popular understanding; yet there is something in the solitary specimen of New England that outvies them all. He has what none else has; he does what none else does. He pierces the crusts that envelope the secrets of life. He joins on equal terms the few great sages and original seers. He represents the freeman, America, the individual. He represents the gentleman. No teacher or poet of old times or modern times has made a better report of manly and womanly qualities, heroism, chastity, temperance, friendship, fortitude. None has given more beautiful accounts of truth and justice. His words shed light to the best souls; they do not admit of argument. As a sprig from the pine tree or a glimpse anywhere into the daylight belittles all artificial flower work and all the painted scenery of theatres, so are live words in a book compared to cunningly composed words. A few among men (soon perhaps to become many) will enter easily into Emerson's meanings; by those he will be well-beloved. The flippant writer, the orthodox critic, the numbers of good or indifferent imitators, will not comprehend him; to them he will indeed be a transcendentalist, a writer of sunbeams and moonbeans, a strange and unapproachable person.

Of Emersons 1st Vol.

Manuscript in private collection. Inscribed in black pencil on two pieces of white wove paper pasted before inscription, totalling approx. 6¾" x 5". The writing suggests a date between 1860 and 1873. The thought suggests the later years of the period.

Of Emersons 1st vol

"Nature" & the Lectures

—nay of his own writings—

—[1] after all these thoughts & themes & statements,[2] good as they are, and welcome & appropriate to certain stages[3] and ages of developement[4]—a certain part of the journey of life & the intellect—[5] it is certain that we pass beyond them, & they become not only useless, but, rather an annoyance—while[6] Iliad & Odyssey, Psalm &[7] idyll of Job, and[8] Lear &[9] Hamlet and even the old ballads as in Walter Scotts Border Minstrelsy[10] return again & again,[11] unflagging unpalling[12] as the sight of mountains or the[13] breeze of the sea shore.[14] (over

[2] Too much intellection—which even his sweetness & manliness cannot make entirely satisfactory

1. Deleted: [*illeg.*]
2. Deleted: "subtle as"
3. Deleted: "of"
4. "v" written over "p" in "development" ; inserted: "—a" above dash before "Certain" ; uppercase "Certain" not reduced, not printed.
5. Deleted: [*illeg.*]
6. Deleted: "the Ill"
7. Deleted: "[*illeg.*] the [*illeg.*]"
8. Deleted: "Lear & P"
9. Deleted: "Richard 2d—yet return" ; inserted: "Hamlet" above "chard" in "[*del.*] Richard"
10. Preceding eleven words inserted above and to the right of "return" above "[*del.*] yet return"
11. Deleted: "unfl"
12. Inserted above "unflagging"
13. Deleted: "air" ; inserted: "breeze" above the deletion and "of"
14. Preceding seventeen words in five lines with irregular indentations.

Of Emerson.

Manuscript in LC (#59). Inscribed in black pencil on verso of a printed appeal from the United States Christian Commission. Dr. Sarah Ann Evans of Kansas City Metropolitan Junior College (Longview Campus) has pointed out that the commission moved to the address printed on the appeal January 28, 1863. WW joined the commission January 20. His feelings toward Emerson were probably particularly warm in January 1863, for Emerson had provided him with letters to Salmon P. Chase, W. H. Seward, and Charles Sumner. First printed in Edmund Wilson, ed. *The Shock of Recognition* (NY, 1949), I, 272.

of Emerson

his quality,—his meaning[1] has the quality of the[2] light of day, which startles nobody you cannot put your finger upon it, yet there is nothing[3] more palpable, nothing[4] more wonderful, nothing[5] more vital and refreshing. There are some things in the expressions of[6] this[7] philosoph, this poet, that are[8] full mates of the best, the perennial masters, & will so stand in fame,[9] the centuries &[10] America[11] in the future, in her own[12] long train of poets & writers[13] while knowing more vehement & luxuriant ones, will I think[14] acknowledge nothing[15] nearer this this[16] man, the actual[17] beginning of the whole[18] procession[19] & certainly nothing purer, clearer, sweeter, more canny, nor, after all, more thoroughly her own &[20] native.

1. Preceding two words inserted above "has the"
2. Deleted: "da"
3. Deleted: "grander" ; inserted: "more palpable" above the deletion and "nothing"
4. Deleted: "so" ; inserted above: "more"
5. Deleted: "so"
6. Preceding three words inserted above "this" and "[*del.*] con"
7. Deleted: "con"
8. Deleted: "certainly the"
9. Inserted: "[*del.*] & the centuries"
10. Deleted: "in"
11. Deleted: "will"
12. Inserted above "lo" in "long"
13. Preceding nine words inserted above "the future, while knows"
14. Preceding six words inserted above "ment" in "vehement" and "acknowledge nothing"
15. Deleted: "before"
16. Inserted: "nearer" above "[*del.*] before" and "this"
17. Inserted above and to the right of "this" over "be" in "beginning"
18. Inserted above "proc" in "processing"
19. Preceding seven words inserted above "& certainly nothing"
20. Preceding three words inserted above "ughly" in "thoroughly" and "n" in "native"

The most exquisite taste & caution[21] are in him, always[22] saving him[23] his feet from[24] passing beyond the limits; for he is transcendental[25] of limits, & you see underneath[26] the rest a secret[27] proclivity America may be, to dare & violate & make escapades.

21. Deleted: "is" ; inserted above: "are"
22. Inserted above "sav" in "saving"
23. Inserted: "his feet" above "him"
24. Deleted: "going" ; inserted above: "passing"
25. Inserted: "of [*del.*] to [*illeg. del.*] limits" above "ntal " in "transcendental" and "&"
26. Deleted: "also"
27. Deleted: "wish" ; inserted: "proclivity, [*del.*] nature [*ins.*] America may be" above the deletion and "to dare &"

Emerson.

Manuscript in LC (#79, #262). Inscribed in a column in black pencil on a cardboard scrap. On recto "Literature" in black ink, cancelled. On verso "Literature" in black ink. Probably a label for the miscellaneous items listed. The date must be about 1867.

Emerson Idaho—(Capt. Mullen)[1]
printed in New York in 1856[2] [:] To the Working Men &c[3]
on A simpler table ex from "Joubert"[4]
Sword-Calls[5] Freiligraths criticism[6]

1. Captain John Mullen. See "Idaho. Capt. Mullen's map." This entry indicates a date after 1863, when Mullen's map of a military road from Ft. Benton, Mont., to Walla Walla, Wash., was published.

2. Preceding six words in three lines to left of brace.

3. No trace has been found of this title. Could it refer to "The Eighteenth Presidency!"?

4. WW read Arnold's "Joubert" or extracts from it in 1864. See "with the fever of." Joubert, as Arnold describes him, was abstemious. He is not mentioned in WW's "A simpler system of the Table."

5. WW projected a poem of this title in 1863 or 1864. See "Sword Calls."

6. Freiligrath's critique was published in 1867. See "Add*resses*."

They Are Not Patriotic.

Manuscript in LC (Feinberg #734). Inscribed in black ink and red ink on white wove sheet, 10″ x 7⁹/16″. Letterhead of Department of Justice Office of the Solicitor of the Treasury, 187—. Blue rules ½″ apart. The derogatory remark about "abolitionism" deleted at the end suggests that WW had been warming over a prewar animosity, which he realized was anachronistic. The date is after 1870. Printed in facsimile in G. M. Williamson, *Catalogue of a Collection of Books . . . by Walt Whitman* NY, 1903(/).

They are not patriotic[1]
Of Emerson, (& the New England set)[2] in Life, in[3] its grand[4] turbulence[5]: in the United States[6] with all its multitudinous noise & practical business & politics,[7] and vehement and oceanic crowds,[8] rushing to and from the trains, and voices[9] as of squads and regiments and[10] armies,[11] endlessly gesticulating & talking in every key, especially the loud ones, is painful to them, grating upon their ears, their nerves, & they shun & abuse it. They teach, and maintain in their writings[12] a proper demeanor, &[13] seriously condemn laughing. They[14] secretly, (and not always secretly) despise the[15] idea of patriotism[16] & think it fine to[17] substitute[18] some other ism in its place.

1. In red ink above letterhead.
2. Above the text.
3. Inserted above "L" in "Life"
4. Inserted above "its"
5. "ce" written over "t"
6. Preceding six words inserted above "lence" in "turbulence" , deleted "and" and in right margin; deleted: "in" ; deleted from insertion: "and" ; inserted above "all": "with"
7. Preceding five words inserted above "noise and vehement"
8. Deleted: "and"
9. Deleted: [*illeg.*]
10. Preceding four words inserted above "in armies" and deleted "talking"
11. Deleted: "talking" above "gestic" in "gesticulation" ; inserted: "endlessly"
12. Preceding five words inserted above "teach, a proper"
13. Deleted: "denounce"
14. Single parenthesis deleted.
15. Deleted: "idea"
16. Deleted: "and have a in its place [*ins. and del.*] bit in place of it, are strong on abolitionism [*"ism" del.*] or some have some ism"
17. Preceding five words inserted above deleted "ism" and deleted "generally" ; deleted: "generally"
18. "e" written over "ing"

Get Emerson's Remarks.

Manuscript in Huntington. Inscribed in black ink on slip of white wove paper, $3^{13}/_{16}''$ x $6^{15}/_{16}''$. Blue rules. Embossed "Congress. . . . ." On July 10, 1872, Emerson read his lecture on " 'Character' or 'Greatness' " to the Amherst student body. The text has not been recovered, but it is suggestive that WW knew about an event that could not have been front-page news even in the more literate papers of the nineteenth century. The date is 1872.

Get Emersons remarks on "Greatness" ?at Amherst—June 1872

I Do Not Feel.

Manuscript in Texas. Inscribed in black ink and, as noted, black pencil. It may well be that this is not one MS or notes for the same essay, since the paper of [*1*] and [2] is not identical. The two MSS are not together in Texas. However, the writing in the first paragraph of [2] seems identical with that of [*1*], and certainly both leaves deal with "culture." [*1*] is on light blue wove paper, 9⅛" x 7¹⁵/₁₆". Blue rules on recto only, ⅜" apart. [2] (A) is on white wove paper, 7" x 7⅜". Blue rules approx. ½" apart. (B) pasted on scrap, approx. 7⅞" x 4½", irregularly scissored on left edge. The writing of the pasted-on scrap is extremely irregular, but it might have been inscribed at a time when WW was in ill health or as he held the paper in his hand or on his knee outdoors. The content of this MS seems to be related to *DV* in its attack on culture. The genteely "cultured" side of Emerson often annoyed WW and in *DV* (*Galaxy* version) he criticizes Emerson for it, although he calls him "the noblest voice in America" (*Prose 92,* II, 395, ll. 1003–1004*n*). The writing suggests a date in 1872.

[1]I [2]do not[3] feel to write, & do not write[4] in deprecation of Culture, or literary or scholastic acquirements, or the esthetic. I know perfectly well[5] that, as they have redeemed him from the merely natural state,[6] they now form an essential part of the glory of civilized man,[7] elevate him,[8] are indispensable to keep him elevated[9] clothe him with[10] his brightest attractions, &, if not above all else, as much as any thing else,[11] make nations & times[12] illustrious.[13]

Yet it is true[14] so far,[15] that the theories of culture, so far, as construed &

1. False start at top of leaf: "I dare not say".
2. Deleted: "must" ; inserted above: "do"
3. Deleted: "say a" ; inserted above: "feel to"
4. Preceding four words inserted above "write in"
5. Deleted: "h"
6. Preceding ten words inserted above "well" and "[*del.*] h" and "that" and "[*del.*] they are" ; deleted: "they are the make" ; inserted and deleted: "have come to" above "[*del.*] the" ; inserted: "they now form" above the deletion and "make"
7. Deleted: "redeem him from the merely natural state"
8. Inserted and deleted: "& that" above the wordspace between "[*del.*] state" and "elevate"
9. Preceding six words inserted above "elevate him, . . . clothe"
10. Deleted: "his or" ; inserted: "his" above wordspace between "[*del.*] his or"
11. Preceding eleven words inserted above "make nations & times"
12. Deleted: "most"
13. Deleted: "I know not if"
14. Preceding four words inserted above "[*del.*] not if" and "So far" . "So" not reduced to lowercase, not printed here as capital.
15. Deleted: "they"

practised,[16] have remained,[17] & to-day remain,[18] absorbed in interests &[19] tendencies not those of Democracy[20]—& that their spirit[21] has never either cordially accepted[22] the idea of American Personalism,[23] nor earnestly contributed toward it.

[2] Not even from Emerson, finely as he presents it,[24] does it cease to bore[25] us, and[26]

We must not complain of him for this, but thankfully accept him as he is[27]

For the[28] very highest of literature[29] untrammels us frees us entirely from Literature (Emerson[30]/

[31]even in the hands of the very highest talkers, nothing is so ?[32] as advise about ? good manners

16. Preceding nine words inserted on two lines in pencil above deletion and "have remained" . Order of whole sentence debatable.

17. Deleted: "in the interest of the Feudal"

18. Deleted: "in the interest engaged" ; inserted: "absorbed" above "gaged" in "engaged"

19. Deleted: "vitalities" ; inserted above: "tendencies"

20. Deleted: "not those a [*not del.*] of a true American Personalism [*space*] and show no signs" ; inserted and deleted above: "with no present indication"

21. Inserted and deleted in pencil: "so far in These States" ; deleted: "does not neither" ; inserted and deleted: "does yet" above "[*del.*] neither" ; inserted: "has never either" above "cordially" and "acc" in "accepted"

22. Deleted: "not [*ins. above* "con" *in* "contributes"] indeed contributes any nor is recipr tributed toward Amer" ; inserted in pencil: "the idea of" above "[*del.*] Amer" and "Am" in "American"

23. Changed from "Personality"

24. Deleted: "does it cease"

25. Deleted: "s"

26. Irregular scrap pasted on.

27. Irregular writing in black ink. Remainder of scrap in very irregular black pencil writing.

28. Deleted: "highest" ; inserted above: "very highest"

29. Deleted: "[*illeg.*] to" ; inserted: "untrammels us" above "ature" in "literature" and deletion.

30. Not identified.

31. Deleted: "of"

32. Deleted: "as those talkers"

His Idea of God.

Manuscript in Duke (25, #31). Inscribed in black pencil with some ink emendations on white wove paper, 10⅛" x 8⅛". Blue rules ½" apart on recto. The writing and the severity suggest a date after 1873, an opinion in which Ghodes and Silver concur. First printed *FC&I,* 28–29.

His idea of God (as in the oversoul)[1] is not the modern[2] Scientific idea, now rapidly advancing, far more[3] sublime[4] & resplendent, and reflecting[5] a dazzling light, upon Democracy its twin,[6] put the old old[7] Oriental idea of God,[8] taken up by the Ecclesiasticism of the middle ages, and still continued by the[9] fossil churches of the present day/[10]

([11]he has a large[12] substratum of Greek and Latin and also[13] of English—. with some German and other—but[14] says little of America, and it[15] not only plays no important figure in his writings as a whole, but hardly appears there[16]/

It[17] is certain that the time comes when all[18] merely intellectual writing, however fine,[19] and has been passed beyond, and ceases to attract or nourish.[20]/

1. Inserted: "as in the oversoul" above "God . . . is not" . In column at right deleted: "is beautiful & tender & orthodox"
2. Inserted above "Scien" in "Scientific"
3. Preceding two words inserted above "sublime"
4. Deleted: "& more"
5. Deleted: "a" ; inserted and deleted above: "its" ; inserted above: "a"
6. Preceding two words inserted in ink above "cy" in "democracy" and "but"
7. Inserted above "O" in "Oriental"
8. Deleted: "inherited" ; inserted: "taken up" on the next line above "by the"
9. Deleted: "principal" ; inserted above: "fossil"
10. The preceding thirteen words are written in three lines deeply indented at left and right.
11. Curved line at left of entire passage.
12. Inserted above wordspace between "a" and "substratum"
13. Inserted above "of"
14. Deleted: "it"
15. Deleted: "hardly" ; inserted above: "not only"
16. Preceding seventeen words indented as above (*n*10).
17. Preceded by pointing hand.
18. Deleted: "fine"
19. Written over [*illeg.*]; deleted following: "tires"
20. Preceding five words indented as above.

Emerson[21]—the poems

—it is all[22] crystal, all a glassy clear stream of thought distilled, we want—not a bit of[23] Homeric, Shakespearean, Rabelaisian red blood, heat, brawn, animality—as in

21. Preceded by deleted: "of"

22. Deleted: "ch"

23. Preceding two words inserted; "Homeric, Shakespearean Rabelaisian" brought up on an arrow. WW's original intention seems to have been "We want blood heat, brawn, animality as in Homer, Shakespeare Rabelais"

Nevertheless It Must Be.

Manuscript in Texas (Hanley). Inscribed in pencil on white laid scrap 3⅓″ x 5½″. The writing, which is rather loose, suggests a date after 1873.

Nevertheless it must be distinctly admitted that Emerson[1] serves Democracy, thog indirectly—He opens the gates. There is[2] much that Democracy has in common with Feudalism—

1. Deleted: "profit"
2. Deleted: "not such an"

No Patriotism in Him.

Manuscript lacking. Text from thermofax of typed transcript made available by Emory Holloway, who could not identify his source. It seems to bear some relation in its anglophobia and insistence on patriotism to "They are not patriotic" that Feinberg dates 1875.

No patriotism in him. A taint of having consulted authorities. The English dread of being quizzed, a certain formality and limit as of one who has never lost a clergyman's metes and bounds. Of course the amount of what Emerson gives us is better than the old conventionalism. We want freedom, faith, self-support, clearness. What have we?

Instead of the storm beats, the wind blowing, the savage throat, the ecstasy and abandon of the prairie, the dashing sea, we have always a polite person amid a well dressed assembly, in a parlor, talking about Plutarch, Astronomy, good behavior, the impropriety of laughing &c and evidently dominated by the English. A certain snobbishness even.

As to His Conservatism.

Manuscript in Brown. Inscribed on scrap of white wove tablet paper. Blue rules, ⅜" apart. On verso note from "Albert" [Johnston?] requesting a copy of *SD* and passing on news that "Folks are now in Paris & happy" . The genial tone suggests the Emersonian passages of 1880 at the end of *SD* and may have been planned for them, especially "By Emerson's Grave." The writing is shaky. The date is probably 1882.

As to his conservatism and non-democracy, they fit him[1] well, and I like him all the better for[2] both.[3] I guess we all like to have,—[4]I am sure I do,—some one who presents[5] those sides of a thought, or possibility, & different from our own view—different, and yet with a sort of home-likeness,—[6]yet a tartness and contradiction, offsetting the case as we[7] view it,[8]—and construed from[9] tastes and proclivities not[10] at all our own.

1. Deleted: "all the"
2. Deleted: "them"
3. The entire sentence inserted at top of leaf.
4. Parentheses before and after following sentence deleted.
5. Deleted: "the" ; inserted above: "those"
6. Deleted: "and with" ; inserted: "—yet" above "[*del.*] with"
7. Deleted: "like to"
8. Deleted: "and" ; inserted: "—[*ins.*] *and* construed" above the deletion and "from"
9. Deleted: "the point of view" ; inserted above: "tastes and proclivities"
10. Deleted: "of" ; inserted: "[*del.*] immediately at all" above "not . . . our own."

It Would Seem.

Manuscript in LC (#218, #1979). Inscribed in pencil on inside of envelope of Philadelphia *Times.* With it is a clipping from the *West Camden Post* for August 12, 1890 denying the story attributed to Emerson by Woodbury that WW appeared at a dinner party in NY in his shirt sleeves and rebuking conservative members of the Emerson set for denying that Emerson admired WW. The date is 1890.

It would seem that the right name & spelling must be *Talks with Ralph Waldo Emerson* by Charles J Woodbury pub'd by The Baker & Taylor Co: New York.

(Literature).

Manuscript in Texas (Hanley). Inscribed in column in sprawling hand in black and red ink as noted on yellow laid paper 8" x 5⅞". At top: *"Emerson"* deleted. A label for one of WW's pinned bundles, possibly for "Poetry To-Day in America" (1881) or "American National Literature" (1891). Emerson is mentioned only in the former and in a footnote. "The American Iliad" is not identifiable, but possibly he was thinking of *LG.* The large sprawling writing with a very broad-nibbed pen suggests that the label at least is very late.

(Literature) (in Washington previous to '73) *National Literature* scraps good[1] *All sorts*[2] — scraps *Emerson* largely (very sharp) *Literature to-day in America & generally* *America's Iliad* (lots & lots of scraps[3]

1. Entry in red ink. Fist pointing to next entry.
2. Pointing fist. All further underlining in red ink.
3. Entry in red ink.

The Song of Hiawatha.

Manuscript in Duke (29, #1). Inscribed in black pencil in hanging indentation on a rather stiff white paper with offset of two printed columns on verso, approx. 9¼" x 5½". The reception of *Hiawatha* in 1855 was everything that the reception of *LG* was not. Nevertheless, WW always ranked Longfellow with Bryant and Emerson among the major American poets. Cf. "The Bible Shakespeare" and "Death of Longfellow" *SD, PW* 92, I, 284–286. A visible dot covered by the beginning of the "e" of "enough" suggests that WW modified his first opinion by the addition of the last two words. The writing suggests an early date. First printed in *N&F,* 127 (Pt. III, #156; *CW,* IX, 156–157).

The Song of Hiawatha by H. W. Longfellow—A pleasing ripply poem—the measure, the absence of ideas, the Indian process of thought, the droning metre,[1] the[2] sleepy, misty,[3] woody character, the traditions, pleased me well enough.—

1. Preceding three words inserted above "thought, the"
2. Written over [*illeg.*]
3. Preceding two words inserted in the left margin and above "woody"

Ossian—Thoreau.

Manuscript not found. Text from *N&F,* 160 (Pt. IV, #24; *CW,* IX, 227). WW had undoubtedly read Thoreau's remarks on Ossian in the copy of *A Week* which Thoreau had given him in 1856. See Feinberg *Cat.,* 128 and Trent *Cat.,* 68, 78. Stovall, *Foreground,* 119*n,* thinks this MS is a label for WW's clipping from *A Week*. For Ossian see "Ossian?—for Note." The date is probably 1856.

Ossian—Thoreau. Macpherson 1737–1796.

Wm. Gilmore Sims.

Manuscript not found. Text from *N&F,* 132 (Pt. III, #174; *CW,* IX, 166). Stovall, *AL* 26, says the quotation is from *United States Magazine,* 4 (June, 1857), 352. WW had reviewed Simms's *Views and Reviews* in the *Eagle,* December 18, 1847.

Wm. Gilmore Simms. Notice in Emerson's United States Magazine, June '57.

"The man of great and commanding genius, who leaves his mark upon the ages, inevitably takes his stand-point of observation outside of that which is current and approved by his contemporaries. He in effect represents posterity more than his compeers. He has an omniscient perception by which he separates the dross from the crucible and finds the pure gold" etc. etc.

W. G. Simms—born Charleston, S. C., April, 1806—now 51 years old— is a true Southerner, florid, warm, of rich nature, defends slavery etc., is a copious writer—rather too *wordy,* overloads his descriptions—too *self-conscious*—his descriptions, characters etc. are good—well drawn.

American Poets.

Manuscript in Morgan. Inscribed in pencil, black ink, and purple crayon as noted on gray-brown wove paper, approx. 9½" x 6⅛". The writing suggests a date in the 1850s, but the deleted passage (*n* 12) is in a less firm hand and was printed in 1891. On verso is an apparently unpublished poem, "After certain disastrous campaigns," beginning: "Answer me, [*del.*] traitor year of repulses!" which suggests a date in the early 1860s.

AMERICAN POETS

It might be[1] demanded worth while[2] [*illeg.*][3] that[4] I should weigh[5] the[6] Poetry and Poets[7] of the Present age[8] at home and abroad from the point of view of my own theories.[9] I can only say that Tennyson in England, and Bryant,[10] Whittier, Emerson,[11] and Longfellow in America[12]

1. Deleted: "da"
2. Preceding two words inserted in purple crayon above "demanded"
3. Deleted: "[*not del., redundant*] that I should, from the point of view of my own estimate and theories" ; inserted above, not deleted in error: "[*illeg.*] [*del.*] genuine part of this [*del.*] essay letter"
4. Inserted above "I"
5. Deleted: "and sum up"
6. Deleted: "Poets and"
7. Preceding two words inserted above "y" in "Poetry" and "of the"
8. Deleted: "in Great Britain and America"
9. "ies." written over "y" ; deleted: "and estimate"
10. Deleted: "Em"
11. Deleted: "and"
12. Paragraph in black ink, cancelled in black ink. See "Old Poets," *GBMF, Prose 92,* II, 660, ll. 70ff.

Whittier.

Manuscript not found. Text from facsimile in Thomas Donaldson, *Walt Whitman the Man,* facing 85. Inscribed in a shaky hand. Date is probably late.

Whittier toward conclusion—a genial friend to whom some of the foregoing remonstrates Why condemn says to me—Seems to me,[1]

Supposing[2] all these your[3] points well taken, why[4] condemn Whittier? At least why[5] should he not express himself, just as he has—and

1. Deleted: "you"
2. Original opening: "Even supposing"
3. Inserted.
4. Deleted: "not"
5. Deleted: "not [*illeg.*] not"

With the Names.

Manuscript in LC, 287. Inscribed in purple crayon on three leaves of faded white wove notebook paper, 6⁹/₁₆″ x 4³/₁₆″. Leaves glued together. See *"American Poets"* for a similar list from a much earlier period. The writing, the use of purple crayon and some of the names suggest a late date. See "Old Poets," *GBMF, Prose 92,* II, 660, ll. 70ff.

With[1] the names of[2] our so-far noblest poets Bryant, Emerson, Whittier, Longellow I should put on the roll at any rate immediately below the others[3] Edgar Poe and Bret Harte though the scope of their song is limited and its direction special

I[4] have said before that all poetry is to be welcom'd—that each of its contributions[5] means something[6] stands for an actual something (or the hiatus of something which is[7] always significant[8]) (All actual facts are divine things was a favorite maxim of Frederic call'd the Great)—and is the expression of the positiveness or negativeness of somebody or some class! Therefore the times, and lands may good naturedly accept even the poetry of Bayard Taylor Stedman[9] Stoddard Aldrich Winter

Often fine thoughts fine incidents finely-express'd

1. Inserted and deleted at top of leaf: "If I had need to name my broad land's powerfulest scene" "T would not be yours N"
2. Preceding three words inserted above "our so"
3. Preceding two words inserted above "low" in "below" and wordspace before "Edgar"
4. False start precedes: "The"
5. Preceding dash and five words inserted above "welcom'd . . . means something"
6. Deleted: [*illeg.*]
7. Inserted and deleted: [*illeg.*] following "is"
8. Preceding four words inserted above "thing" in "something" and "All actual"
9. Inserted above "Stod" in "Stoddard" . The original omission is curious, for Stedman was the sole genteel poet who consistently supported WW. The others had little good to say or were aggressively hostile.

VIII. English Writers.

As to Shakespeare's.

Manuscript not found. Text from *N&F,* 94 (Pt. III, #42; *CW,* IX, 88). The spelling "Shakespeare" may be Bucke's error, for WW preferred "Shakespere." Stovall, (*AL,* 26, 345) says it was probably made on reading "Translators of Homer," *Whig Review* (October, 1846), Bucke's clipping #404.

As to Shakespeare's translations—they are the translation of so much beef and bread into vital human body and soul.

Shakespeare Born.

Manuscript in Virginia (Barrett). Inscribed in black ink on pink wove paper, 9⅞" x 5¾". Hanging indentations as noted. The sources of WW's notes have not been discovered. Stovall ("Whitman's Knowledge of Shakespeare," *SP,* 49 [1952], 665) notes that [he died] "in the 53d year of his age" is the phraseology of Rowe's Life as reprinted in Malone's *Plays and Poems,* I. The phrase is, however, a cliché. Mr. Philip Weiss of Western Illinois University has noticed striking echoes in the language of the quotation and the language in Henry Hallam's *Introduction to the Literature of Europe in the Fifteenth, Sixteenth and Seventeenth Centuries* (London, 1839). Weiss used a London, 1855, edition, III, 308–310. Hallam went through several reprints in London and NY, and WW might well have consulted it as a standard handbook. The resemblances are striking, but not identical. Nor is the drift of the treatment of Shakespeare's pessimism the same. One gets the impression that WW is quoting someone who had borrowed from Hallam, or, since his use of quotation marks is not systematic, he was quoting from memory. The pink wove paper indicates a date after *LG* (1855). First printed *N&F,* 94 (Pt. III, #'s 43–44; *CW,* IX, 88–89.

Shakespeare[1] born April 1564 (was one of 8[2] childr[en?] [*Shakespeare*][3] died in the 53d year of his age—1616 Married, (on or subsequent to,) 28th Nov. 1582. first child christened 26th May 1583[4] wife had twins early 1585—no more children afterward.
went to London 1586/ is heard of three years afterward as a sharer in the Blackfriars theatre[5]

Shakespeare—first folio edition, (one vol. nearly 1000 pages), complete collection of Comedies, Histories & Tragedies published by his associates and first editors Heminge & Condell 1623 (7th year after Shakespeare's death.)/

. . . . "During the next eight or nine years—from the first year of the 16th century to about 1609 or '10—*from the poet's thirty-seventh to about his forty-sixth year*—his genius rose at once to its highest point of culmination.—It was the era of his tragic power, of *his resistless control over the emotions of terror and* of *pity*—and of his deepest and most gloomy philosophy.—This was the period when he appeared as *"the stern censurer of man,"*—when his deeper insight into the human

1. Thick, dark italic lettering. Cf. "Memory" and "Edmund Spenser."
2. "8" in thick, dark writing.
3. Ditto mark in MS.
4. "5" in thick, dark writing.
5. Preceding seventeen words in left margin.

heart led him to dark and sad views of human nature—sometimes prompting the melancholy philosophy of Hamlet, sometimes bursting forth in the fiery indignation of Timon and Lear.—It was during this period that he most impressed upon his style that character which we now recognize as peculiarly Shaksperian, by *crowding into his words a weight of thought until "the language bent under it."*—His *versification becomes, like his diction, bolder, freer, careless of elegance, of regularity and even of melody,— a sterner music, fitted for sterner themes.* |

Ben Johnson born 1574—was a working bricklayer (Plutarch, English trans. from a French one in the reign of Queen Elizabeth.)[6] Shakspeare evidently did not anticipate[7] the fame that was to follow him(?)[8]—also was indifferent about fame—did not even see to the printing of his plays and poems, or even correcting them, when misprinted.—He minded his thrift, was hospitable lived on what he made

6. In a loop at top, bottom and right after first line of entry on Jonson in thick, dark writing.
7. Preceding three words inserted on two lines above deleted [*illeg.*].
8. Inserted in pencil above dash.

Published Venus & Adonis.

Manuscript in Virginia (Barrett). Inscribed in black ink, black pencil, and red crayon on green wove paper, 9½" x 4¾". Number "8" at upper right in another hand. Stovall, *SP,* 49 (1952), 665, thinks that this may be based on Collier's 1844 *Works,* I, cxix–cxxvi. The paper indicates this was written shortly after the publication of *LG* (1855), probably in 1856. First printed *N&F,* 95 (Pt. III, #46; *CW,* IX, 90–91).

Published Venus & Adonis—1593 [*Published*] Tarquin & Lucrece[1] 1594 Pilgrim 1599 Sonnets 1609[2]

Shakespeare (1586)[3] *commenced at* 27 years of age, in London—was already the father of three children—never seems to have amoured his wife afterward—?nor did they[4] live together:—(This last is not so certain — they possibly lived sociably in the same house, after S. settled in Stratford.)/

As a young man must have been a great pet with everybody—/[5]

Richard Burbage—young man—his friend—the "star" of the company—the original actor of the leading Shakesperian characters.— Burage died 1619—was the original Hamlet[6] Macbeth Brutus Coriolanus Shylock Romeo Prince Henry Henry V Richard III Lear Pericles Othello Burbage must have been a superb man He left children—two sons.[7]/

1. Stovall, *SP,* 49 (1952), 665, says that this title for the *Rape of Lucrece* was common in WW's time. Probably a bowdlerization.
2. Four entries in column in black pencil.
3. Inserted above "com" in "commenced"
4. Deleted: [*illeg.*]
5. Sentence in hanging indentation.
6. Sentence in hanging indentation. Following names of leading roles in three columns.
7. Preceding sentences one above the other at left of list of characters. Each set off by curved line at left.

The *Sonnets* [8]
Shakespeare wrote his "sugar'd sonnets" early—probably soon after his appearance in London—the beautiful young man so passionately treated, and so subtly the thread of the sonnets, is (?) without doubt, *the Earl of Southampton*—who made Shakespeare the magnificent gift of a thousand pounds—Southampton was nine years the youngest—[9] the ancient Greek friendship, seems to have existed between the two.

("Venus and Adonis" is dedicated to Lord Southampton, and styled by the[10] poet[11] the "first heir of his invention".—This—the "Lucrece"—and the sonnets—all precede his great dramas.—[12]

Spenser, his contemporary, already alludes to him in 1791 (Shakespere then only 27 years old,) as a superior writer "whom nature's self had made, to mock herself" —and as "our pleasant Willy."[13]
(Spenser was doubtless intimate with Shakespeare and knew what he had in him.[14]

8. Written in left margin. Following entry in hanging indentation. Cancelled with red crayon slash. Large question mark in left margin also in red crayon.
9. Preceding six words inserted above "—the" to "frien" in "friendship"
10. Written over [*illeg.*]
11. Inserted above "the"
12. Preceding entry in hanging indentation.
13. Preceding entry in hanging indentation. Large red crayon question mark in left and right margins.
14. Preceding entry in hanging indentation.

His Earliest Printed Plays.

Manuscript in Duke (30, #6). Inscribed in black pencil, black ink, and red pencil as noted on white laid paper, approx. 7⅞" x 4¼". Vertical blue rules approx. ⅜" apart. Hanging indentions, unless otherwise noted or printed. WW has turned the leaves on their sides. Floyd Stovall, "Whitman's Knowledge of Shakespeare," *SP,* 49 (October, 1952), 636–666, points out parallels of substance and phraseology with the biography of J. Payne Collier in his *Works of William Shakespeare* (London, 1844), I. Only those passages *not* indebted to Collier are noted here. Stovall thinks that WW may have used Veazie's 1865 Boston reprint of Collier ("Reading Shakespeare"), but it seems likely that he used an earlier edition, such as Redfield's 1853 Collier. The writing suggests that this was written in the 1850s, and all dateable entries [*12, 14*] point to a date late in 1856. Whether the echoes of "Crossing Brooklyn Ferry" preceded its publication in *LG* (1856) in September (?) of that year cannot be determined, but the echoes are too close to be mere coincidence. Aside from their relation to the dating, these passages are worth further thought. Was WW subconsciously (or consciously) identifying his generic "Myself" with Shakespeare? No source for WW's curious insistence that Shakespeare was indebted to the *Iliad* has been found. (See "Homer and Shakespeare.")

MS first published in *N&F,* 85–88 (Pt. III, #27; *CW,* IX, 71–77). [*15*] is in facsimile in *Manuscripts . . . of Walt Whitman,* Sale #4251, American Art Association Anderson Galleries (NY, 1936), Lot 46.

[1] His earliest[1] printed plays 1597 (Romeo & Juliet Richard 3d & Richard 2d[2]/
Chapman's trans. of Homer, printed 1600.[3]/

The gift of the £1000, was without much doubt, made about 1593,[4] when Southampton was 20 years old, and Shakespeare 29—?I suspect earlier than that?/[5]

1596—his sone Hamnet died, in the 12th year of his age./[6]

1. Written over [*illeg.*]

2. Titles in column at right.

3. Written on two lines at left in pencil under "His earliest printed" . Stovall, *AL,* 26, 341, says it is probably from "Translators of Homer," *American Whig Review* 4 (October, 1846), Bucke's clipping #404.

4. The "3" written over "4"

5. Curved line across leaf. Whole entry in block paragraph. One wonders what WW had in the back of his mind when he wrote the last sentence. It is written, as if a later entry, on two lines under "peare" in "Shakespeare" and "29" , and it is not based on Collier.

6. Rule across leaf.

1598 To this year, only five of his plays had been printed—although he had been a public writer for twelve years.—(*Positively,* he was by certain parties, more or less numerous, adjudged already to deserve a place among the great masters, as early as this date—1598[7] (in the 35th[8] year of his age)/[9]

The printing of Shakspeares dramas was without his instigation or assistance—It is thought quite certain[10] *he was indifferent to their appearance in print*—and did not mind even the blunders and omissions that marred them [:] probably for the same reason that Forrest would not like to have his plays in print now)/[11]

1598—Now, (12 years after going to London,) he returns to Stratford, purchases and lives in one of the best houses of the place—[12]"New Place"

1601 his father died, aged 71—his last years were probably comfortable.

[*3; 2 blank*] 1600?? As the first translations (worth mentioning) of the Iliad and Odyssey were published in 1675, Shakespeare was probably not intimate with those poems.[13]/

Queen Elizabeth no doubt often saw Shakespeare as an actor, and applauded him.

1603 James 1st of England & VI of Scotland commenced—previously of course Queen Elizabeth reigned.—[14]

James 1st must also have seen him[15]

1607 Susanna, his eldest daughter, aged 24, was married to John Hall, "gentleman"—a physician.—

1608 his mother died—a little previous, his brother died.—the mother was probably over[16] 70 years of age.

7. The "5" is written over another number.

8. The "35" is written over another number.

9. In the MS the parenthesized phrase is at the right on two lines in a loop represented by the parentheses.

10. Preceding two words written above "thought"

11. Preceding seventeen words written in pencil on three lines at right after a brace. Not from Collier. The tragedian Edwin Forrest (1806–1872) refused to allow the printing of plays written for him in order to control the performing rights.

12. Dash written over smeared letter.

13. Written at the top of the leaf on three lines in pencil. See, however, [*11*], below, and "Homer and Shakespeare."

14. Facts but not language from Collier.

15. Circled at left. Not from Collier.

16. Deleted: "y"

Shakespeare, at this time, 1608[17] seems[18] to have had his reputation at its height.—

£400 a year is supposed to have now been his income. 1608/[19]

Burbage died worth £300 a year.—/[20]

about 1607[21]—(15 years after the "Venus and Adonis,) Lord Southampton still befriends Shakespeare—writing a letter to the Lord Chamberlain in behalf of him and Burbage

[5; 4 *blank*] 1600 and for some time before and after, *juvenile companies* were much patronised—They must have been very good companies too.—[22]

Shakespeare owned in both the Globe and Blackfriars theatre.

—Bought and sold, bargained, was thrifty, borrowed money, loaned money had lawsuits[23]—

Richard, his youngest brother, died in 1612—aged 40

His brother Gilbert two years his elder, probably resided in Stratford in 1612—and before & afterward

His sister Joan, (5 years younger than he) married William Hart, hatter,—they called their first child "William."

His daughter Susannah made him a grandfather when he was 45 years old./

1605 Had a chancery suit

[7; 6 *blank*][24] Did right and wrong—was entrusted with commissions—lost by fires,[25] thieves, cheats—committed follies, debaucheries, crimes—

17. Written over another number.
18. Written over [*illeg.*]
19. Rule across leaf.
20. Rule across leaf.
21. "7" written over another number.
22. The last sentence, which is not mentioned by Stovall, is probably not from Collier.
23. Preceding two words inserted in red pencil above and following the dash. The information but not the words are in Collier. For a similar passage (both suggestive of "Crossing Brooklyn Ferry," sec. 6, ll. 65–77) see below.
24. Illegible mark, perhaps £, in upper left corner. Block paragraph. Cf. "—Bought and sold . . ." (*n*23) above. Scrap of newsprint on [6].
25. Stovall suggests that "commissions" and "fires" refer to Shakespeare's commission to use his influence against the enclosure of the commons and the burning of the Globe. The rest of the note is not supported in Collier.

1616—Feb.; his daughter Judith married to Thos. Quiney a vintner.—Judith had 3 children She died 1661–2[26]/

Made his will—signed it twice with unsteady hand Made an[27] effort with firmness on the final signature "By me William Shakespeare"[28]/

(Death—at the age of 52

Death. "Shakespeare, Drayton & Ben Johnson had a merrie meeting, and, it seems, drank too hard,—for Shakespeare died of a fever there contracted." Rev. John Ward's Diary.

His wife Anne outlived him she died 1623/

His last lineal descendant died 1670

[9; *8 blank*] See Shakespere vs. Sand—printed following/[29]

The half-length upon his monument (erected anterior to 1623,) "conveys[30] the impression of a cheerful, good[31] tempered, somewhat jovial man."

(*It is evident to me, beyond cavil, that Shakespeare, in his own day, and at death, was*[32] *by many placed among the great masters, and acknowledged.*)[33] and yet the florid style of praise was applied to everybody and almost everything in those times.[34]

"He was a handsome, well-shaped man, very good company, and of a very ready, and pleasant, and smooth wit." Aubrey.

Some think Shakespeare was lame, and, for that reason, retired from the stage—came perhaps, from some accident.—

"gentle" is the epithet often applied to him.

26. Rule across leaf.

27. "n" added to "a" ; deleted: "final"

28. Rule across leaf. Block paragraph. Entry brought up from below "Rev. John Wards Diary" on loops and arrows.

29. Preceded by a pointing hand in pencil. The clipping, which is not now with the MS, is identified by Stovall as by G. W. Peck, *American Whig Review* (May, 1847). It contrasts the "common sense and wholesome realism" of Shakespeare's characterization with that of modern French novelists, especially George Sand, then in high disfavor among the respectable.

30. Possibly altered to "conveyed"

31. Deleted: "natured"

32. Written over another word.

33. A large pencilled question mark in the left margin seems to apply to the entire parenthesized entry.

34. Preceding seventeen words crammed at right on four lines following *"acknowledged"*

?at that[35] time was not it's signification "like a gentleman" "of highblooded bearing"?

Fuller speaks of the "wit combats between Shakespeare & Ben Jonson at the Mermaid club.

"Myriad minded Shakespeare."

[*11; 10 blank*] Evidently he was familiar with the Iliad./[36]

His autograph is in a translation of *"Montaigne's essays"*—he then must have been familiar with Montaigne.—/

"Venus & Adonis" passed through six editions, in Shakespeare's lifetime, and a number more afterwards.

Sonnets—first printed 1609.

Milton admired and loved Shakespeare—writes praises of him.—/

But yet he charges harshly against Charles 1st that the monarch had a copy of Shakespeare in his cabinet for his constant use./[37]

The character of the bastard Falconbridge,—his[38] gloating pleasure over the fact that he is the *bastard of a king* rather than the legitimate son of a knight—What was this but either from a sentiment now repudiated or[39] to please the aristocracy?—Yet what was it also but a true depicting of those days?—a true depicting also of[40] thousands of men's minds these days?/[41]

Shakespeare is much indebted to the ancients—Hamlet's soliloquy, "To be or not to be" is taken almost verbatim from Plato—)?is this so?[42] To the Iliad, every one of his best plays is largely indebted.—[43]

35. Deleted: "was" ; inserted above: "time was not"

36. In smaller pencil writing at top of leaf. Not from Collier. See [3] above.

37. Entry in pencil, preceded by pointing hand. Not from Collier. Stovall, *AL,* 26, 342, says it is probably from an extract from Isaac Disraeli in L. Herrig's *British Classical Authors,* which WW knew and clipped, or, alternatively, from Disraeli's *Amenities of Literature,* III, 214, which he reviewed in the *Eagle,* March 9, 1847.

38. Deleted: "animal" ; inserted above: "gloating"

39. Preceding eleven words inserted in pencil above "was this but to please"

40. Written over another word.

41. Rule across leaf.

42. Query written over an erasure to right of quotation, which is set off, and probably applies to the entire entry. None of the entry is from Collier; Stovall says it is directly from John and William Langhorne's edition of *Plutarch's Lives* (NY, 1844), v.

43. Entire entry in a darker ink than the rest of the MS. See [3], above.

[*12*] See Emerson's Shakespeare[44]

[*13*][45] Shakespeare put such things into his plays as would please the family pride of kings and queens.—and of his patrons among the nobility.—[46] He did this for[47] Queen Elizabeth, and for James the 1st.—His renderings of many phases of character[48]—The rabble, Jack Cade, the French Joan, the greasy and stupid canaille that Coriolanus cannot stomach, all these[49] fed the aristocratic[50] vanity[51] of the young[52] noblemen and gentlemen and feed them in England yet.—[53] Common blood is but wash—the hero is always of high lineage.—/ Doubtless in so rendering humanity, Shakespeare strictly rendered what was to him[54] the truth,—and what was the truth.—[55] The class of mechanics, tailors, salesmen,[56] attendants, 9c, in Europe then perhaps even now, are they or are they not[57] properly reflected by such reflections as Shakespeare gives of them?—

[*14*][58] Illustrated London News.
Oct. 25, 1856

a paper read by William Henry Smith, author of "Was Lord Bacon the author of Shakespeare's Plays?"—"What Pope says of some of the Plays of Shakespeare is probably[59] true of all—that they were pieces of unknown authors, or fitted up for the theatre while under his administration,—revised and added to by him."

It seems according to Malone that "the London Prodigal" was acted at his theatre and afterwards printed with his Shakespeare's[60] name on the title page—

44. Preceded by a pointing hand. *Representative Men* (Boston, 1850). Followed by two unidentified clippings probably from newspapers: "Shakespeare as a Man" and "Shakespeare's Stage," the latter a selection from G. W. Thornbury's *Shakespeare's England* (London, 1856).

45. Block paragraph.

46. Preceding seven words inserted on two lines above "and queens.—"

47. Deleted: "the"

48. Preceding seven words inserted on two lines above "—The rabble"

49. Deleted: "[*ins. above* "m" *in deleted* "marked"] are marked, in his renderings of them with the as he renders them, take mean and please [*ins. above* "ease" *in* "please"]feed"; inserted: "fed" above wordspace between "[*del.*] please" and "the"

50. Spelling "aristicratic" corrected.

51. Deleted: [*illeg.*]

52. Possibly "gay"

53. Preceding six words and punctuation inserted above "and gentlemen" . Deleted: "Family" ; inserted above: "Common" . Redundant dash not printed.

54. Preceding four words inserted in pencil above "tly" in "strictly" and "rendered the"

55. Preceding five words and dashes inserted in pencil above "The class of" and "mecha" in "mechanics"

56. "smen" written over [*illeg.*]

57. Preceding five words inserted in pencil, "they" following "are" and "or are they not" above "properly" and "ref" in "reflected"

58. In black pencil. Along left margin: "Jan '57— Smith continued these lectures" in a loop.

59. Deleted: "of"

60. Inserted above "name"

and, though he had never written a line of it he was indifferent to the cheat and to the printer's impudence.

—Bacon, according to W.H. Smith, was most probably the real[61] author—he goes on with his reasons therefor, some of them very curious and plausible, especially a contemporary[62] letter to[63] Viscount St Albans saying "the[64] most prodigious wit that ever I knew of[65] my nation, or[66] of this side of the sea, was of your Lordship's name, though he be known by another."

[15] *Overcoloring.*

Many little things are too much overcolored, in Shakespeare—*far too much.*— The features of beloved women, compliments,[67] the descriptions of moderately[68] brave actions, professions of service[69] and hundreds more, are painted too intensely. It is no answer to this, to say that a lover would so state the case about a woman he loved, or that a strong rich nature would be apt to describe incidents in that manner; and[70] that Shakespeare is therefore[71] correct in so presenting them.—Immensely too much is unnaturally colored—the sentiment is piled on, similes, comparisons, defiances, exaltations,[72] immortalities,[73] bestowed upon themes certainly not worthy the same,—thus losing proportion [74](Also,??[75] most of the discursive speeches of the great and little characters are glaringly inappropriate, both words and sentiments such as could not have come from their mouths, in real life[76] and therefore should not in the plays.[77]—) Yet on great occasion the character and action are perfect.— This is what saves Shakespeare—Is he imitative of Homer? If so, where and how?

61. Inserted above wordspace between "the and author"
62. Inserted above "a" and into the right margin.
63. Deleted: "calling Bacon" ; inserted above: "to Viscount St. Albans saying"
64. What seems to be a minute scrap of newsprint above.
65. Deleted: [*illeg.*] "any" ; inserted above: "my"
66. Deleted: "the"
67. Inserted in pencil above "women"
68. Inserted above "of brave"
69. Preceding three words inserted in pencil above "ns," in "actions," and "and"
70. Deleted in pencil: "therefore" ; inserted in pencil: "that" above "th" in "[*del.*] therefore" in "[*del.*] therefore"
71. Inserted in pencil above "corr" in "correct"
72. Deleted: "divinities,"
73. Deleted: "are all" ; inserted: "bestowed" above "[*del.*] all"
74. Preceding three words inserted above "the same,—"
75. Question marks inserted; deleted: "many" ; inserted above: "most"
76. Preceding three words inserted in pencil above "ths" in "months" and "and"
77. Preceding three words inserted in pencil above "t.—" in "not.—" and "Ye" in "Yet"

Richard Burbage.

Manuscript in Duke (36, #28). Inscribed in black pencil on proof (?) paper, but thinner and smoother than that of "Reading Shakespeare," approx. 5⁵⁄₁₆" x 5⅝". Hanging indentation. The writing seems to be WW's handwriting of the 1850s.

Richard Burbage, principal owner in theatre, & principal actor of first parts, must have been quite a character—he was quite rich—died in 1619—(worth £300 a year)

I Think it Probable.

Manuscript in Virginia. Inscribed in black ink on verso of blue Williamsburgh tax blank. The date is therefore 1857. Delia Bacon had proposed the Baconian theory in *Putnam's Monthly* (January, 1856) and in *The Philosophy of the Plays of Shakespeare Unfolded* (1857). Bucke and O'Connor were both Baconian zealots, but evidently WW had been corrupted before meeting them. (See "His earliest printed plays.") He never quite committed himself, perhaps because he didn't care, perhaps because he felt that it would be unfitting for the Poet of Democracy to deny that a simple country boy could become a great poet. "Shakespere—Bacon's Cipher" (1891), despite the title, is about mystic meanings. First printed by Bucke as part of "His earliest printed plays" in *N&F,* 85 (Pt. III, #27; *CW,* IX, 70).

I think it probable or rather suggest it as such[1]that Bacon (& perhaps Raleigh[2] had a hand in Shakespeares Plays—how much, whether as furnisher, pruner, poetical illuminator, knowledge infuser,—what he was or did, if anything, it is not possible to tell with certainty

1. Preceding six words inserted by a line and caret from above "it probably"

2. Preceding three words and parenthesis inserted on two lines above "Bacon" . In 1888 he expressed the belief that the plays were written by a committee or by various persons who used Shakespeare as a front (Traubel, IV, 52–56, 449).

Homer and Shakespeare.

Manuscript in Virginia (MacGregor). Inscribed in black ink with some pencil insertions on pink wove paper, 9¾" x 4⅞". The first eight lines are written over six erased lines in pencil. For WW's knowledge of Shakespeare, see "Shakespeare born." J.A. Buckley's translations of the *Iliad* and of the *Odyssey* and lesser pieces were both published in London in 1851 and in NY in 1856 and were several times reprinted. The *National Union Catalog* does not list a one-volume edition. WW owned a copy of Buckley's *Odyssey* (London, 1863), which he received as a gift in 1865 (Feinberg *Cat.*, #363), but he seems to have already read it or have planned to read it as early as 1857 (marginalia at Middlebury College, *N&F,* 158 [Pt. III, #18; *CW,* IX, 222]). He also read Pope's translation, possibly earlier, and two notebooks of 1872 in the Feinberg Collection (Feinberg *Cat.*, #42) note that he had read William Mumford's translation of 1846, which he found inferior to Buckley's. The linking of Homer and Shakespeare, with a plea for an improved modern poetry, which appears in the draft prefaces of the 1860s, is a Whitmanesque cliché. For further notes on Homer and Shakespeare see "His earliest printed plays." Homer and Shakespeare were the greatest, of course, of the national poets whom WW admired (e.g. *DV, Prose 92,* II, 366*n*.) The paper and writing suggest a date of 1856. First printed *N&F,* 111 (Pt. III, #92; *CW,* IX, 123–124).

(both are objective)[1]
Homer and Shakespeare deserve all[2] the reward that has been bestowed upon them.—They did what was to be done, and did the work divinely[3] Homer poetized great wars, persons, events, throwing together in perfect proportion—a perfect poem, noisy, muscular, manly, amative[4] *an amusement, and excitement.*—a sustenance and health.[5]

Shakespeare, the gentle, the sweet, musical, well-beloved Shakespeare,[6] delineated characters; They are better done represented[7] by him than by any other poet, at any time.—Kings, traitors, lovers,[8] ambition, perplexed persons[9] youth old

1. Written in black pencil above "Shakespeare" and "des" in "deserve"
2. Inserted: "the [*del.*] great reward" above "all . . . that has"
3. The smaller size of the writing and the placement of the last four words on two lines in the left margin suggest that the two preceding sentences were inserted as an afterthought.
4. Preceding four words inserted above "ct" in "perfect" and *"amuse"* in *"amusement"*
5. Preceding four words inserted in pencil.
6. The preceding seven words inserted on two lines above "are" in "Shakespeare" and "delineated *characters;"*
7. Inserted above "done" as an alternate.
8. Deleted: "men"
9. Preceding two words inserted above "him" in insert in *n* 10.

age, &c he[10] easily reflects.—He, through them, delivers many profound[11] thoughts—many poetical,[12] subtle fancies—many involved, rather elaborate, unnatural[13] comparisons.—Well may Homer remain, and Shakespeare remain.[14]

Could Shall[15] there not be a poet of America, doing no less than they, but different from[16] more than either of them?—Stamping *this age,* and so all ages, in his poems?—Feeding character with a strong clean meat? Riveting the passing incidents, sentiment, persons, tendencies, visible things, landscapes, voyages, politics, Manhattan Island, the Yankee, the Californian, all American features and leading facts, in poems?—(?Bequathing the most precious of all works in literature to the future American woman and man?)[17]

10. In pencil. The preceding twelve words inserted in ink above "other he"
11. Deleted: "subtle" ; comma not deleted, not printed.
12. Deleted: "sweet" ; inserted in pencil: "subtle" above "swe" in "[*del.*] sweet"
13. Deleted: "similes"
14. Cramped writing suggests that preceding sentence was inserted.
15. Inserted above "Could" as alternate.
16. Preceding seven words inserted above "ca" in "America" and "doing more than"
17. The parentheses and the first question mark are in pencil.

Reading Shakespeare.

Manuscript in Duke (36, #28). Inscribed in black pencil on heavy coarse proof(?) paper, approx. 8⅛" x 5⅜". As Stovall *SP,* 49 (1952), 666, points out, Veazie was a publisher, and that edition is a reprint of Redfield's 1853 reprint of John Payne Collier's eight-volume edition of the same year. In *N&F,* Bucke has questioned the incorrect date of the First Folio with "[?1623]." First printed *N&F,* 142 (Pt. III, #181; *CW,* IX, 189). The MS was written in Washington in 1865.

Reading Shakespeare Sept. 1865 Washing/[1] Edition in 8 vols of *Wm. Veazie, Boston, 1859*/[2] *The Text regulated by the Folio of 1632* (Portrait from the Monument in Stratford Church)/[3]

Ben Jonson's Eulogy—very fine & sounding

"He was not of an age, but for all time." —"a good Poet's *made* as well as *born*"[4]/

Shakespeare *born*

about 23d April 1564 (died 1616)——

began his theatrical career in London (about) 1586/ (was owner in *two* theatres *Globe* and *Blackfriars*

1. In upper right corner. Centered rule.
2. Rule across leaf.
3. Rule across leaf.
4. Rule across leaf.

[*Illeg.*] Speaking.

Manuscript in Duke (36, #28V). On recto "America has been called." Inscribed in pencil on white wove paper like that of "Slavery—the Slaveholders—." Blue rules ⅜" apart. Cancelled. The "leader" of this "graceful" school is not identifiable, but Tennyson comes to mind. The writing and paper suggest this was written in the 1850s.

[*Illeg.*] speaking [*illeg.*] best way of speaking[?] of his graceful and talented school, so numerous both[?] in Great Britain and America.—

The[1] eleves of this[2] graceful[3] talented school are numerous both in Great Britain and America, yet we shall speak of their leader[?] as the best way of speaking of them. His eleves are perhaps more numerous in New York, Cincinnati and Charleston than they are in other cities[4] graceful and talented writer.— He is the[5] artificial phases of modern society

1. Original opening deleted: "Many of"
2. Deleted: "school are"
3. Probably a word torn off at left.
4. Deleted: "He is the poet of the highly published" Words trimmed at left.
5. Words trimmed at left.

Old Original Rude Ones.

Manuscript in Texas. Inscribed in black pencil with some emendations in black ink on a white wove scrap, 8″ x 5½″. First printed by Herbert Bergman, "Whitman and Tennyson," *SP* 51 (July, 1954), 498. No date can be assigned.

old original[1] rude ones, yet,[2] with[3] greater artificial[4] charm of beauty & polish—[5] (as if only one took the lions or[6] sea-cliffs, or[7] Krakens,[8] old[9] [*illeg.*] &[10] wrought beauteous[11] first-rate, gold & silver images of them,[12] for the library, or[13] bouoir,[14] far more welcome[15] to respectable[16] citizens & their wives & daughters[17] than any[18] real Krakens or any lion[19] savagery whatever—or any[20] lion literature either;)—

1. Preceding two words inserted on two lines above "rude"
2. Inserted and deleted: "making all allowances" above "yet, with [*del.*] their"
3. Deleted: "their"
4. Inserted above "charm"
5. Inserted and deleted: [*illeg.*] above "as"
6. Preceding three words inserted above "ok" in "look" and "sea-"
7. Deleted: "lions" ; inserted above in black ink: "Krakens"
8. Deleted: "or"
9. Deleted: "some grandest savagest objects" . The "est" and "st" are insertions.
10. Deleted: "made" ; inserted above: "wrought" ; inserted and deleted: "the" above "bea" in "beauteous"
11. Deleted: [*illeg.*]; inserted: "first-rate, gold & silver" above the deletion and "images"
12. Preceding two words inserted in ink above "ages" in "images"
13. Preceding two words inserted above "the" and into the left margin.
14. Deleted: "or parlor-mantel—therefrom—which said [*ins. above*] china images [*del.*] would [*two words ins. and del. above* [*del.*] would"] certainly [illeg."
15. Deleted: "in the parlor of [*ins.*] most" ; inserted: "to" above deleted "in"
16. Deleted: "folks"
17. Preceding six words inserted above deleted "folks" and "than any"
18. Inserted: "real" above "lions" ; deleted: "lions" ; inserted: "Krakens" above "lions"
19. Preceding two words inserted in ink above "sava" in "savagery"
20. Deleted: "real"

The Great Themes.

Manuscript in LC #279(*l*). Inscribed in black ink and black pencil on white wove paper, 10″ x 7¾″. Blue rules on recto, ½″ apart. The writing is WW's of the 1860s and the reiterated insistence on the abstraction "Democracy" points to the same period or later. The author being rebuked might well be Tennyson, but cannot be identified.

The[1] great themes of the Literatus are[2] as common as the air, the light, the destinies, the pride[3] love of man & woman, and come home to all, like life & death. This[4] writer is noble, but dainty.[5] Not that he is of no value, for he is of measureless[6] value. But[7] he picks and[8] rejects. Strictly speaking he belongs to the aristocracy[9] Much is in[10] his writings, and the young men of America are probably[11] are[12] debtors to[13] them more, far more than to those of [*illeg.*] authors.[14] But the lesson of Democracy, &[15] the lesson of the infinite and all-embracing amplitude of Nature & the Democracy of Nature & the application of that lesson to man,[16] are not in them.[17] He sometimes seems as if he would bravely

1. Deleted: "final" ; inserted above: "great"
2. Deleted: "as unspent and"
3. Preceding three words inserted in black pencil above "e" in "the" and "love of"
4. Deleted: [*illeg.*]
5. Deleted: "He is of" ; inserted and deleted: "Strictly speaking he" above deleted "he" and "Not" and "th" in "that"
6. Deleted: [*illeg.*]
7. Deleted: "The [*illeg.*]"
8. Inserted above wordspace between "picks" and "rejects"
9. Preceding seven words inserted in black pencil above "jects" in "rejects" and "his writings"
10. Deleted: "him" ; inserted above: "his writings"
11. Deleted: "in"
12. Deleted: "of"
13. Deleted: "him" ; inserted above: "them"
14. Preceding twenty-one words inserted between lines. Deleted new paragraph beginning: "The infinite man"
15. Preceding five words inserted; preceding four words in pencil; following "The" not reduced to lowercase in MS.
16. Preceding sixteen words inserted on two lines above "the infinite" ; deleted: "is" ; inserted above deleted "is" : "are"
17. Deleted: "And the analogies of Democracy, wanted in subtlest fields pined for" "And the spirit of"

approach these[18] armored[19] themes, where they stand[?] threatening in full panoply,[20] & do battle with them—but he never really does.[21] Then he is,[22] to speak it plainly, too genteel & conventional—too dandified—no Juvenal, or Rabelais, or[23] blurting Hebrew prophet.[24] After their[25] intellection, dainty suprciliousness seems with all the health & sweetness[26] be the unseen background of character to these writings[27]

18. Deleted: [*illeg.*] ; inserted: "these themes where they stand threatening."
19. The emendation described in *n*18 leaves "armored" isolated, but this seems the proper location.
20. Preceding three words and comma inserted. An isolated "Themes," deleted.
21. Succeeding words in black pencil brought down from upper margin on asterisks.
22. Deleted: "too"
23. Deleted: "Heb"
24. Preceding twenty-nine words in black pencil written diagonally at lower right of leaf.
25. Deleted: [*illeg.*]
26. Preceding six words inserted in black pencil.
27. Preceding sentence separated from preceding at lower left corner of the leaf by a line above and at right.

16th Century Queen Mary.

Manuscript in LC (#60, sheet #264). Inscribed in black ink and black pencil on a white wove scrap, 9⅜" x 5⅜". Tennyson's *Queen Mary* was published in England and the US in 1875. On July 24 WW wrote him about it, mentioning the criticism of Thomas Jefferson, on nineteenth-century medievalism, but remarking "I did not know till I read it, how much eligibility to passion, character and art arousings was still left in me in my sickness & old age" (Corr., II, 335). Bergman implies that he may have read not the play but, rather, the very full critique and excerpts in the NY papers. He also attributes the notes ("Era of Queen Mary," "of the 16th Century," "Q. Mary) The 16th," "Wolsey," "Queen Mary of England," "Henry 8th," "[*illeg.*] Richard 2d" preserved with this MS in LC to an interest aroused by the play. Date, 1875. First printed in Bergman, *SP,* 51, 497.

Queen Mary 16th Century

Out of this century to undoubtedly came the distinctive shaping & coloring of Skakspere's[1] genius.

Queen Mary, like so many fine[2] plays, poems, romances, &c, is undoubtedly open to the[3] severe criticism of Jefferson on the[4] general scope of Walter Scott, namely[5] that[6] while it fails to give at all[7] the life of the great mass of the people,[8] then & there, it picks out the[9] life of a few great persons, & gives that life[10] deceptively The same criticism can be made, from our point of view, against Skakspere. Yet,[11] as all art is a compromise.[12] It is the trick (& probably[13] should be so) of the good portrait painter, who first[14] gives a good likeness and then to present his subject at[15] the best, adds to or leaves off without scruple

1. Here and below the spelling is distinctly "Skakspere" . Possibly O'Connor had convinced him that not only the traditional vowels were wrong but also the consonants.
2. Inserted above "ny" in "many"
3. Deleted: "sarcastic" ; inserted above: "severe"
4. Deleted: "writings" ; inserted above: "general scope"
5. Inserted above "that"
6. Deleted: "it picks out"
7. Preceding two words inserted above "the"
8. Inserted and deleted: "of the time [*illeg.*]" ; inserted: "then & there" above "people"
9. Deleted: [*illeg.*] ; inserted above: "life"
10. Deleted in pencil: "falsely" ; inserted above in pencil: "deceptively"
11. Inserted and deleted in pencil: [*illeg.*] above "as"
12. The text continues in pencil.
13. Inserted above "should"
14. Inserted above "gives"
15. Deleted: "its"

Tennyson Dec. '78.

Manuscript in Texas (Hanley). Inscribed in black pencil on half-sheet of white wove notepaper, 9⅛" x 4⅞". Blue rules, 5/16" apart. This MS, with *"Tennyson* have been reading," "Tennyson residuum scraps," "the old, original rude ones," "comes it," and "the primary point," all originally in the T.E. Hanley Collection, are notes for an essay or lecture on Tennyson. Possibly "Tennyson loves to haunt" was part of this group. All are written in a similar handwriting and are dateable, or appear to be dateable, to 1878. Although none of these manuscripts appears to have been used in print, they are typical of WW's difficulties with Tennyson.

Even more than Emerson, to whom he felt an uneasy filial tie, and Carlyle, who was a worthy but not dangerous opponent, Tennyson was the contemporary who troubled WW. At the beginning of his career he announced anonymously in "An English and an American Poet," *American Phrenological Review* (October, 1855 and in *LG* [1856]) that he was about to replace the kind of poetry Tennyson represented and kept saying the same thing for the next twenty years. By 1870, he seems not to have been so sure. Possibly his growing awareness that his country was not accepting him led him to a number of mildly foolish efforts to promote himself. (See "We suppose.") He also grasped at the possibility of an English audience developed by the Rossetti selections and worked it for all it was worth ("Introduction to the London Edition.").

For all these reasons he felt a deep need for Tennyson's approbation and in 1871 sent him books through a mutual acquaintance (*Corr.,* II, 125–126). Tennyson was courteous and understood the *Leaves* well enough to pronounce that they had "go" (an all-purpose word for American energy). WW was immensely and pathetically proud of this approbation from the Highest Source, but fortunately did not quote it on the spine of *LG*.

The details of the relationship of the two poets are laid out by Herbert Bergman, "Whitman and Tennyson," *SP,* 51 (July, 1954), 492–504. See also Stovall, *Foreground,* 258–264. MS first published in Bergman, *SP,* 51, 502.

Tennyson Dec '78[1]

Tennyson's[2] poems are certainly[3] not Democracys poem's—nor helpers to[4], or believers in,[5] or illustrators of Democracy—[6] any more than Shakspere's pro-

1. Written at upper right.
2. Deleted: "works" ; inserted above: "poems"
3. Preceding four words inserted above deleted "He is" and "not" and "Democ" in "Democracys" . Original openings deleted: "Though his" , "Alfred [*illeg.*]" , "He is"
4. Inserted above "rs" in "helpers"
5. Inserted above "rs" in "believers"
6. Deleted: "no" ; inserted above: "—any" . Redundant dash not printed.

ductions,[7] or Carlyle's—at least they are not designed[8] by their authors[9] to be so.[10] Yet to me the whole thee are[11] important for their profoundest[12] Democratic[13] help, in spite of themselves.[14] Tennyson has indeed[15] done[16] one service to the age in some respects the geaest service—[17] he has express'd certain characteristic[18] colorings of our century—certain glistening lights[19] and shades, ([20]our age while moral & manly at the marrow[21] is largely reminiscent, ennuyeed, languishing,[22] love-sick with elegance,)[23] not alone among artists, perhaps better than any other.[24] Democracy,[25] I say, needs[26] all[27] such masters bring—refinement,[28] poetical glow, and the[29] best force-specimens & personalities[30] of the past, as in Homer,[31] Shakspere, Walter Scott[32] and A T.—needs the

7. Inserted above "pere's" in "Shakespere's"

8. Deleted: "at all"

9. Inserted above "there . . . to"

10. Preceding twelve words inserted on a line above "Carlyle's . . . Yet to me the whole"

11. Deleted: "dear, not only to my own personal taste, but" ; inserted: "[*del.*] very important" above "are" and deleted "taste, but"

12. Preceding two words inserted above "Democratic"

13. Deleted: "service" ; inserted above: "help"

14. Deleted: "As to me"

15. Inserted above "s" in "has" and "d" in "done"

16. Deleted: "the" ; inserted above: "one"

17. Preceding six words and dash inserted above "service" and deleted "the age &c" and "he has" ; deleted: "the age &c"

18. Deleted: [*illeg.*]

19. Deleted: "sheens"

20. Deleted: "that"

21. Preceding seven words inserted above "des" in "shades" and "our age . . . is"

22. Inserted.

23. Inserted and deleted: [*illeg.*]

24. Preceding nine words inserted on two lines above "Democracy,"

25. Deleted: "continually [*illeg.*] to be to-day"

26. Deleted: "always" ; inserted above: "all"

27. Deleted: "the strong [*ins.*] special help"

28. Deleted: "and the"

29. Inserted above wordspace between "and" "best"

30. Preceding two words inserted above "ens" in "specimens" and "of the"

31. Inserted above "in" and "S" in "Shakspere"

32. Deleted: "and Tennyson and" "rude" ; inserted above: "and A.T.—needs" . See "*Shakespeare and Walter Scott."

Tennyson / Residuum Scraps.

Manuscript in Texas (Hanley). Inscribed in black pencil and blue crayon on half a page torn from side-bound notebook. Rounded lower right corner. Blue rules, ¼″ apart. Probably a label for other Hanley notes on Tennyson. The date is probably 1878.

Tennyson / residuum scraps /[1] Much silk & velvet spangled with pearls,[2] but[3] enough of[4] oak & hard wood, & sometimes the finest steel let alone gold & silver

1. Preceding words in blue crayon. Deleted: "Silk." "It" "There is"
2. Preceding three words inserted above "velvet but"
3. Deleted: "there is"
4. Deleted: [*illeg.*]

Tennyson Have Been Reading.

Manuscript in Texas (Hanley). Inscribed in black pencil with black ink emendations on scrap of white wove side-bound notebook, 6 11/18" x 4". Blue rules ¼" apart. Bottom scrap, 5" wide, has blue rules 5/18" apart. Possibly designed for a lecture. See "Tennyson Dec '78." Date 1878. First printed in part in Bergman, *SP,* 51 (July, 1954), 498.

Tennyson

have been reading—handy new edition of Alfred Tennyson's poetry.[1]—full of[2]
heroic knights, lords, Kings—Arthur and his braves, Geraint,[3]
— gentle and subdued ladies[4] sometimes pretty sly,[5] ambitious, love-sick Guinevere, Enid, Vivien, Lady Clara Vere de Vere,[6]
debonair,[7] royal laurate, indeed, this Tennyson[8]—fit for[9] the Victorian
court, the Queen, elegant lords & ladies—dedicates his best to[10] Royal Consort Albert[11]
— Merlin,[12] Oriana, the Northern Farmer, Elaine, "To the Queen," Lucretius, Godiva,[13] the Merman and Mermaid, Ulysses,[14] In Memorian to AHH,[15]
the Northern Farmer, in his Yorkshire lingo, exquisite in drawing & color—[16]
perhaps the piece in the collection[17] call'd 'the Brook' a fair[18] sample of his gen-

1. Written above and around the title on three lines. There were five American one-volume editions in 1877–1878.
2. Deleted: "brave"
3. Space of perhaps three lines below.
4. Deleted: "Guin"
5. Deleted: "loving" ; inserted: "ambitious, love-sick" above "pretty sly" and deleted "loving"
6. Space to end of line and for one line below. Deleted after space: "courtly"
7. Deleted: "he is the"
8. Preceding three words inserted above "ate" in "laureate" and "fit for"
9. Deleted: "a"
10. Deleted: "the"
11. Space of perhaps two lines below.
12. Deleted: "Ulysses, Marianne" ; inserted: "Oriana" above deleted "Marianne"
13. Inserted above "s," in "Lucretius," and "the"
14. Inserted above "aid," in "Mermaid," and wordspace following.
15. Beginning of pasted-on scrap.
16. Deleted: "but"
17. Preceding three words inserted above "piece call'd"
18. Deleted: "average"
19. Preceding two words inserted above "his . . . middle"

eral &[19] middle-average, (the plot, or[20] to its effect, repeated[21] in half a dozen [2] other[22] poems,)[23] — But the Idylls of the
King, amid much[24] mannerism,[25] and involution,[26] showing his[27] flush power & muscle.
The lately published[28] plays,[29] in my opinion, much[30] the same.
(I will read you the read Northern Farmer)[31]

20. Deleted: "about the"
21. Deleted: "in various" ; inserted: "in" above "us" in "[*del.*] various"
22. Inserted on an angle above "po" in "poems"
23. Deleted: "his well known Enoch Arden among the rest"
24. Deleted: "verbal"
25. Deleted: [*illeg.*]; inserted above: "and"
26. Deleted: "and verbal polish,"
27. "his" inserted above "showing" ; inserted and deleted: "fullest [*illeg.*] following "[*ins.*] his" ; deleted: "fine [*illeg.*] his" ; inserted and deleted: "his ripen'd" above "[*del.*] his" and "power" ; inserted in ink: "flush" above "ower" in "power" . The plays were probably *Queen Mary* (1875) and *Harold* (1877), or possibly also *The Cup and the Falcon* (1879). *Beckett* was published in 1884.
28. Inserted above "plays"
29. Deleted: "do too"
30. Inserted in ink above "n," in "opinion," and "t" in "the"
31. Scrawled below on three lines within braces.

Tennyson Loves.

Manuscript in Rutgers. Inscribed in black ink and black pencil on white wove notepaper, 8″ x 5″. Blue rules ⅜″ apart. On verso, note from Whitelaw Reid, editor of the NY *Tribune,* December [?] 28, 1878. First printed in Bergman, *SP,* 51, (1954), 502–503.

Tennyson[1] loves to haunt old castles,[2] to deal with[3] them and their inmates. But don't he take[4] persons & plots sometimes[5] from low life? and don't he[6] render them very finely too? Yes; but[7] in the loftiest, daintiest[8] spirit of aristocracy—[9] the very salt of "good birth".—[10]

1. Originally a title; brought down on an arrow. Deleted: "—he"
2. Preceding four words inserted above "loves to deal" and "wi" in "with"
3. Inserted above following deleted "kings and courts" in pencil: "them and their inmates." Deleted in pencil: "kings and courts, [*del.*] & Earls, Bishops, Knights, Princesses, noble ladies, &c. [*del.*] I ["N" *ins.*] ever [*ins. above* "er" *in* "never"] indeed [*del.*] have has there been a more "aristocratic" poet, [*two words del.*] from the [*ins. above* "the"] with closest affiliations of his plots [*del.*] with [*ins. above* "with"] to "high blood" "
4. Deleted: "characters" ; inserted above: "persons"
5. Deleted: "in" ; inserted above: "from"
6. Preceding two words inserted above "and" and "re" in "render"
7. Deleted: "it is that" ; inserted and deleted: [*illeg.*] ; inserted: "in [*ins. in pencil*] the" above deleted "that"
8. Deleted: "(in [*two words del.*] some a [*ins. above deleted* "some"] one [*del.*] sense [*ins.* "sense" *above deleted* "sense"] most democratic)" . It would be interesting to see how WW justified this paradox.
9. Inserted and deleted in pencil: "it is with" above "the very"
10. Deleted: "that these very plots are conceived & characters painted [*preceding eight words del.*]" ; inserted and deleted in pencil: "low life plots & characters too" above the deleted "very plots are conceived" ; inserted in ink: "are always seasoned." above "[*del.*] painted" and into the right margin.

[*Illeg.*] Comes It That.

Manuscript in Texas (Hanley). Inscribed in black pencil on three scraps: [1] tan laid, [2 and 3] pasted on white wove. Blue rules, 5/16" apart. Overall dimensions approx. 5½" x 5¼". The date is approx. 1878. First published in part in Bergman, *SP,* 51 (1954), 503.

[*Illeg.*] comes it that such a poet as Tennyson is[1] to-day the most read and absorbed of any of his kind [*illeg.*] America?[2]

Instead of having any thing in common with either politics, or vulgar[3] work-aday world,[4] this land of[5] ten million ballots (black an white) the Victorian Laureate[6] not implies, but *is*[7] the monarchy on every page, the feudal principle, caste, lords & ladies owning & ruling, ([8]yet perhaps many by right of superior physical and moral qualities, heroism, bravery, beauty[9] manners, generosity,[10] purity) the mass of[11] people serving as children serve their[12] olders,[13] & betters.

Then a principal

1. Deleted: [*illeg.*] ; inserted above: "to-day"
2. Deleted: "Let us take the [*illeg.*]" . End of first scrap.
3. Deleted: [*illeg.*]
4. Preceding six words inserted above "tead" in "instead" and "of having anything" and "ei" in "either"
5. Deleted: "equality" ; inserted: "ten million ballots (black and white)" above the deletion and "the Victorian Laureate"
6. End of second scrap.
7. Deleted: "inequality aristocracy" ; inserted: "the monarchy" above and "on every page" below "[*del.*] inequality"
8. Deleted: [*illeg.*]; inserted above deletion and "many" : "Yet perhaps"
9. Preceding two words inserted above "heroism" and "man" in "manners"
10. Deleted: "bravery"
11. Deleted: "the"
12. Deleted: "wisers"
13. Deleted: [*illeg.*]; inserted above: "betters"

The Primary Point.

Manuscript in Texas. Inscribed on two scraps of heavy wove cream paper, 8[11]/16" x 4½" and 7⅜" x 4[11]/16", pasted together on darker coarse white paper. First scrap in ink, second in pencil. At top, in an unidentified hand: "On Tennyson." The unsteady writing suggests this was written in the 1870s or 1880s. First scrap printed by Herbert Bergman, "Whitman and Tennyson," *SP,* 51 (1954), 501–502.

the[1] *primary* point of[2] the man's excellence is the[3] indisputable, though very subtle,[4] identity of his verse with[5] the narrow[6] British Islands,[7] their[8] composite Anglo-Saxo-Norman stock, spirit & history. Artificial as they are,[9] his poems are the[10] flowers of his own race and land.[11] He filters the past & brings it down to to-day. In[12] entirely different ways from Shakspere's; yet[13] his utterance is nothing, if not feudal and[14] English.][15]

English[16] social[17] life, of the highest[18] range, (a melancholy, affectionate, heroic, very dainty[19] breed)[20]pervades it[21] like an invisible scent—the idleness, the

1. Present opening preceded by: "[*illeg.*] I am not sure but to my mind" , which appears to be deleted.
2. Deleted in pencil: "this" ; inserted in pencil above: "the"
3. Deleted: "curious"
4. Preceding three words and comma inserted above "table" in "indisputable" and "identity"
5. Inserted and deleted: "his own race and [*illeg.*]" above "verse with"
6. Inserted in pencil above "Bri" in "British"
7. Deleted: "the"
8. Deleted: "Saxo-N" ; inserted above: "composite"
9. Preceding four words inserted in pencil above "history . His" ; uncorrected capital "H" in "His"
10. Inserted and deleted: "scented and ripe (is it [*preceding two words del.*] are they [*preceding two words ins.* above deleted "is it"] too ripe?)" above "poems are the flowers"
11. Deleted: "and are As much as Shakspere" ; inserted: "He filters . . . to-day." above "race and land" and "[*del.*] and are"
12. Deleted: "an"
13. Deleted: "they" ; inserted: "his utterance is" above "[*del.*] they" and "are" and "not" in "nothing" ; uncorrected "are" not shown; "s" removed from utterances"
14. Preceding two words inserted above "not" and "En" in "English"
15. End of first scrap.
16. Preceded by [*illeg.*] deleted word written diagonally.
17. Deleted: "is"
18. Inserted: "est" on "high"
19. Preceding two words inserted above "heroic"
20. Parenthesized words inserted above "social life of the highest range"
21. Deleted: "all through"

traditions, the delicate manners and mannerisms,[22] the stately ennui—the yearning of[23] love,[24] a spinal-marrow[25] inside of all—the costumes, old brocade, or silk and satin—[26] the old houses and furniture—the lasting oak, no mere [*illeg.*][27]—the traditions every where—some mouldy secrets [*illeg.*]—with[28] the verdure, the ivy on the walls, the moat,—the English landscape outside[29] the buzzing fly[30] in the sun inside the window pane

22. Preceding two words and comma inserted above "manners, the"
23. Preceding three words inserted above "ennui—"
24. Deleted: "like an [*illeg.*]" ; inserted: "a spinal-" above the illegible deletion.
25. Deleted: "pervading"
26. Preceding eight words inserted above "[*del.*] pervading" and "all—the old houses"
27. Preceding six words inserted above "and furniture—the traditions"
28. Preceding five words inserted above "everywhere the"
29. Preceding four words inserted in ink above "walls, the moat the"
30. Deleted: "behind" ; inserted: "in the sun inside [*ink*]" above "fly" and deleted "behind"

"Still Lives the Song.

Manuscript not found. Text from *N&F,* 167 (Pt. IV, #52; *CW,* X, 15). Stovall, *Foreground,* 115, identifies the source as Margaret Fuller's *Papers on Literature and Art* (1846), the quotation being from Sterling's "Alfred the Harper." Stovall, however, assumes that the addendum printed by Bucke "The Word is become Flesh" is part of this MS, whereas the scriptural quotation is on a separate slip in Duke. He may well be right in interpreting it as having reference to WW's identification of himself with his poetry. There is, however, no evidence of any connection between the two MSS other than Bucke's habit of running separate MSS together. The date is probably in the late 1840s.

"Still lives the song tho' Regnar dies." —*John Sterling.*

Keats' Poetry.

Manuscript not found. Text from *N&F,* 109 (Pt. III, #87; *CW,* IX, 120). Stovall (*AL,* 26, 348) suggests that it derives from a review of *Hyperion* in *American Whig Review,* 14 (October, 1851), 320 (Bucke #54); see "Bells and Pomgranates." Since it was a Bucke MS, the date is probably in the 1850s. First printed in *N&F.*

Keats' poetry is ornamental, elaborated, rich in wrought imagery, it is imbued with the sentiment, at second-hand, of the gods and goddesses of twenty-five hundred years ago. Its feeling is the feeling of a gentlemanly person lately at college, accepting what was commanded him there, who moves and would only move in elegant society, reading classical books in libraries. Of life in the nineteenth century it has none any more than the statues have. It does not come home at all to the direct wants of the bodies and souls of the century.

(1854) Alexander Smith's.

Manuscript in Middlebury. Inscribed in black pencil on white wove leaf, approx. 9½" x 5¼". Alexander Smith (1830–1867), a Scots poet and essayist, was satirically labelled a member of the "Spasmodic School." WW quotes the passage about "the great, forthcoming poet" in "An English and an American Poet," a review of *LG* (1855) and Tennyson's *Maud* (1855) in the *American Phrenological Journal* (October, 1855). Bayard Taylor (1825–1878) became one of WW's *bêtes noirs* in the 1870s. The date is 1854 or later. First printed in *N&F,* 127 (Pt. II, #'s 154–155; CW, *IX,* 156).

(1854)

Alexander Smith's Poems—"A Life Drama" and minor pieces.—

There is one electric passage in this poetry, where the announcement is made of a great forthcoming Poet, and the illustration given of a king who, about dying, plunges his sword into his favorite attendant, to send him on before.—

Alexander Smith is imbued with the nature of Tennyson.[1] He is full of what are called poetical images—full of conceits and likenesses;—in this respect copying after Shakespeare and the majority of the received poets.—He seems to be neither better or worse than the high average.—

Bayard Taylor's Poems more resemble N. P. Willis's than any others.—They are polished, oriental, sentimental, and have as attributes what[2] may be called their psychology—You cannot see very plainly at times what they mean although the poet indirectly has a meaning

1. Inserted: period; deleted: "a good deal.—"
2. Deleted: [*illeg.*]

1855—I Have Looked.

Manuscript in Duke (30, #4). Inscribed in black pencil with black-ink emendations on tan wove paper, approx. 9⅛" x 5½". Stovall, *AL,* 26, 352, reports a clipping (Bucke #389) on Massey with the MS. Massey (1821–1907) was of working-class origin and self-educated. He was associated with the Chartist and Christian Socialist movements. First printed *N&F,* 127 (Pt. III, #157; *CW* IX, 157). The date is 1855.

1855— I have looked over *Gerald Massey's Poems* London.—[1] They seem to me zealous, candid, warlike,—intended, as they[2] are, to get up a strong feeling against the British aristocracy both in their social and[3] and political capacity.—Massey, I hear, is a youngish man, a radical, an editor now I believe in one of the provincial towns.—His early life laborious, a workman in a factory I think.—

1. Inserted above dash and period after *"Poems"* . Redundant period and dash not printed.
2. Deleted in ink: "surely"
3. Deleted in black ink: "governmental" ; inserted above in black ink: "political"

? Hallam D'Israeli.

Manuscript at Rutgers. Inscribed in black ink and black pencil on pink wove paper, approx. 9¾" x 5⅞", cut at left edge. Written around an unidentifiable clipping giving the ages of eminent men. Dates are one above the other opposite braces. Stovall *AL,* 26, 357–358, identifies the source as an unidentified edition of Louis (or Ludwig) Herrig's *The British Classical Authors*. Some names are omitted, and some dates vary from Herrig and those accepted today (e.g. *Oxford Companion*), but the arrangement is Herrig's. See also the closely related "Letters of Junius." The paper, the date, 1855, in the MS, and the information in the clipping establish the date as 1855. First printed *N&F,* 159 (Pt. IV, #22; *CW,* IX, 224).

? Hallam D'Israeli[1]	Chaucer	born 1328 died 1400
	John Gower	born 1325 died 1409
	Gawin Douglas Scotch John Wickliffe	1474 1522
Samuel Rogers, 96, died. Dec. 1855.[2]	(with Chaucer)	1324 1384
	Sir Thomas More	1480 1535
1855)	Sir Edmund Spenser	1558 1598
	Christ. Marlowe	1562 1592—
? Bulwer	Shakespeare	1564 1616—
born 1784	Ben Johnson	1574 1637

1. Two preceding names upper left.
2. Written in pencil above clipping. Following items in column at right.

		Phil Massinger	1584 1640
		Sir Philip Sidney	1554 1586[5]
Sir Walter Raleigh	1552 1618	Jos. Addison	1672 1719?[6]
Francis Bacon	1561 1626	Saml. Johnson	1709 1784
Milton	1608 1674	Jonathan Swift Daniel Defoe Henry Fielding	1667–1745 1663–1731 1707–1754
Saml Butler Hudibras	1612 1680	Lawrence Sterne Tobias Smollet—	1713–1768 1721–1771
John Dryden	1631[3] ?1700	Oliver Goldsmith Henry Mackenzie— David Hume—	1729–1774 1745–1831 1711–1776
John Locke	1632 1704	Edward Gibbon— Wm. Robertson	1737 1721–1793
John Bunyan	1628 1688	Dr. Hugh Blair— Philip Dormer Stanhope Earl Chesterfield	1729–1774 1694–1773
Alex. Pope	1688 1744[4]	Lady Mary Wortly Montagu Edmund Burke—	1690–1762 1730–1797 (over)[7]
	1855)	?Bulwer	1784[8]

3. Deleted in pencil: [*illeg.*]

4. First "4" over [*illeg.*]. Beneath deleted: "? 86 years old" . Following names in column at right, separated by vertical line from preceding.

5. Following items in column at left below clipping and below line across leaf.

6. Question mark in pencil opposite both dates.

7. Preceded by "over" ; followed by a fist pointing right. Verso blank.

8. Both written to left of clipping in which "Bulwer" is parenthesized in pencil.

Letters of Junius.

Manuscript in Rutgers. Inscribed in black ink and black pencil on pink wove paper, 9¾" x 5⅝", cut at the left, torn at the right. On verso is "Rei ne cke". Inscribed neatly but bizarrely in columns as indicated in notes. The names, like those in the closely related "? Hallam D'Israeli," are from Louis Herrig's *The British Classical Authors*. The paper, the writing, and the relation to "(? Hallam D'Israeli)" establish the date as 1855. First printed *N&F,* 159 (Pt. IV, #22; *CW,* IX, 224–225.

Letters of Junius——1769—70—71

("Transition School")

	James Thomson——	1700—1748
	William Cowper——	1731—1800
Ellegy in Church Yard	Thomas Gray——	1716—1771
	William Collins——	1720—1756
	Mark Akenside——	1721—1770
Ossian	James Macpherson	1737—1796
	Thos Chatterton[1]——	1752—1770
Reliques of Ancient Poetry	Dr. Thos. Percy——	1755
	Robert Burns——	1759[2]—1796
("Modern Literature")	(—Sir Jas. Mackintosh——	1765—1832
	James Montgomery——	Born 1771
	Sir Walter Scott——	1771—1832
	H.K. White——	1785—1806
	Robt Bloomfield——	1766—1823
	Ann Letitia Barbauld——	1743—1825
	Lord Byron——	1788—1824
	Percy Bysshe Shelley——	1792—1822
	Geo. Crabbe——	1754—1832
	Thos. Campbell——	1777—1843
	Thos. Moore——	1780
	Robt. Southey——	1774—1843
	Wm Wordsworth——	1770—1850
	Saml. Taylor Coleridge	1773—1834

1. In pencil: "43" . WW's hand?
2. Inserted in pencil and deleted: "?" above "9"

	Felicia Hemans— ————	1794—1835	
	L.E. Landon— ————	1802—1838	
	T.B. Macaulay— ————	1800 still living	
Scotch	Jas. Hogg— ————	1772—1835	
	Robt. Tannahill— ————	1774—1810	
	Allan Cunningham— ————	1784—1842	
	Wm. Motherwell— ————	1797—1835[3]	
Novelists	Ann Radcliffe— ————	1764—1823	Hazlitt
	Maria Edgeworth— ————	1771	1780—1830
	? Edward Lytton Bulwer— ——	1784	Chas Lamb
	Charles Dickens, about	1812	1775—1835
	G.P.R. James— ————	1801[4]	
orators	Wm. Pitt Earl of Chatham	1708—1778	Carlyle
	2d Wm Pitt— ————	1759—1806	born 1795
	C.J. Fox— ————	1748—1806[5]	

Henry Grattan———	1750—1829	Brougham ——	1779
Geo. Canning ——	1770—1827	Peel ————	1788
O'Connell[6] ———	1774—1847		

3. Rule across leaf.
4. Rule across leaf.
5. Following three names at left edge.
6. Three preceding names at right with straight lines left, above, right. Two following names at center with straight lines above, below, and to left.

What Are Inextricable.

Manuscript in Duke (29, #42). Inscribed in black ink on pink wove paper [*1*] 9¾″ x 5⅞″ and [*2*] 9½″ x 5⅞″. On verso of [*2*] is a clipping praising and quoting William Cowper's "Yardley Oak" and inscription "Cowper 1731–1800 an ennuyeed poet" . The paper and writing indicate a date in 1855 or in 1856. First printed *N&F,* 107 (Pt. III, #77; *CW,* IX, 114–116).

What are inextricable from the British poets are[1] the ideas of royalty and aristocracy, the ideas of the[2] radical division of those who serve from those who are served, and[3] a continual recognition of the[4] principles[5] at the bases of monarchy[6] and the societies and beliefs of[7] caste[8].—[9]In the continents of the eastern hemisphere[10] a bard[11] whether ancient or modern has been an attaché to a nobleman or a court, or to[12] the order of noblemen and courts.—The skald, the harper, the[13] troubadour, Shakespeare, the feudal minstrel, the more modern poet, the laureate,[14] all[15] write or did write or speak for those selected persons and at their behest, and for the honor and largesse they gave.—Shakespeare[16] composed altogether for the court and for the young[17] nobility and the gentry;—he had no other audience.—[18]The courts have at all times pensioned eminent poets, and[19]

1. Preceding eight words written above "The ideas aristocracy" . Following "The" not reduced to lowercase in MS.
2. Deleted: "separation" ; inserted above: "radical division"
3. Deleted: "of the idea"
4. Deleted: "great leading"
5. Deleted: "that lie" ; inserted and deleted: "spread" above "[*del.*] lie" and "at"
6. Corrected from "monarchial" ; deleted: "institutions"
7. Deleted: "the"
8. Deleted: "notions"
9. Inserted and deleted: "[*illeg.*] and in" above "In the"
10. Deleted: "the" ; inserted above: "a"
11. Reduced to singular from plural. Deleted: "have always been"
12. Deleted: "that order" ; inserted on two lines above: "to the order of noblemen and courts" . Deleted: "In"
13. Deleted: "th"
14. Probably a reference to Tennyson, who had been named Laureate in 1850.
15. Deleted: "have found written and spoken for them" ; inserted: "write or did write or speak for those selected persons" above the deletion and "and at"
16. Deleted: "wrote" ; inserted above: "composed"
17. Inserted above "the" and "n" in "nobility"
18. Preceding five words inserted above "The courts"
19. Deleted: "does" ; inserted above: "do"

do so to this day.— . . . . . In all times and in all nations it has been the faith of poets to believe in the noblest thoughts and deeds and to express them and to diffuse the love of beauty.— In this we inherit and partake of every one, without distinction of period or place.[20] In this is the common glory of poets, irrespective of period or place.— In this the good of any one is the good of all.— . . . . .[21] Yet is no poet[22] dear to a people unless he[23] be of them and of the spirit of them,[24] a growth of the soil, the water, the climate,[25] the age, the government, the religion, the leading characteristic, a height and individuality for his own nation and days and[26] not for other nations—in Egypt an[27] Egyptian, in Greece a Greek, in Germany a German, in England an Englishman, in[28] the United

[2] Of the leading British poets many who began with the rights of man, abjured their beginning[29] and came out for kingcraft priestcraft, obedience, and so forth.—Southey, Coleridge, and Wordsworth, did so.—

20. Sentence inserted on two lines above "love of beauty—In this"
21. Deleted: "Nor can any" ; inserted above: "Yet is no"
22. Deleted: "be" ; inserted and deleted: "become" above deleted "be" and "dear"
23. Deleted: "represent"
24. Deleted: "—in"
25. Deleted: "the" ; inserted above: "a"
26. Deleted: "f"
27. Corrected from: "and"
28. Reading of two preceding words from *N&F*.
29. Corrected from "begin"

Byron Born At Dover.

Manuscript in Duke (27, #38V). Inscribed in black ink (as noted) and black pencil on right half of "undeniable might." It is probable that, having used the notes in that MS in *LG* (1856), he erased the right half in 1856 for some characteristic notes on literary history. At the bottom is a clipping of London literary gossip endorsed "London Letter. N.Y. Tribune, July 12, '56" . An unidentified clipping, probably also from the *Tribune,* is the source of his notes on Carlyle and Dickens. The date is 1856, after the publication of *LG* (1856). First printed *N&F,* 161–162 (Pt. IV, #27; *CW,* IX, 230). See illustration.

(Byron, born at Dover, Eng, 1788
died at Missolonghi, 1824 aged 36)[1]
Leigh Hunt Shelley Coleridge, Southey[2] Moore, Campbell[3]
Crabbe, Rogers[4] Keats, Wordsworth[5]
(Byron[6] born at Dover, Eng 1788 Died at Missolonghi Greece
1824 aged 37

Bulwer, D'Israeli[7]

Appearance of Carlyle 1827

Appearance of Dickens 1835 (then 23 years old)

1856 Carlyle appeared then nearly 30 years ago[8]/

1. Black ink. Entire entry inside very irregular parenthesis
2. Written side by side.
3. Written side by side.
4. Wirtten side by side.
5. Written side by side.
6. Black ink. Entire entry in curved line around left, above and below.
7. Written side by side.
8. Written across leaf.

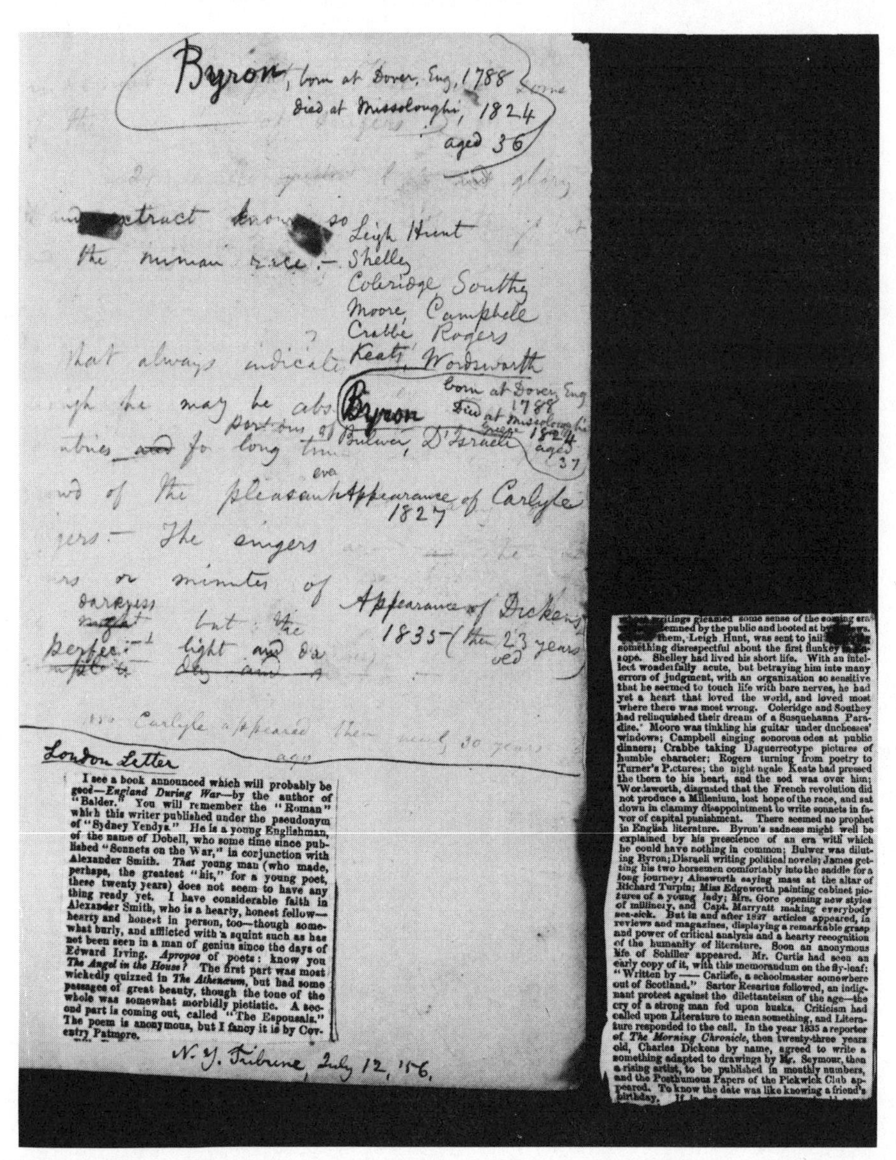

Byron, born at Dover, Eng, 1788
died at Missolonghi, 1824
aged 36

Leigh Hunt
Shelley
Coleridge Southey
Moore, Campbell
Crabbe Rogers
Keats, Wordsworth

Byron born at Dover, Eng 1788
died at Missolonghi Greece 1824
aged 37

portions of Bulwer, D'Israeli

Appearance of Carlyle 1827

Appearance of Dickens 1835 (then 23 years old)

London Letter

I see a book announced which will probably be good—*England During War*—by the author of "Balder." You will remember the "Roman" which this writer published under the pseudonym of "Sydney Yendys." He is a young Englishman, of the name of Dobell, who some time since published "*Sonnets on the War*," in conjunction with Alexander Smith. *That* young man (who made, perhaps, the greatest "hit," for a young poet, these twenty years) does not seem to have any thing ready yet. I have considerable faith in Alexander Smith, who is a hearty, honest fellow—hearty and honest in person, too—though somewhat burly, and afflicted with a squint such as has not been seen in a man of genius since the days of Edward Irving. *Apropos* of poets: know you *The Angel in the House?* The first part was most wickedly quizzed in *The Athenæum*, but had some passages of great beauty, though the tone of the whole was somewhat morbidly pietistic. A second part is coming out, called "The Espousals." The poem is anonymous, but I fancy it is by Coventry Patmore.

N. Y. Tribune, July 12, '56.

...writings gleamed some sense of the coming era ...emned by the public and hooted at by ... them, Leigh Hunt, was sent to jail ... something disrespectful about the first flunkey ...ope. Shelley had lived his short life. With an intellect wonderfully acute, but betraying him into many errors of judgment, with an organization so sensitive that he seemed to touch life with bare nerves, he had yet a heart that loved the world, and loved most where there was most wrong. Coleridge and Southey had relinquished their dream of a Susquehanna Paradise.' Moore was tinkling his guitar under duchesses' windows; Campbell singing sonorous odes at public dinners; Crabbe taking Daguerreotype pictures of humble character; Rogers turning from poetry to Turner's Pictures; the nightingale Keats had pressed the thorn to his heart, and the sod was over him; Wordsworth, disgusted that the French revolution did not produce a Millenium, lost hope of the race, and sat down in clammy disappointment to write sonnets in favor of capital punishment. There seemed no prophet in English literature. Byron's sadness might well be explained by his prescience of an era with which he could have nothing in common; Bulwer was diluting Byron; Disraeli writing political novels; James getting his two horsemen comfortably into the saddle for a long journey; Ainsworth saying mass at the altar of Richard Turpin; Miss Edgeworth painting cabinet pictures of a young lady; Mrs. Gore opening new styles of millinery, and Capt. Marryatt making everybody sea-sick. But in and after 1827 articles appeared, in reviews and magazines, displaying a remarkable grasp and power of critical analysis and a hearty recognition of the humanity of literature. Soon an anonymous life of Schiller appeared. Mr. Curtis had seen an early copy of it, with this memorandum on the fly-leaf: "Written by —— Carlisle, a schoolmaster somewhere out of Scotland." Sartor Resartus followed, an indignant protest against the dilettanteism of the age—the cry of a strong man fed upon husks. Criticism had called upon Literature to mean something, and Literature responded to the call. In the year 1835 a reporter of *The Morning Chronicle*, then twenty-three years old, Charles Dickens by name, agreed to write a something adapted to drawings by Mr. Seymour, then a rising artist, to be published in monthly numbers, and the Posthumous Papers of the Pickwick Club appeared. To know the date was like knowing a friend's birthday. ...

BYRON, BORN AT DOVER. Trent Collection, William R. Perkins Library, Duke University, Cat. p. 27, #38. Notes of 1855–1856. On recto is "Produce great persons" (q.v.). See p. 1779.

Memory.—Nothing makes this faculty so good, as the employment of it.—Locke.

Many trouble themselves about conforming to laws.—A great poet is followed by laws—they conform to him.

Plutarch—born about the year 50 A.C. probably died at 125 A.C.

Notes of Life, books &c. translations when appeared.—

Plutarch's Lives—
Amiot's translation (French) 1558
in Greek text, at Paris,—1624
First English translation—during reign of Queen Elizabeth.
Dryden, with many others in Co. also made a translation "a motley work;"

Plutarch—born in Bœotia, in Greece, about the year 50 of the Christian era
studied (like the general Greek youth)—acquired a great art of memory—read all the books (MSS.) of his time—leaned toward the tenets of Pythagoras.—
was of patrician family—supposed wealthy—
—had two brothers his associates in study and amusements—he always speaks of them with pleasure and affection—
Probably traveled into Egypt—Certainly into Italy
—studied Latin quite late in life—never made much progress
Lectured in Rome—(So Lectures, it seems, there were, even in those days;—quite like the modern fashion, they seem to have been.
Plutarch had a good reputation at Rome.—
—some say he was preceptor to the Emperor Trajan
Notes, in the time of Plutarch, were unknown in literary compositions—this accounts for his digressions and tedious episodes.—
Late in life retired to Chæronea, a philosopher, priest.—
Was married—had five children, four sons & a daughter
had a good wife.
I suppose he attained a good old age.—"a long life"
Most of his writings, with many Lives, are Lost—those that remain being but a portion of what he wrote

MEMORY. Trent Collection, William R. Perkins Library, Duke University, Cat., p. 35, #24. Notes of 1855–1856.

(Keats Died.

Manuscript in Duke (31, #7). Inscribed in black pencil on verso of what appears to be a galley proof of a school grammar, 5" x 4¾". Stovall, *AL,* 26 (1954), 344–345, identifies WW's sources as "The Life and Writings of Percy Bysshe Shelley," *North British Review,* 8 (November, 1847), 116–137. With the MS are "Characteristics of Shelley," *American Whig Review,* 5 (May, 1847), 534–536, a copy of "The Sky-Lark" clipped from Charles Knight, ed., *Half-Hours with the Best Authors* (NY, 1856, 1859 etc.) and two other clippings. First printed *N&F,* 92 (Pt. III, #35; *CW,* IX, 84).

(Keats died 1821)[1] *Shelley, born 1792*—died 1822 *stock, English* gentry (must have been quite such another as *T. L. Harris*[2] went to Eton & Oxford 1810 figure slight tall, stooped,[3] aspect youthful screamed loud in talking when enthusiastic/[4] head small, hair long, & bushy/[5] generous, benevolent, pure/[6] early riser—in winter evenings lay on the rug before the fire and sleep curled round, like a cat—/[7]fed simply—liked bread & raisins/ expeld from college 1811—/married same year separated 1813—wife died married 2d, 1816/ was[8] not healthy—or rather not rudely so.[9]

1. In upper right corner with lines at side and bottom represented by parentheses.
2. Harris (1823–1906), an American Christian mystic, who in trances composed long poems on the theme of celestial love. According to Stovall they were written under Shelley's influence.
3. Preceding two words inserted above "ght" in "slight" and "aspect"
4. Rule across leaf.
5. Rule across leaf.
6. Rule across leaf.
7. Deleted: "never distinguished flowers"
8. Deleted: "never" ; inserted above: "not"
9. Preceding eight words in lower left corner with line above and to right.

Milton—1608.

Manuscript in Duke (35, #27). Inscribed in black ink over partly erased "Poet, bard, minstrel " after the material had been used (see "undeniable might"). On verso: *"Burns* born 1757 died 1796 aged 39" . The date 1574 rather than 1572 or 1573 for Jonson's birth suggests that WW got his information from Louis Herrig, *British Classical Authors* (1855). The date is 1856, probably after the appearance of *LG* (1856). First printed *N&F,* 163 (Pt. IV, #30; *CW,* X, 8).

Milton—1608–1674 Contemporary of[1] (Horace & Byron[2]
Ben Jonson 1574–1637
Dryden 1631–1710
Bunyan 1628–1688

followed by Alexander
Pope—1688–

1. Deleted: "Shakespeare—1564–1616" above "Ben Jonson 1574–1637"
2. In upper right corner following "1674" set off by line around

Dryden.

Manuscript in Duke (29, #12). Inscribed in black pencil on pink wove paper, 9¾" x 5⅞". Verso bears impression of numerous parallel horizontal lines and two vertical serrated lines. Attached to the bottom are clippings giving sketches of Jeremy Taylor, Smollett, Pascal, and Franklin from *Half-Hours with the Best Authors*. The date is probably 1856 or 1857. First printed *N&F,* 113 (Pt. III, #101; *CW,* IX, 127–128).

Dryden 1631 to 1701

Dryden seems to have been of vigorous make, sharp-tempered—used his poetical talent to make money, show up his enemies,—those of the opposite party, noblemen, politicians, &c.— He sings a good deal in the inflated, distressingly classical style of those times

Geoffrey Chaucer.

Manuscript not found. Text from *N&F,* 92–93 (Pt. III, #37; *CW,* IX, 85–87). Stovall, *AL,* 26 (1954), 345, says drawn from "Chaucer," *North British Review,* American edition, 10 (February, 1849), 158–177, in Bucke's list of articles (#327). It appears that WW's source was also Charles Deshler, *Selections from the Works of Geoffry* [sic] *Chaucer,* (NY, 1847). (He also reviewed a book by Deshler, *Chaucer and Selections from His Poetical Works,* as Stovall points out [see *UPP,* I, 127], possibly the same book.) The MS has verbal echoes of pp. 5–29 of the book first cited above. WW, however, disagrees with Deshler's ranking (p. 29) of Chaucer with Homer and Shakespeare. The last entry is no doubt pure WW. The date *may* be as early as 1847, but it is more likely from his period of intense self-education between 1855 and 1860.

Geoffrey Chaucer, born 1328, died 1400 aged 72, parents citizens of London. Contemporary of Froissart, Walter de Manny, King Edward and Queen Phillippa.

Chaucer is supposed to have seen and conversed familiarly with Petrarch.

He received in the 39th and 44th years of his age two grants or annuities from the King.

He cultivated his own growth out of that of the Italian and Provençal poets.

Appointed by the King Comptroller of the customs of wool, wool-fells and hides—income £ 1,000, equal to about $15,000 now.

After death of Edward III. held similar favor and kindness under Richard II.

Wickliffe was his contemporary and friend. Chaucer sat in Parliament 1386.

Personally (aged 30) "of a fair and beautiful complexion, his lips red and full, his size a just medium, his air polished and graceful." Married at 37 to the daughter of a Hainault knight.

Of course in Chaucer's time the language of the court and of learned and refined persons, especially of poetical-disposed genteel persons must have assimilated to the French and mostly was French, coming on to them from William the Conqueror and his nobles and their descendants.

Spencer copied Chaucer 200 years after his time.

Of all Chaucer's poems Driden preferred Palamon and Arcite.

As great as Spencer and Milton very easily—and no obstinate quarrel about Dante; but wait awhile before putting him with Homer or Shakespeare.[1]

1. Bucke's notes: "Marginal note. The writer in magazine has said: 'Chaucer must be classed with Homer and Dante, with Spencer, Shakespeare and Milton.' "

Doubtless at that time no one knew or thought those persons heroes or those wars and politics important. Also Chaucer alone of eminent English poets seems to have been above adulating royalty and nobles for gain's sake.

There has been hardly a poet in the English language since 1400 but imitates Chaucer more or less.

Driden founded the school under which Pope's style comes. Driden's forte was satire—his poems all have it more or less—visibly or invisibly.

Chaucer was humorous—perhaps as humorous as Shakespeare.

Chaucer was plainly a strong wholesome man with large perceptive organs, friendly, amative, of independent spirit—possessed of the true English tastes, rude, fond of women, fond of eating and drinking, not to be quelled by priestcraft or kingcraft.

Oliver Goldsmith.

Manuscript in Duke (30, #3). Inscribed in black pencil on white paper from pocket ledger, 5¾" x 3⅜". Blue rules, 5/16" apart; vertical red rules. Stovall (*AL*, 26, 348) describes it as a paraphrase, with a few quotations, of Macauley's essay on Goldsmith in *Encyclopedia Britannica* (8th ed.) which WW could have read in *Harper's Magazine*, 14 (April, 1857), 633–639. The date is probably 1857. First published *N&F*, 108–109 (Pt. III, #84; *CW*, IX, 118–119).

Oliver Goldsmith

born at Pallas, (Ireland) Nov. 1728

father a curate & small farmer—moved to Wesmeath £200 a year educated Trinity College, Dublin thoughtless, heedless, credulous,—gambled, was helped to money—lost it—/ at 24 went to Edinburgh to lectures—thence to Leyden——at 27 with a smattering of medical knowledge wandered through France,[1] Switzerland—Flanders, Italy—returned to England—lived in low life from 30 to 36—a literary hack—then better known & better off—then prosperous received sums of £200, £300, £600 &c for his poems, histories & plays—/
as a talker, frivolous, weak, no good—/
as a writer and compiler, wonderfully *ignorant*
[2] was a gambler still—got deeply in debt, £2000—preyed upon his mind—/

Associates regarded him with kindness and contempt/
he was envious, and showed it—/
income last 7 years of his life £400 a year/
died 3d April, 1774—in his 46th year/
he sometimes felt keenly the sarcasm which his wild blundering talk brought upon him.

1. Deleted: "Italy"

Gower, Born 1326.

Manuscript not found. Text from *N&F,* 92 (Pt. III, #36; *CW,* IX, 85). The date, like that of many of WW's notes on his reading, is probably the late 1850s.

Gower, born 1326, died 1402, was an intimate friend of Chaucer who calls him "the moral Gower." Seems to have been a devout churchman. Rich and orthodox—"one of the fathers"—with Chaucer.

Shakespeare, Wordsworth.

Manuscript not found. Text from *N&F,* 158 (Pt. IV, #20; *CW,* IX, 223). See Stovall, *AL,* 26 (1954), 357.

Shakespeare, Wordsworth, Scott, Milton, Byron, Hume, Swift, Addison.

Chaucer, Spencer and Milton were full-blooded Cockneys. Shakespeare alone was not a Londoner although a long resident.

1356. The first English book—*"Sir John Mandeville's Travels."*

1385. Polychronicon—a sort of jumble of history. For to those dates there was no English Literature—hardly even for many years afterwards. The English language was not thought of as fit for the learned or for poets.

Samuel Johnson.

Manuscript in Virginia (Barrett). Inscribed in pencil on pink wove paper, approx. 8⅛" x 5⅞". Stovall, *AL,* 26 (1954), 349, identifies the source as Macaulay's essay on Johnson (1856) for the *Encyclopedia Britannica* (6th ed.) which was also printed in *Harper's Magazine,* 14 (March, 1857), 483–497. The word "purblind," however, is used only in Carlyle's "Boswell's Life of Johnson." The paper suggests a date after 1855, but 1857 is quite late for pink wrapper stock. First printed *N&F,* 111–112 (Pt. III, #93; *CW,* IX, 124–125).

Samuel Johnson 1709 — 1784[1]/

Was born in[2] Litchfield, Eng.— Father a bookseller—educated thoroughly—read every thing—went through college—physically queer, scrofulous, purblind, crotchetty, alimentive,—married a vulgar old woman that painted, and wore all sorts of false things—was faithful and fond to the last—"dear Titty"— —went to London—struggled on there *thirty years* through all sorts of privations and starvations—sometimes lucky (a little)—wrote "Idler," "Rambler" &c— "Rasselas" written in a week to make money for his mother's funeral expenses, &c— —wrote Dictionary[3]—had £1500 for it— —edited an edition of Shakespeare, (a poor one)—at last received a pension of £300 a year from the government—/[4]

was always of coarse behaviour,—wrote in a latinized style,[5] not simple and with unlearned instincts,[6] but pompous & full of polysyllables.

1. Line across leaf.
2. Deleted: "Litch"
3. Capitalized over "d"
4. Short line from left.
5. Deleted: "quite elegant and learned"
6. Deleted: "*—his ideal was Milton.*" ; following six words inserted above the deletion.

Carlyle, Born 1795.

Manuscript not found. Text from *N&F,* 161 (Pt. IV, #26; *CW,* IX, 229–230). The relationship between WW and Carlyle, despite the paucity of extended MS reference, was important, for the latter was a principle source of information about German literature, a carrier of what by the 1840s were key Romantic commonplaces, and a challenge to WW's political ideals. See Stovall, *Foreground,* 104–110. See also "*Neibelungen-leid* Song," "Richter born 1763," "Goethe's Complete works," "Goethe," "Employments," "Our own account," "Byron born," "The foregoing remarks," "Two suggestion points," "Carlyle vol. I," "merciless lance-thrusts," "Astronomy"; "New York Dissected," *NYD,* 120; "Carlyle's History of Frederick II," *ISLO,* 68; *Corr.,* passim; "Cedar-Plums like—Names," *SD, Prose 92,* I, 245; "Death of Thomas Carlyle," ibid., 248–262; Appendix, ibid., 337, 350; *DV,* ibid., II, 375, 379; "Poetry To-Da—Shakspere—the Future," ibid., 478; "A Word about Tennyson," ibid., 570; "Elias Hicks," ibid., 647; "American National Literature," ibid., 667; "A Backward Glance O'er Travel'd Roads," ibid., 725; Appendix, ibid., 749, 750, 761, 771. First printed *N&F,* 161.

Carlyle, born 1795, Nov. ('57), aged 62. Dec. '57 Carlyle's Frederick the Great is announced to be now in press.

Leigh Hunt.

Manuscript in Middlebury. Inscribed in pencil on right margin of Item 89, an extract from Leigh Hunt's "What Is Poetry?" pp. 610 ff., clipped from *Half Hours with the Best Authors*. "A good essay." is written at the top and the text has been heavily marked. Although marginalia are excluded from this edition, WW's evident interest in the essay makes it worth noting. The date is July, 1857 and August, 1859. First printed *N&F,* 15 (Pt. #18; *CW,* IX, 222).

Leigh Hunt—born 1784—is he now living? aged 72./ Yes (July '57) he lives, old and in fair condition, in London, aged 73./ Died, Aug., '59/ aged 75.

Edmund Spenser.

Manuscript in Duke (31, #8). Inscribed in black ink on slightly different leaves of white laid paper, approx. 7⅞" x 4". Blue rules ⅜" apart. [2] has "So Lee Mass" embossed at upper right. WW's perfunctory interest in Spenser is discussed and sources for these notes identified by Stovall, *Foreground,* 234. The fragment of embossing: "So Lee Mass" suggests a date of 1859 or 1860, when WW was using paper thus marked. See "What name." First printed *N&F,* 88–89 (Pt. III, #28; *CW,* IX, 77–79).

Edmund Spenser: [1]

born about 1553—died 1599./
was an intimate friend of Sydney (Philip) who was killed by a wound at the battle of Zutphen [2]/
Wrote adulatory verses on Queen Elizabeth—"(great Gloriane,)"/
Raleigh was Spenser's next friend, after Sydney.[3]
had a pension of £50 from the Queen, and the actual Laureateship [4]/
he danced attendance, like a lackey, for a long time at court,—but without luck.—
He left in disgust at last, and went to his Irish estate,[5] the banks of the Mulla/
Earl Leicester was his patron and friend—[6]/
The E.K. often mentioned by Spenser is supposed to have been *himself*—E.K. has much to say of Spenser's writings—commends them.—[7]/
Spenser took his degrees of B.A. and M.A. at Cambridge in 1573 & 1576[8]
after serving in an Irish secretaryship received from the Queen the profitable grant of property, the Abbey of Enniscortty in the county of Wexford,—making the poet rich—owner of and resident in Kilcolman castle.[9]
[2] There in his castle he must have written or finished[10] in 1588–9—the Fairy Queen—it was published in 1590—("twelve books fashioning twelve moral[11] virtues")/

1. Inked heavily.
2. Hanging indentation.
3. Hanging indentation.
4. Hanging indentation.
5. Deleted: "on"
6. Hanging indentation.
7. Rule across leaf.
8. Hanging indentation. Rule across leaf.
9. Hanging indentation. Rule across leaf.
10. Preceding two words inserted above "en" in "written" and "in"
11. Inserted above "elve" in "twelve" and "virtues"

was married when 40 (or over)/
Kilcoman castle attacked by insurgents.— Spenser and his family fled—one of his children burned to death—the castle being fired.—[12]/
A flight from Ireland—
Poverty ensued.— comparative poverty anyhow/
Lived a year in London/
Died—was buried in Westminster Abbey.— a monument erected, 30 years after death, by Anne, Countess of Dorset.[13]
In his poems, reverence for purity and goodness, is paramount to all the rest.—/
In person Spenser was small and delicate, and in costume precise, "as became a man of taste."[14] His face had sweetness & refinement—mild almond-shaped eyes, —forehead lofty, but not very wide—was well beloved by contemporaries—who all exempted him from satire[15]
[3] Tone of Spenser's poetry is unworldly, abstracted, contemplative in the highest degree—loving high themes—princeliness, purity, white garments,—rather averse to reality—his personages being only half-real— He is haunted by a morbid refinement of beauty—beauty three times washed and strained—[16]/
No doubt but he was very learned.—/
Even at the time of writing them, Spenser's words, in his poems, were many of them unusual, obsolete, or considered affected and strained.[17]/
Fairy Queen—personages.
Red Cross Knight—"Holiness"
Una—"Truth"
Sans foy—"Faithless"
Arthur—Magnanimity
Orgoglio—"Pride"
Gloriana—Glory—Queen Elizabeth[18]
In the F.Q. are also Despair, Fear, Care, and Mammon.—
First book—a king's daughter applies to a knight—her parents are confined in their castle—a vast and terrible dragon has laid in wait devouring[19] the country, and is now after them— The knight sets forth, encounters a monster, an enchanter, kills the dragon, delivers the king & queen, marries the daughter.

12. Hanging indentation.
13. Hanging indentation.
14. Hanging indentation.
15. Hanging indentation.
16. Hanging indentation.
17. Hanging indentation.
18. In column.
19. First syllable written over [*illeg.*]

Spenser's Single Object.

Manuscript in Virginia (Barrett). Inscribed in black ink on scrap of gray-brown grayed laid paper with quadrilling visible on surface, 4½" x 6⅞". Since it was a Bucke MS, the date is probably in the late 1850s. First printed *N&F*, 167 (Pt. IV, #54; *CW*, X, 15).

Spenser's single object through the vast amplitude and variety of his "Faerie[1] Queene"[2] is "to fashion a gentleman of noble person in virtuous, brave, and gentle discipline"

1. Spelling corrected from "Faery" . Deleted: "Queen"
2. "e" added.

Shakespeare. Milton.

Manuscript not found. Text from *N&F,* 167 (Pt. IV, #51; *CW,* X, 14). Included by Bucke in a jumble of miscellaneous notes.

Shakespeare. Milton. Racine. Corneille. Luther. Goethe. Schiller.

Bells & Pomgranates.

Manuscript in Duke (71). Inscribed in pencil on tan proof (?) paper, approx. 8¼" x 5⅛". The entries on pp. [*1–3*], to "New English Poets" are separated by rules across the leaf. The first three leaves are a rough table of contents for a collection of clippings described in Trent *Cat.,* 71, from which most of the identifications are taken. The earliest date for these leaves is probably 1855, although some clippings are earlier. The other leaves, although in pencil on similar paper, were probably separate from the first three. Bucke, for example, prints them separately. Leaf [*4*] may be after 1860 (see *n*23). Leaf [*7*] may or may not refer to leaves [*1–3*]. These last four leaves were first printed in *N&F* as noted. The dates may be as late as 1860 or 1861. As a final hypothesis, this may have been part of the scrapbook now in the Bayley Collection, Ohio Wesleyan University Library (see "Languages").

Bells & Pomgranates, Robert Browning/
Casa Guidi Windows, Elizabeth Barrett Browning/
Wordsworth*/
Tennyson, Shelley, Keats./
Taylor's Eve of the Conquest.[1]/
Tennyson[2]/
Hyperion of Keats* J.D.W.[3]/
Oliver Goldsmith/
Festus, Manfred, Paradise Lost, Book of Job/
Festus/
Miss Barrett's Poems.[4]/
Lessing's Laoccoön J.D.W.[5]/
Phrenology, a Socratic Dialogue J.D.W.[6]/
Style.— J.D.W.[7]/
American Literature*

1. *Edinburgh Review* 89(April, 1849), 352–380.
2. "Poems of Alfred Tennyson," *Westminster Review* (Amer. ed.), 51(July, 1849), 145–148.
3. J. D. Whelpley, "The Hyperion of Keats," *American Whig Review,* n.s. 8 (October, 1851) 311–322.
4. Ibid., 1 (January, 1845), 38–48.
5. J.D. Whelpley, ibid., n.s. 7 (January, 1851), 21–26.
6. J.D. Whelpley, ibid., 3 (January, 1846), 31–46.
7. J.D. Whelpley, ibid., 2 (October, 1845), 358–364). The clipping is in Rutgers University Library.

(Margaret Fuller.)[8]/
Essay on Critics.—/
Dialogue between Poet and Critic/

[2] [*illeg.*] Poetry/

Provencal & Scandinavian Poets[9]/
Chaucer[10] —American Poets—/
Villemain's Literature of the Middle Ages[?][11]/
Pope. ———[12] Robert Southey./
Characteristics of Shelley./
Shakspeare vs. Sand./
[*illeg.*] Moralists. La Bruyere, Montaigne, Nicole.[13]/
Poets & Poetry of Europe.[14]/
Scotch School of Philosophy & Criticism[15]/
Campbell, (Dr. Beattie's Life of)[16]/
Southey.— Waller and Marvell[17]/
Wordsworth's Prelude.[18]/
Speculative Philosophy of the 19th century/
Keats——— The Raven[19]/
E. A. Duykinck on Literature
for 1845[20]/
[3] Prose Writers of America[21] —
Review of Emerson/
Styles American & Foreign/
America and the early English Poets,/
Thoughts on Reading[22]/
Pleasures of the Pen,/

8. From her *Papers on Literature and Art,* II (NY, 1846). See "Criticism."

9. Note review of Fauriel, et al. *Edinburgh Review* (Amer. ed.) 88 (July, 1848) 1–16.

10. *North British Review* (Amer. ed.), 10 (February, 1847).

11. Review of Villemain's *Literature of the Middle Ages, Westminster Review* (Amer. ed.) 51 (July, 1849), 181–192.

12. Review of Roscoe's edition, *North British Review* Amer. ed.), 9 (August, 1848), 163–182.

13. "The French Moralists," *American Whig Review* 2 (November, 1845), 497–504.

14. Review of Longfellow's *Poets and Poetry of Europe, American Whig Review,* 4 (November, 1846) 496–507 (December), 581–588.

15. Ibid., 2 (October, 1845), 386–396.

16. *Quarterly Review* (Amer. ed.), 85 (July, 1849), 17–18.

17. "Political Poets: Waller and Marvell," *American Whig Review,* n.s. 7 (May, 1851), 411–418.

18. O.W.W., "The Prelude," *American Whig Review,* n.s. 7 (May, 1851) 448–457.

19. Ibid., 1 (February, 1845), 143–146. Poe's poem, but under a pseudonym, "Quarles." It had been published slightly before under Poe's name in N. P. Willis's *Daily Mirror.*

20. Ibid., 146–151.

21. Rev. Rufus Wilmot Grisworld's compilation, *U.S. Democratic Review,* 20 (May, 1847), 384–398. The Emerson item in "New Poetry in New England" which WW annotated significantly. See "The superiority of Emerson's."

22. *American Whig Review,* 1 (May, 1845), 483–496. Immediately preceded by WW's "The Boy-Lover."

New English Poets[23]/
Owen Meredith (Young Bulwer.)
Matthew Arnold
Sidney[24] Dobell
Alexander Smith
Gerald Massey
[4][25] Swedenborg
Rousseau
Montaigne
Cervantes
Richter
Jacob Boehme

[5][26] *Greatest*

Homer Hesiod
Pindar
Tyrtaeus
Virgil
Horace
Anacreon
[6][27] Hafiz
Sadi
Valmiki—(author of Ramayana
Vyasa (Mahabarata)
Ossian
Bards of Wales, Scotland, Ireland—Druids
Chaucer

[7][28] Of the Foregoing two or three pages the lists of names on colored paper[29]
Remember, these are Europeans and[30] Americans—not the whole world's contributions. Each continent, each[31] nation, gives its contributions—every one at any time,[32] as perfect as it can be, considering what preceded it.—

23. *Putnam's Monthly,* 6 (September, 1855), 225–238.
24. *N&F,* 166 (Pt. IV, #51; *CW,* X, 13) See "Leaves of Grass".
25. Ibid.
26. Ibid., 167.
27. *N&F,* 159 (Pt. IV, #22; *CW,* X, 226). On white scrap. Hand pointing left at top center.
28. Following seven words inserted on two lines
29. Preceding seven words inserted in ink on three lines at right following "pages"
30. Inserted in wordspace after "Europeans"
31. Written over [*illeg.*]
32. Preceding three words inserted above "as" and "per" in "perfect"

They Say Milton's.

Manuscript in LC (#46, sheet #746). Inscribed in black ink on a scrap of white laid paper with red-blue-red vertical rule 1¼″ from left and blue rules ½″ apart. Hanging indentation. Milton draws the parallel with Aeschylus himself in the preface to *Samson Agonistes*. The paper suggests a date in the late 1860s (see "Carlyle vol. 1").

They say Milton's Samson Agonistes gives the best English analogy of Eschylus—in metre, abruptness, general form & spirit—

British Born Died.

Manuscript in Texas (Hanley). Inscribed in black ink and blue crayon on white wove paper, approx. 8″ x 6¼″, torn neatly at the edge. On verso of [5] is "every page teems with" (all deleted). The source has not been discovered, but obviously it was a popular self-culture handbook like Louis Herrig's *The British Classical Authors* or L.D. Jones's *Memoria Technica*. (See "Language. Religion. Numismatics.") The writing suggests this was written in the 1860s.

British	Born		died[1]
Mary queen of Scots	1540		1587
Spenser	1553		1599
Sir Walter Raleigh	1552		1613
Shakspeare ———	1564		1616
Lord Bacon	1561		1626
Sir Edward Coke	1549		1634
Ben Jonson	1575		1637
Milton ———	1608	———	1674
Bunyan	1628		1688
George Fox ———	1624		1690
Robert Barclay	1648		1690
Dryden ———	1631		1700
Locke ———	1663	———	1704
Sir Isaac Newton	1642		1727
Pope ———	1688	———	1744
Swift	1667		1745
Junius's[2] Letters	1769	to	1772
Lord Chesterfield	1694		1773
Goldsmith	1728		1774
Hume ———	1720	———	1776
Dr. Johnson	1709		1784

[2]

British	born	died
Adam Smith ———	1723	1790

1. Preceding three words laid out as column headings.
2. This and the four following names checked at left in blue crayon.

Sir Joshua Reynolds ——	1723	1792
Robertson ——	1721 ——	1793
Gibbon[3]	1738	1794
Burns ——	1759 ——	1796
Byron ——	1787	1824
Sir Walter Scott	1771	1832

Dutch[4]

Erasmus	1467 ——	1530
Arminius	1560	1609
Grotius ——	1583	1641
Hooft ——	1581 ——	1647
Kats poet, *very popular*	1577 ——	1660
Vondel (—the highest poet tragedies best)	1587	1679
the Elizevir family printers	1592	1680
Hubert Poot, (a sort of Burns)	1689	1732
Hoogvleit (pious poet took the Bible for his subject—one of a class of poets)	1687	1763

[3]

German [:][5]	born	died
Zimmerman	1728	1794
Lavater ——	1741	1801
Klopstock ——	1724	1803
Kant[6] ——	1724	1804
Schiller ——	1759[7] ——	1805
Fichte[8] ——	1762	1814
Kotzebue ——	1761	1819
Jean Paul Richter	1763	1825
F. Schlegel ——	1774	1829
Hegel[9] ——	1779	1831
Niebuhr ——	1776	1831

3. This and the three following names checked at left in blue crayon.
4. Above names.
5. Written sideways on left margin outside brace on all the German names.
6. Checked at left in blue crayon.
7. Long dash and date deleted and rewritten slightly above.
8. Checked at left in blue crayon.
9. Checked at left in blue crayon.

Goethe[10] ———	1749	1832
Zschokke	1774	1847

French[11]

Montaigne	?1553	1592
Cardinal Richelieu	1585	1642
Descartes	1596	1650
Pascal	1623	1662

[4]

French[12]

Rochefoucalt ald[13]	1613	1680
P. Corneille	1606	1684
Madame de Sevigné	1627	1696
Racine ———	1639	1699
Fenelon ———	1651	1715
Rollin ———	1661	1741
Montesquieu ———	1689	1755
Rousseau[14] ———	1712	1778
Voltaire ———	1694	1778
Buffon ———	1707	1788
Volney	?1757	1793

Swedish[15]

Swedenborg[16] ———	1689	1772
Linnæus ———	1707	1778

[5]

(?Artists, also?)	born	to	died
Galileo, (It.) ———	1564	....	1641
Salvator Roza			died 1673
Cervantes [Sp]	1547		1616
Lope de Vega [*Sp*][17]	1562		1635
Calderon [*Sp*]	1600		1687
Luther ———	1483		1546
Melancthon	1498		1560

10. Checked at left in blue crayon.
11. Centered heading.
12. Above names.
13. Written above.
14. This and the three following names checked at left in blue crayon.
15. Centered heading.
16. This name and Linnaeus checked at left in blue crayon.
17. WW used ditto marks.

Hans Sachs[18]	1494	1576
Boehme		died 1695
Opitz	1597	1635
Puffendorf	1632	1694
Liebnitz	1646	1716
Mosheim	1695	1755
Wolf	1679	1766
Winkelman	1707	1768
Lessing[19]	1729	1781
Frederick the Great	1712	1786

18. "Sachs" also written lengthwise in blue crayon opposite name.
19. This and following name checked in blue crayon at left.

The Picture.

Manuscript in LC (#79, sheet #755). Inscribed in pencil on white wove scrap. An equestrian drama based on Byron's poem, *Mazeppa,* was popular in the first half of the century. WW saw it in 1833 or 1834 (Stovall, *Foreground,* 62), and it is hard to imagine his not seeing the sensational version in which his friend Adah Isaacs Menken appeared in June, 1861. No date can be assigned.

the picture of the
big white cat with
the frog on his back
Mazeppa

On Poems.

Manuscript in Folger (Black Box 106 Whitman). Inscribed in black pencil on stiff white wove paper torn on fold at left edge. Cf. "The Bible Shakespeare" for another possible plan for a lecture. The writing suggests a date in the 1860s or early 1870s.

on Poems[1]
The Hebraic poems—(the Bible) with readings—the Book of Job dominating
The Hindu poems with readings
The Homeric poems with reading
The Medieval poetry
?The Nibelungen
Ellis's English &c Metrical romances
Shakespeare
with readings. (over)

1. Original beginning of title deleted: "Course of lectures"

Astronomy.

Manuscript in Texas (Hanley). Inscribed in black pencil on white wove scrap, approx. 4¼" x 4". Blue rules, 5/18" apart. The article on Carlyle's *Reminiscences* is "A Study of Carlyle" by the author of "The Moral Influence of George Eliot by One Who Knew Her," *Contemporary Review,* 39 (April, 1881), 584–609.

Astronomy

— mention "the Swan" flying down the Milky Way (not far from Job's Coffin)

get Contemporary Review for April '81 for a strong article on Carlyle's *Reminiscences*

An Ossianic ¶.

Manuscript in Middlebury. Inscribed in brownish ink on tan wove paper 10″ x 5½″. A clipping, identified by Stovall (*Foreground,* 115) as from Margaret Fuller's "Things and Thoughts in Europe. No. V" in the NY *Tribune* (September 30, 1846), reads:

> For about two hours I saw the stars, and very cheery and companionable they looked; but then the mist fell, and I saw nothing more, except such apparitions as visited Ossian on the hill-side, when he went out by night and struck the bosky shield, and called to him the spirits of the heroes and the white-armed maids with their blue eyes of grief. To me, too, come those visionary shapes; floating slowly and gracefully, their white robes would unfurl from the great body of mist in which they had been engaged, and come upon me with a kiss pervasively cold as that of death. What they might have told me, who knows, if I had but resigned myself more passively to that cold, spirit-like breathing!

Ossian was one of the national or "bardic" poets whom WW was fond of citing as being among the masters. He told Traubel in 1888 that he had always had a copy but had never read it "with any great fervor" (Traubel, II, 17). His relationship to Ossian is discussed by Stovall, *Foreground,* 115–120. See also "Ossian—? for Note Preface" and "Ossian-Thoreau."

Since it is reasonable to assume that WW made these notes at the time the clipping, which is too small to be filed conveniently, was published, this must be one of his earliest bits of advice to himself about style and, as such, a significant indication that his mature style was developing in 1846. First printed in *N&F,* 97 (Pt. III, #51; *CW,* IX, 94–95).

An Ossianic ¶: Margaret Fuller, benighted and alone[1] on Ben Lomond.—/[2]

Ossian must not be despised—it means that kind of thought and character growing among a rude, combative illiterate[3] people, heroic, dreaming, poetical, on mountains, *not* on rich lowlands, *not* with placid gods and temples, *not* with[4] cultivated benevolence, conscientiousness, agreeableness, or constructiveness.—

How misty, how windy, how full of diffused, only half-meaning words! —How curious a study! —(*Don't fall into the Ossianic,* by any chance.)

1. Reading from *N&F*. Upper right corner torn.
2. Clipping pasted below heading to left of MS text.
3. Inserted in pencil.
4. Deleted: "a"

?Can it be a descendant of the Biblical poetry?—Is it not Isaiah, Job, the Psalms, and so forth, transferred to the Scotch Highlands? (or to Ireland?)[5]/

? The tremendous figures and ideas of the Hebrew poems,— are they not *original*?—for they are certainly great— (Yes they are original[6]

5. Parenthetical statement in pencil. Entire entry inserted.
6. Sentence in pencil.

Ossian—? For Note Preface.

Manuscript in Duke (36, #28). Inscribed in purple crayon and black pencil on two scraps of white wove paper, approx. 4¼″ x 6¼″, as described in the notes. There is an apparently earlier version of the beginning of this MS also in Duke (36, #28) which has the additional entry in blue crayon: "Read Ossian a while this morning" The writing and use of blue and purple crayon in both suggests the last years of WW's life. See "An Ossianic ¶" and "Ossian—Thoreau." First printed *N&F,* 141 (Pt. III, #178; *CW,* IX, 187–188.)

Ossian—? for Note Preface

For all their restorations—perhaps something worse[1] there[2] is to me such[3] so much race (to use[4] an old[5] Scotch word) of the[6] pre-historic primitively[7] Irish and Caledonian thought and personality in these poems—*[8] notwithstaning their[9] general mistiness and gossamer character,[10] (they always[11] bring up to me the long trailing drape of the[12] moss hanging down so profusely[13] on the live-oaks in Florida or Louisiana, and slowly moving to the twilight[14] breeze)—I have had[15]

1. Original opening word deleted: "Though" ; preceding seven words inserted on two lines above the deletion and "There is to me such "[*del.*] a"
2. Reduced from uppercase in MS.
3. Deleted in black pencil: "a [*illeg.*] or a" ; inserted in black pencil: "so much" above illegible deletion.
4. Deleted: "the" ; inserted above: "an"
5. Deleted: "Sch"
6. Deleted: "the old" ; inserted in black pencil: "the pre-historic" above the deletion and "primitive" in "primitively"
7. Deleted: "simple [*illeg.*] antique"
8. Inserted passage from leaf 2 begins.
9. Converted from "the"
10. Deleted: "of the poems"
11. Deleted: "remin"
12. Deleted: "wild"
13. Preceding four words inserted above "moss on the live"
14. Inserted above "the" and "br" in "breeze"
15. Inserted above wordspace between "have more"

more or less[16] good from[17] what they give out. It[18] like the reminiscence of an[19] odor shut up for ages in some venerable chest. A witty friend of[20] mine calls them[21] "the *real ghosts* of poems."

16. Deleted: "enjo"

17. Deleted in black pencil: "them" ; inserted following in black pencil: "what they give out." End of leaf 2. Return to leaf 1.

18. Deleted: [*illeg.*]

19. Deleted: "some" ; inserted: "an" above "me" in "some"

20. Deleted: [*illeg.*]

21. Inserted above "lls" in "calls"

IX. German, French, Italian, Spanish, Scandinavian and Classical Writers.

Neibelungen-Leid Song.

Manuscript in Middlebury. Inscribed in pencil on brownish tan wove paper approx. 9³/₁₆" x 5⁵/₁₆". Each entry in hanging indentation. Folded creases on left edge. Notes from Carlyle's "The Nibelungen Lied," *Critical and Miscellaneous Essays,* Centenary Edition II, 216–272. William A. Little, "Walt Whitman and the *Nibelungenlied," PMLA,* 80 (1965), 562–570, attempts to reconstruct WW's knowledge of the *Nibelungenlied,* which derived perhaps completely from secondary sources. (See also Stovall, *AL,* 354.) Little's account seems fundamentally correct, although the full MS evidence was not available. The facts seem to be as follows. Probably WW's earliest real acquaintance with the epic was through an anonymous review of several works on Provençal and Scandinavian Poetry in *The Edinburgh Review,* 88 (1848), 13–18. WW's marginalia on the article can be dated between 1855 and 1856 (Little, 564) and was printed in *N&F,* 160–161 (Pt. IV, #24; *CW,* IX, 228). (See also *n* 1 below and "Our own account of this poem." The essay by Carlyle provided WW with a comprehensive critical account of the poem as well as a summary of the plot. In this MS, the notes on the major characters, rather than the minor characters, suggests to Little (564) that they represent WW's first acquaintance with the details of the plot. WW's other main source, and for German literature and philosophy in general, was Joseph Gostwick's *German Literature* (see "Our own account"), from which he drew criticism and translations of the poem. A reference to Gostwick in "[*illeg.*] Dick Hunt" occurs between an entry dated December 20, 1856 and an entry dated January 7, 1857. Some of his notes on Carlyle are on pink *LG* wrapper, (see "Rei nec ke") which WW used in 1856. Thus, WW probably read the article by Carlyle in 1856 (see "Carlyle, born 1795"). Though not discussed by Little, a translation of Claude Fauriel's *History of Provencal Poetry,* one of the books reviewed in *The Edinburgh Review,* was published in 1860, a work which included a long and vivid plot summary, giving WW his most detailed knowledge of the characters and their actions. For WW's notes on Fauriel see "The *Nibelungen Leid."* It is not known whether WW ever read the poem itself, which was first translated into English in 1848. See also "Mr. & Mrs. Fitz," dated 1860, which mentions Karl Simrock who translated the epic into modern German. Each of WW's sources adopted a slightly different version of the German names which, though WW is also inconsistent in his spelling, is sometimes helpful in identifying his source. See "Ethnology," "The Nibelungen," "Author of the Neibelungen leid," "The celebrated old German poem," "Our own account of this poem." "The *Nibelungen Leid,"* "Niembsch Lenau," "Literature," "A Backward Glance O'er Travel'd Roads," *Prose 92,* 722. First printed in *N&F,* 91 (Pt. III, #33; *CW,* IX, 83). (Gene Edward Veith, Jr.)

Neibelungen—leid Song of Neibelungen

author unknown it is objective, like the Iliad[1] Song of the

Probably[2] dates back to about the 6th or 7th Century but the date when it was written as now, is the *13th century* /

Carlyle supposes it to be about the third redaction (digestion) from its[3] primitive form[4] out of myths,[5] acts, traditions, or what not.—/

Characters

Siegfried—the hero, a warrior, king, full of courage—the usual type-hero, as seen, duly followed, in all modern novels and plays.

Chriemheld—a beautiful princess, sister of three kingly brothers,[6] of Worms, in time Siegfrieds[7] wife

Gunther, the principal of the three brothers[8]

Brunhilde, a brave, vindictive, relentless woman—Gunthers wife/

Hagen, a brave warrior

Etzel (king of Hun-land Chriemhilde's second husband) supposed to be the historic Attila died 450 a D.[9]/

In their present shape these poems Heldenbuch, and Neibelungen, cannot be older than the twelfth century.—[10]/

The poet himself is unknown—he probably *made up* the poem in the thirteenth century.—[11]/

1. This description of the poem is from the article in the *Edinburgh Review*. Cf. WW's marginalia on the article from *N&F*, 160–161 (Pt. IV, #24; *Cw*, IX, 228): "Subjective—out of the person himself. Objective—of other persons, things, events, places, characters. As the *Iliad* is profoundly objective, *Leaves of Grass* are profoundly subjective."

"Subjective or lyric, objective or epic, as for instance the *Iliad* is notably objective but *Leaves of Grass* are profoundly subjective."

"Song of the" written under "like the Iliad"

2. Deleted: "composed" ; inserted above: "dates back to"

3. Written over [*illeg.*]

4. Inserted: "out of" to left of and above "m" in "myths

5. Deleted: "poems" ; inserted above: "acts"

6. "b" written over [*illeg.*]

7. "g" in "Siegfrieds" written over [*illeg.*]

8. "thers" written over [*illeg.*]

9. Rule across leaf.

10. Rule across leaf.

11. Rule across leaf.

The Nibelungen.

Manuscript in Duke (33, #18). Inscribed in pencil on white laid note paper, chain-lines ⅛″ apart, mottled texture, approx. 3¼″ x 4⅞″. Blue rules on recto, ⅜″ apart. Embossed stamp. Mounted on inside cover of *Voices From the Press* (NY, 1850). Printed in *FC&I,* 23. (Gene Edward Veith, Jr.)

The Nibelungen

vast passions of man, with play of heat & cold & storm, like undercurrents, or volcanos, or stormy seas.

Author of the Neibelungen Leid.

Manuscript in NYPL (Berg). Inscribed in pencil on white woven butcher paper faded brownish, 2¼″ x 5 13/16″, all corners trimmed. Paper identical to that of "Hans Sachs" and "Ferdusi, and the primeval," both notes from Carlyle's *Critical and Miscellaneous Essays,* which suggests that this information WW also obtained from Carlyle, probably from "The Nibelungen Lied," *Critical and Miscellaneous Essays,* II (Centenary Edition), 267. See "Neibelungen-leid" and, for Carlyle, "Carlyle, born 1795 " This probably was written in 1856. (Gene Edward Veith)

Author of the Neibelungen Leid [:][1] composed, as now extant, about the 13th century, but dating back with its written germs may be in the 6th century

1. Text following on six lines in a brace to the right of the first five words.

The Celebrated Old.

Manuscript in Duke (36, #22). Inscribed in black ink on two irregular scraps of white wove paper, corners clipped, approx. 4⅜″ x 7⅞″ and 5⅛″ x 7⅞″, at one time pinned together. For WW and the Nibelungenlied see "Neibelungen-leid Song." The text is a paraphrase of Joseph Gostwick, *German Literature* (Philadelphia, Lippincott, 1854), 18–19. Gostwick (1814–1847) was a respected scholar, translator, and popularizer of German writing, and his *German Literature* was one of the most important sources for WW's knowledge of German literature and philosophy. See W.B. Fulghum, Jr., "Whitman's Debt to Joseph Gostwick," *AL,* 12 (1941), 491–496 and Stovall (*Foreground,* 195–196 and passim). WW's annotated copy was sold as Item 616 in the Donaldson Sale in 1899. See *Walt Whitman at Auction,* 5. The confusion about Gostwick's name persisted here, for it was given as "Goshek." For Gostwick see also "our own account of the poem," "Barthold Niebuhr. 1776," "Frederick Schlegel 1772–1829," "Sunday evening lectures," "Kant," "[*illeg.*] Dick Hunt." The writing is the looser writing of the 1860s, but WW's hand seems to have changed in the late 1850s. See, for example, "A Visit to the Opera," which is from 1858 or after. It is possible that WW was preparing another "authoritative" article for *Life Illustrated.* Probably "Our own account" is part of this attempt. The date, in any case, is the very late 1850s or early 1860s. First printed, *N&F,* 141 (Pt. III, #177; *CW,* IX, 187). (Gene Edward Veith, Jr.)

The celebrated old German poem we are going to make a running sketch of,[1] is traceable back to the Twelfth Century, when,[2] or soon after when, it was probably put in the shape transmitted to[3] modern times, by some[4] rhapsodist whose name is now[5] unknown.— Yet it is quite certain that this remarkable epic, long antedates even that far off period.— How much further back, though, it is impossible to tell, with any certainty.[6]

Of the many critical theories,[7] about the construction of the Nibelungen, the most plausible is that[8] the ballads or versions floating about, were collected by the

1. Perhaps an allusion to "Our account of this poem."
2. Inserted: "or soon after when," above "n," in "when," and "it was" and "pro" in "probably"
3. Deleted: "us"
4. Deleted: "writer or" ; inserted above: "rhapsodist"
5. Inserted above "is" and the wordspace following.
6. End of first scrap.
7. Following six words and punctuation inserted above "itical" in "critical" and "theories the"
8. Deleted: "there were many" ; inserted: "the" above "e" in "[*del.*] "the"

rhapsodist[9] before alluded to,[10] during the Twelfth or Thirteenth Century, and fused into one connected Epic.— The critics say they can tell the connecting passages; and they point to marked differences of style, and contradictions.—[11] The Nibelungen is thus, by high authorities, stated to[12] have been formed from[13] ballads belonging to several ages, but having a general principle of union and character, and[14] thus comes to be united upon the thread of one main plot.—

9. Deleted: "just" ; inserted above: "before"
10. Following six words and punctuation inserted above "and fused into one"
11. New paragraphing corrected with a line and WW's notation "run on" enclosed in curved line.
12. Deleted: "be a series of" ; inserted above: "have been formed from"
13. Inserted and deleted: "this" following "from"
14. Inserted: "thus comes to be" following "and united"

Our Own Account.

Manuscript in Duke (23, #20). Inscribed in black ink and some pencil on four leaves of white wove paper: [*1*] two scraps formerly pinned together, 12″ x 7¾″, [*2*] 10″ x 7 11/16″, [*3*] 13⅝″ x 7 13/16″, [*4*] 11⅞″ x 7 11/16″. Leaves numbered in pencil, not by WW. See "Neibelungen-leid Song. " William A. Little, "Walt Whitman and the *Nibelungenlied,*" *PMLA,* 80 (1965), 565–570, discusses this MS in great detail. The introduction in [*1*] Little shows to be derived from *The Edinburgh Review,* 177 (1848), WW's second paragraph from p. 22, and his third paragraph from p. 14. The poetry on [*2*], the opening three stanzas of the Fourteenth Adventure of the *Nibelungenlied,* is WW's paraphrase of Joseph Gostwick's literal translation in *German Literature* (Philadelphia, 1854), pp. 31–32*n* (see "The celebrated old German poem" and Stovall, *AL,* 26, 354) and *Foreground,* 193–194. On [*3*] and [*4*] is a rendition of the last fourteen stanzas of the Thirty-ninth Adventure, based on Gostwick's verse translation, pp. 30–32. The writing indicates that this was written in 1858 or slightly later. Printed in *FC&I,* 20–22. (Gene Edward Veith, Jr.)

[*1*] Our own account of this poem, "The German Iliad," being but a fragment, and more intended to[1] furnish the reader, in one or two specimens, a glimpse of the old verses, by a free translation of them, we refer those who[2] desire a[3] complete resumé of the Nibelungen, to Carlyle's[4] essay of that name—to which, however, we are *not* indebted for our own article in any particular.— The translations we give are original in this article.—[5]

Like all the[6] productions of the earlier northern bards, German or Scandinavian, the poem is not subjective, but eminently objective.— It[7] gives definite[8] characters,[9] good or bad,— it relates what is done or said.— All is narrative; no sentiment, or reflection, or corollary.—[10]

1. Deleted: "give" ; inserted above: "furnish"
2. Deleted: "a"
3. Deleted: "fuller"
4. Deleted: "article" ; inserted above: "essay" . For WW's indebtedness to Carlyle for his knowledge of the *Nibelungenlied* see "*Neibelungen-leid* Song." For a discussion of WW's disclaimer see Little, 565–566 (see also "Carlyle, born 1795").
5. End of first scrap.
6. Deleted: "poems" ; inserted above: "productions"
7. Written over a blotted "T"
8. Inserted above "char" in "characters,"
9. Inserted: "good or bad,—" over "s,—" in "characters,—" and "it"
10. New paragraph indicated by WW's symbol.
11. Deleted: "charac strength of the"

¶ We have said that the spinal[11] connection of the piece is Pagan; yet,[12] as we have it,[13] a clumsy attempt is made to Christianize[14] many of the Characters.—[15] The Knights go to mass; and there is, in general, the same change as[16] that attempted with some of the old architecture and sculptures in Rome, by chopping off a little here and there, and[17] altering the names from Jupiter[18] or Mars[19] or Minerva to St. Peter and[20] Michael and the Virgin Mary.—

[2] Before the vesper hour, lo! a great movement of knights in the court-yard,
To engage in a tournament, for the royal pastime.—

Looking on, among the rest, there sat the two wealthy queens,
And talked of the heroes[21] worthy of praise.

Then said the beautiful Queen Kriemhilde,
"My husband is the most noble, and by right this kingdom, and the rule of it, is his."

Then said the lady Brunhilde, "Nay,
The King,[22] your brother, is most noble—If none were living but you and your man,
Then[23] what you say might be—but not while Gunther lives."

[3] First went the queen to Hagen, and, looking upon him with hatred,
"Restore," said she, "before it is too late, my Nibelungen treasure,
Then Gunther and yourself may[24] return to your own country."

Then out spoke Hagen, perfectly fearless,
"It is in vain, for I have sworn[25] the treasure shall remain buried,
As long as[26] one of Gunther's royal family is alive;
Therefore ask me no more—but do with me what you will."

12. Deleted: "in"
13. Deleted: "many of"
14. Deleted: "the"
15. Deleted: "Some of"
16. Deleted: "has been" ; inserted: "that" above "[*del.*] "been"
17. Deleted: "changing" ; inserted above: "altering"
18. Deleted in pencil: "and" ; inserted above in pencil: "or"
19. Inserted and deleted in pencil: "and" ; inserted in pencil: "or" ; inserted: "Minerva" above "to St."
20. Deleted: "St."
21. Deleted: "most"
22. Inserted: "your brother," above "king, is most"
23. Deleted: "it" ; inserted: "what you say" above the deletion and "migh" in "might"
24. Inserted and then smeared out: "freely" above "may"
25. Deleted: "that" ; inserted: "the" above at the right.
26. Deleted: "any" ; inserted above: "one"

Then turning to a follower, Kriemhilde commanded him
To go to the cell where Gunther was imprisoned, and dispatch him, and bring the head thither.

Soon Hagen, with horror, with distress in his heart,
Saw the servant appear, with the bloody head of Kriemhilde's brother.

He looked at it a moment, and then with stern resolution, to the queen
"Gunther," said he, "is dead—and Gernot and Giselher, thy brothers all, are dead,
And I shall soon follow them—yet, she-wolf,
I tell you not the hiding-place of the gold and gems."

[*4*] "So be it, then," said Kriemhilde, "one useful thing, at any rate, you have restored to me,
The sword, the weapon of my noble Seigfried."

With that, she drew Seigfried's sword from the scabbard,
And struck off the hero's head with her own hands,
And Etzel cried aloud in horror, to see what was done.

And at the same time, ancient Hildebrand,[27] springing to his feet,[28]
Exclaimed, in frenzy, "Shall such a warrior fall by the hand of a woman?
Then thus I revenge him!"

And swiftly drawing a dagger, he smote the queen in the side,
And Kriemhilde fell, dying, and her kinspeople gathered round her.[29]

Without avail,[30] therefore, was shed the blood of many valiant princes, and their followers
And over the[31] lost and the dead, Dietrich and Etzel, left alone, lamented.
Thus love doth evermore bring dole and sorrow,
And thus ends the Song of the Nibelungen.—

27. Deleted: "risin [*?*]"

28. Smeared out: "cried" ; next line begins "Cried" , which is deleted and "Exclaimed" inserted above.

29. Next line begins "Thus," deleted; uppercase "W" written over lowercase in "without"

30. Deleted: "ran" ; inserted above: "was shed" ; inserted and brought into place by curved line: "therefore," above "avail"

31. Deleted: "dying and" ; inserted above: "lost and the"

The Nibelungen Leid.

Manuscript in LC (Feinberg #831). Inscribed in black ink on good quality white wove paper, 7⅞" x 5", torn from bound notebook and tied together with a pink tape. WW did not line up all the torn edges, so that some leaves are torn at bottom. Vertical rules ⅜" apart, except where noted, and embossed with capitol (?) as noted. Notes from C.C. Fauriel (1772–1844), *History of Provençal Poetry,* trans. G.J. Adler (New York, 1860). WW had read a review of Fauriel's book in *The Edinburgh Review,* 88 (1848). See "Neibelungen-leid Song." The date, from the publication date of the book and from the large loose handwriting, is in the 1860s, perhaps, from the embossing, when WW was in Washington during and after the war. (Gene Edward Veith, Jr.)

[*1*] *The Nibelungen Leid* /

(Nibelungen[1]—[:][2] Nibel–ie–fog lungen[3]—land Leid[:][4] song—lay—poem) /real author unknown / arranged—12th Century—(or perhaps first half 13th Century)/ see pp. 195–220—Fauriel/

[*7; 2–6 blank*[5]] The[6] motive idea of the epic is revenge, a woman's revenge, which after[7] slumbering for twenty years[8] at last breaks out[9] & satiates itself in a scene of[10] slaughter worthy[11] to[12] culminate[13] & end this powerful chant of action,[14] strife, jealous[15] bitterness, smouldering hatred, strong animal emulation & passion, & wholesale angry fighting &[16] war—(Likeness to Iliad, also a poem of moodness & revenge[17]

1. Inserted over [*illeg.*] spelling attempt.
2. Brace, pointing right. The etymologies do not seem to be from Fauriel.
3. Initial letter overwritten.
4. Brace pointing right. Final letter in "leid" written over [*illeg.*].
5. Printed rules on [*4,5*] extend only about 1" across leaf.
6. Deleted: "active" ; inserted above: "motive"
7. Preceding two words inserted above "slumbering"
8. Deleted: "only to" ; inserted above: "at last"
9. Inserted: "& [*illeg. del.*] satiates itself"
10. Deleted: "blood &"
11. Inserted and deleted: "to end" ; inserted: "to" following the deletion.
12. Inserted and deleted: "be the" following "to"
13. Inserted, "e" written over "tion" in "culmination." Inserted and deleted: "[*not del.*] & end of" ; inserted: "& end"
14. Deleted: "quarrel, ambition" ; inserted: "strife" above "[*del.*] quarrel"
15. "y" of "jealousy" struck out; deleted: "revenge" ; inserted above: "bitterness,"
16. Preceding three words inserted above "war"
17. The preceding does not seem to be from Fauriel and is probably WW's critical comment. His notes from Fauriel follow, the parenthetical remarks being WW's comments.

[*9; 8 blank*] Contains 6000 verses (I suppose *lines*)/

The Story—

toward middle of 5th century existed kingdom of Burgundia, along the Middle Rhine—capital Worms (pr. Vurms)[18]—King Gunther, with two younger brothers Gernot & Giselher—a great Chief & vassel Hagen— —Sister of the King &c—Chrimhild—(the motive personage—the pivotal person of the story)[19]/

then another Kindom Niderland, or[20] the Lower country. —King Sigmund—the son SIEGFRIED—he (Siegfried the epical hero of those times)[21] had conquered the treasures of the Nibelungen—& buried them in a cavern—had a wondrous sword & a cap producing invisibility [*11;10 blank*] Siegfried seeks Chrimhild—goes[22] to Gunther's court does him varies services—wins for him Brunhild a famous Amazon & queen—wins by his invisibility, &c.[23] her virginity, (a curious passage to modern notions, but[24] a pivotal part of the plot of the poem.)—[25]

Siegfried marries Chrimhild—the jealousy &c of the imperious Brunhild—Siegfried is treacherously assassinated by Hagen, to satisfy Brunhild—

[*13;12 blank*] Chrimhild remains at Worms, very rich from the Nibelungen treasure[26]—but Hagen machinates & steals them from her—time passes

—13 years elapses from the assassination of Siegfried—

—Now appears in[27] the poem Attila, King of the Huns, suing for Chrimhild to be his wife—also RUDIGER margrave of Bechlare on the Danube his the King's[28] representave & spokesman

[*15;*[29] *14 blank*] Chrimhild refuses once & again—but at last consents to mary King Attila[30] in the expectation of thus winning vengeance—She marries Attila,[31] is received at Vienna, goes to her new kingdom—seven years pass away—

—Still,[32] still, harping on her wrongs—she plans an invitation for her broth-

18. Parenthetical words inserted above "ms" in "Worms—"

19. Parenthetical insert written to right, possibly written later (on three lines) with a finer-nibbed pen.

20. Deleted: "of"

21. Preceding eight words inserted, possibly later with a finer-nibbed pen on three lines above "—had conquered the"

22. Initial letter written over [*illeg.*].

23. Preceding four words inserted above "wins her virginity"

24. Deleted: the" ; inserted above "a"

25. Fauriel's delicacy prevents clarity here, and WW is understandably misled. Siegfried substitutes himself for Gunther, who had been rejected and bound hand and foot by his powerful bride on their wedding night, but Siegfried swears to keep the king's honor and, after subduing Brunhild, takes only her girdle and ring—but not her virginity.

26. Blot at end of word, perhaps a deleted "s"

27. Blotted, perhaps over [*illeg.*]

28. Preceding two words inserted above "his"

29. Embossed. Traces of writing from [*17*] soaked through.

30. Deleted: "under a"

31. Overwritten.

32. Initial letter written over "T" [*?*]

ers, Hagen &c. to come & make a visit to Attila's court—they are invited & accept— (the adventure with the sirens on the [*17;*[33] *16 blank*] banks of the Danube— —the priest thrown overboard—[34]

Volker, a Burgundian[35] warrior & minstrel, with Gunther
Huns [:][36] Rudiger, of the Huns, receives them, feasts them &c. in his city Bechlare
Dietrich, of Verona Hildebrand his servant & warrior
Orteliebe, boy,[37] the son of Attila & Chrimhilde[38] [*18–30 blank*][39]

33. Embossed.

34. The sirens predict that only the priest will survive the adventure. Hagen tries to thwart the prophecy by drowning their chaplain, who, however, is saved by a miracle.

35. Inserted above "a warrior"

36. Brace, with an extension, marking all subsequent entries on the page, which are in hanging indentation.

37. Inserted above wordspace between "Oteliebe . . . the"

38. Orteliebe is mentioned on p. 211 in connection with the beginning of the bloodshed.

39. Embossed: [*19*], [*21*], [*23*], [*25*]. No rules: [*22*], [*24*], [*26*], [*27*].

Goethe's Complete Works.

Manuscript in Duke (33, #17). Inscribed in black pencil and black ink as noted on pink wove paper, approx. 9¾" x 5¾". A Roman "I" opposite the second entry may be by another hand. The source appears to be Carlyle's various essays on Geothe (Stovall, *AL,* [1954], 26, 347 and *Foreground,* 129–137). For other comments on Goethe see "Goethe 1750–1832," "Goethe from about 1750," "Schiller—born 1759," "These I believe," "Miss Harriett N Swallow"; *Corr.,* IV, 129, 259, 260, 391*n*; "Poetry To-day—Shakspere—The Future" *Prose 92,* II, 485; "Lacks and Wants Yet," "Notes Left Over," ibid., 533, "Robert Burns as Poet and Person," ibid., 559, "Notes (such as they are) Founded on Elias Hicks," ibid., 628; "Old Poets," ibid., 660, "American National Literature, ibid., 664, "A Backward Glance O'er Travel'd Roads," ibid., 664. There is no evidence that WW read any Goethe, although he probably did so in Longfellow's *Poets and Poetry of Europe* (1845) and Frederic H. Hedge's *Prose Writers of Germany* (1848). The date is after July, 1855. First published in *N&F,* 105 (Pt. III, #75; *CW,* IX, 110–111) as part of a "made-up" essay on Goethe.

Goethe's Complete works, last complete edition of his own revision, 1827–8, a short time before his death.— Goethe born 1750—died 1832.[1]

Carlyle, in reviews and otherwise, seems to have been the introducer of Goethe and the principal German writers, from 1827 onward 10 years[2]

Goethe — (reading Carlyle's criticisms on Goethe.) over leaf[3]

Here is now, (January 1856) my opinion of Goethe: Had I not better read more of Goethe, before giving an "opinion"?[4]

He is the most profound reviewer of Life known.— To him life, things, the mind, death, people, are all studies, dissections, exhibitions.— These[5] he enters upon[6] with unequalled[7] coolness and depth of penetration.—[8] As a critic he stands apart from all men, and criticises them.— He is the first great critic, and the fountain of modern criticism.—

1. Hanging indentation.
2. Hanging indentation. Cf. a similar acknowledgement of Carlyle in "Richter born 1764."
3. At right edge of leaf in large loop. See [2].
4. At right in black ink, boxed by straight lines above, below, and to left. Probably a later insertion.
5. Deleted: "departments"
6. Deleted: "in modes not comparable with any previous excellence but"
7. Deleted: "grandeur and" ; inserted above: "coolness and"
8. Deleted: "In the work of" ; inserted: "As" above "[*del.*] work"

Yet Goethe will never be[9] well beloved of his fellows. Perhaps he knows too much. I can fancy him not being[10] well beloved of Nature for the same reason.— A calm and mighty person whose anatomical considerations of the body are not enclosed by superior considerations, makes the perfect surgeon and operator upon the body upon all occasions.— So Goethe operates[11] upon the world . . . . his office is great . . . . what indeed is greater ? — He shall have the respect and admiration of the whole.— There is however what he cannot have from [any.][12]

[2] Goethe

Carlyle vaunts him as[13] showing that a man can live[14] even these days as "an antique worthy." This vaunt[15] Goethe deserved—he is indeed a cultivated German aristocrat, physically[16] inextricable from his age and position, but morally bent to the Attic spirit and its occasions two thousand and more years ago;— That is[17] he;[18] such are his productions.—[19] The assumption that Goethe passed through the first stage of darkness and complaint to the second stage of consideration and knowledge.—and thence to the third stage of triumph and faith—this assumption[20] cannot pass,[21] cannot stand amid the[22] judgments of the soul.—[23] Goethe's was the faith of a physical well-being,—a good digestion and appetite—[24] it was not the faith of[25] the masters, poets, prophets, divine persons.—[26] Such faith he perhaps came near, and saw the artistical beauty of,—perhaps fancied he had it—but he never had it

[3] *Goethe*—1750–1832

His first literary productions fell in his 23d year
Sorrows of Werter in his 25th year[27]
in 1776—Goethe was seen by the heir-apparent of Weimar
Soon after invited to court—and accordingly settled at Weimar

9. Deleted: "dear to men" ; inserted: "well beloved of his fellows" above deleted "to men" and "Perhaps"
10. Deleted: "dear to" ; inserted above: "well beloved of"
11. Deleted: "with"
12. Inscription runs off the bottom of the leaf. Bucke's reading.
13. Deleted: "having [*illeg.*]"
14. Preceding four words inserted above "even these"
15. Inserted above wordspace before "Goethe" and over "G" in "Goethe"
16. Inserted above "inextric" in "inextricable"
17. Deleted: "his"
18. Deleted: "and"
19. Deleted: "All" ; "the" capitalized.
20. Deleted: ", in the"
21. Deleted: "and remain permanently" ; inserted: "cannot stand" above deleted "and remain"
22. Deleted: "accepted"
23. WW is dismissing Goethe from the Romantic canon. Deleted: "His"
24. Preceding five words inserted on two lines above "being—it" . Redundant dash not printed.
25. Deleted: "phro" ; inserted: "the masters" above "ro" in "[*del.*] phro" and "poets"
26. Deleted: "Of" ; "such" capitalized.
27. Sentence begins at left edge of leaf, "Sorrows of Werther" having been inserted in pencil in right margin.

(Goethe was tall, handsome, every way personally attractive) had the title of Legations-rath.—
(some time after) By degrees whatever was brightest in Germany had been gathered to this little court.
There was a classical theatre under Goethe and Schiller
There Wieland taught and sang.
In the pulpit, there, Herder.[:][28] ? was this about [29]
Goethe had risen until at last he was appointed Minister (I suppose Chief)/

So[30] Goethe lived amid princely persons, all ceremonies, etiquets, ranks, ribbons, caste, the classics, refinements, taxes, money plenty, deference,— all that belongs to a petty German court,[31] and the minutest observances of the same, with exact precedence and routine for every thing.— arranged art exhibitions, palace-building, laws for the university and so on

[5; *4 blank*][32] Goethe 1750–1832

Goethe's poems, competitive with the antique, are so because he has studied the antique.— They appear to me as great as the antique in all respects except one.— That is, the antique poems were growths[33]— *they* were[34] never studied[35] from antiques.—
Goethe's *Wanderjahre* vandryahre[36] was published in his 72d year.— (Sorrows of Werter in his 25th)[37] It's characters illustrate, (in dialogue and incident) a philosophical theory of the Christian religion, finely spun.— The orthodox statements of Christ, the crucifixion, &c are re-stated — "the sun hiding its head when He died," — &c/

Feb. 18 '56—There is one point of the Goethean philosophy which[38] without appeal and forever incapacitates it from suiting America or the forthcoming years;— It is[39] the cardinal Goethean doctrine too, that the artist or poet is to live in art or[40] poetry alone apart from affairs, politics, facts, vulgar life, persons, and things— seeking his "high ideal."—/

Feb. 22. Goethe is never carried away by his theme—he is always master.— He is the head person saying to a pupil Here, see how well this can be done.

28. Brace at right of this and preceding entry.
29. [*Illeg.*] date deleted.
30. Pointing hand in left margin.
31. Deleted: "with" ; inserted above: "and"
32. In upper right corner, "2" in another hand.
33. Underscore deleted.
34. Inserted above "ne" in "never"
35. Deleted: "there" ; inserted: "from"
36. Inserted above *"Wanderjahre"*
37. On four lines in left margin surrounded by bracket.
38. Deleted: "at once" ; inserted: "without appeal [*ink over an erasure*]" above "and forever"
39. Deleted: "that"
40. Written over [*illeg.*].

Goethe.

Manuscript in Duke (33, #16). Inscribed in black pencil, with black-ink emendations on yellow wove paper: [*1*], approx. 9¾" x 5⅜"; [*2*], 9⅞" x 5½". Right edges irregular and somewhat tattered. Stovall (*AL,* 26, 347) says that this MS was WW's original observations, which are repeated in "American National Literature" (1891). See "Goethe's Complete Works." The date is probably late 1856. First published in *N&F,* 106 (Pt., III, #75; *CW,* IX, 113–114) as part of a "made-up" essay.

Goethe—from about 1750 to 1832.
Schiller died 1806—born 1759

Goethe is the result of a well-ordered[1] polished, learned state, not physically great, acknowledging[2] etiquette,—of moving mainly among gentlemen and ladies of culture, and taking it for granted that there is nothing[3] better than[4] culture.— The[5] educated mind has[6] pleasure in Goethe's works—many, perhaps all[7] of them. Still questions arise: Why do not [*?*][8] uneducated minds also receive pleasure from Goethe? Is he really an original creator, or only the noblest of imitators and[9] compositors? Would[10] he have written any thing, without the studies of the antiques? Is a man or woman invigorated, made[11] cleaner, grander [*2;*[12] *3 blank*] sweeter, by his poems? or more friendly and less suspicious? Has he raised any strong[13] voice for freedom and against tyranny— Has he satisfied his reader of immortality? I am convinced that Goethe has not[14] the indefinable something that is Nature itself—his Nature is the Nature of school[15]

1. Deleted: "and"
2. Deleted: "sta culture and"
3. Deleted: "better" ; inserted above and deleted: "more needed" ; inserted above "[*del.*] more needed" : "better [*del.*] better"
4. Deleted: "gentlemen and ladies of"
5. Deleted: "mind" ; inserted above "[*del.*] mind" and deleted: "cultivated" ; inserted below "cultivated" "and above "mind": "educated"
6. Deleted: "almost boundless"
7. Preceding two words inserted in ink above "many of" ; comma inserted.
8. Deleted: "uncultivated" ; inserted above: "uneducated"
9. Preceding two words inserted above "of" and "comp" in "compositers"
10. Inserted in ink above "Would" : "C" perhaps as an alternate reading ("Could").
11. Deleted: "purer[?]" ; inserted above: "cleaner"
12. Blank, except for pasted-on clipping of highly unfavorable comments about Goethe which identifies him with Walshingham in John Sterling's "The Onyx Ring" 1837–1838; Boston, 1856.
13. Deleted: [*illeg.*].
14. Deleted: "to me"
15. Sentence crammed in at top of leaf. There is no indication as to where it is to be inserted.

What Goethe was, it[16] is doubtless best that he was.— It is also eligible, without finding any fault with him, to inquire what he was not.— He could not have been what he was without also being what he was not.—[17] To[18] the little court of Wiemar,—[19] to the poetical world,[20]—to the learned and literary worlds,[21] Goethe has a deserved greatness.— To the genius of America he is neither dear nor the reverse of dear. He passes with the general crowd upon whom the American glance descends with[22] indifference.— Our road is our own

16. Deleted: "was" ; inserted above "[*del.*] was" and "best": "is doubtless"
17. Sentence inserted above "was not.——. . . the little court of"
18. Inserted above dash; following "The" not reduced to lowercase.
19. Deleted: "and" ; inserted above wordspace and deleted: "to" ; inserted: "to" above "[*del.*] and"
20. Deleted: "and" ; inserted above: "—to"
21. Deleted: "may all take attitudes"
22. Deleted: "a certain blending of [*preceding two words ins. and del.*] curiosity and"

Niembsch Lenau.

Manuscript in Middlebury. Inscribed in black pencil (entry on Lenau) and brownish black ink on tan wove scrap, 9⅜" x 5⅝". On verso "The secret is here." Niembsch Lenau (1800–1850), Austro-Hungarian poet, lived in Ohio, between 1832 and 1833. A Mr. Held and Charles Held are mentioned in "16th Sept," *DN,* III, 778 and "[*illeg.*] Dick Hunt" [*11*]. Stovall, *AL,* 26 (1954), 348, traces the comment on the *Niebelungenlied* to Gostwick's *German Literature* (see "Neibelungen-lied Song") and (ibid., 360), the comment on Dutch literature to Longfellow's *Poets and Poetry of Europe*. The date is in the 1850s. First printed in *N&F,* 107–108 (Pt. III, #6, 79–82), 166 (Pt. IV, #46), *CW* IX, 116–117, X 12.

Niembsch Lenau (Nicolaus Strehlenau

Hungarian (died 1853—insane an idiotic and animal—from love aged 35)[1]

Tankó, the horse-herd a popular poem life of a Hungarian horse-herd, scenes, characteristic adventures,—common life—real life.—[2]/

conversation with Mr. Held about German poet. *his talk*[3] as follows:

Frieligrath (frī le grät) a democrat—impulsive when he meets any one, or as he walks the road, or at a meal, &c &c. he composes—he improvises easily—Rickert, Uhland, Kinkel, Hoffman, Heine, Xavier?[4]/

Shakespeare depicts actual life, Schiller the ideal Goethe mixes both actual and ideal[5]/

Nīēbelunen[6] Lied— scene much[7] in the city of Worms and environs—Siegfried fifth century much of it dialogue, passed on from one character to another, flowing out./ Only experts in antique German can get along with the Neibelunen[8]—it is as[9] far different from modern German as the Saxon preceding Chaucer is from the present English./[10]

Dutch Holland, Belgium [:][11] Netherlands — Have a literature, poets, historians, essayists, — first-raters—/

See over

1. Parenthetical comment in upper right corner. Deleted: [*illeg.*]
2. Rule across leaf.
3. Fist pointing down to "Freiligrath" paragraph below, which presumably is the information from Mr. Held.
4. Rule across leaf.
5. Entries in column.
6. WW cancelled the "g" in "Niebelungen"
7. Inserted.
8. The "g" has been deleted.
9. Inserted above wordspace between "is far"
10. Rule across leaf.
11. "Holland" and "Belgium" are at left of the brace written respectively, on the line above and the line below the line in which "Dutch" is written. They are connected to "Dutch" by short lines.

Schiller—Born 1759.

Manuscript in Duke (34, #20). Inscribed in black pencil on yellow wove paper, approx. 9½" x 515/16". The yellow paper may be left-over stock from endpapers of *LG* (1855). Stovall (*AL*, 26, 347–348) says that the notes on Schiller are from Carlyle's "Schiller" in *Critical and Miscellaneous Essays*. He further (360) says that the notes on Klopstock and Lessing, except for Lessing's being a Jew, are from a review of Longfellow's *Poets and Poetry of Europe* (see "Bells and Pomegranates") and that the names and order of poets are the same as in Longfellow's anthology. On verso is pasted a clipping of a newspaper review of Lewes's life of Goethe endorsed *"Goethe* from 1750 to 1832 *as* a *Young Man* Also In *Old Age*" . In 1885 WW noted the page number in Lewes of the passage in the clipping describing Goethe's youthful beauty ("Miss Harriett H Swallow"). The date is probably 1855 or slightly later. First printed as two MSS in *N&F*, 106, 166 (Pt. II, #76, Pt. IV, #45; *CW*, IX, 114, X, 12).

Schiller—born 1759—died 1806.[1] aged 47[2]

Of the last 15 years of his life, not an hour could have been entirely free from pain.—Was helped by Goethe, aided to emoluments.—They two were friends—had frequent and learned correspondence.—(It is published)/

Klopstock, (patriotic extremely and enthusiast and very religious
Lessing, (Jew, critical,)—both flourished from 1750 onward—before Goethe/

Later poetical successors, since Goethe and Schiller,
Tiēck (teek)
Çhamisso (shamisso)
Ûhland (Ooland)
Schûlze (shûltzė)
Rûckert (rook urt)
Heīnĕ (hī ne)
Hoffman (tall in person)
Freiligrath (frī le grât) something like the English Tennyson and
the American Bayard Taylor

1. "O" inserted over [*illeg.*].
2. Preceding two words written below "1806."

Zschokke.

Manuscript in LC (#77, sheet #s 603–605). Inscribed in black pencil on yellow wove paper: [*1*] 10⅝" x 6½", [*2*] 10⅞" x 6⁵/₁₆", [*3*] 10⅛" x 6⁷/₁₆". Hanging indentations. The foliation is WW's. Heinrich Zschokke (1771–1848), German tale-writer, had a certain popularity in translation in the 1840s. WW probably read his *Autobiography* in the London, 1845, translation. The yellow paper, possibly *LG* (1855) endpaper stock, and the writing suggest a date in the late 1850s when WW was educating himself.

Zschokke

Probably no autobiography ever permanently deceived mankind.—[1]

The life of Man is interesting and striking enough to stand by itself unwarped[2] by the merit[3] of the Author, or the celebrity of the Statesman.—[4]

Zschokke, born 1770

Commenced preface to "Autobiography" 1840, (in 70th year,) "I thought that I was alone with God in world, and that He was educating me in the School of Life, until I should be fit to live at home in Heaven with Him.— For me He had built this wonderful place, (the Earth,) and all which I saw, men, women, children, animals, were all moved about solely for me and in my presence, being without life or motion when I was away.— Whenever I came God hastened to continue the wonderful spectacle for me, to teach and educate His child.—[5]

Z 2

I had learnt to feel at home and cool amid all the changing vicissitudes of fortune —to laugh in adversity and remain cautious in prosperity;—to dispense with ease and superfluity—to live independent and frugal.—[6]

1. Verbatim from translator's preface to *Autobiography,* iii.
2. "d" deleted after "un"
3. "it" inserted over [*illeg.*].
4. Adapted from translator's preface, *Autobiography,* iv.
5. Almost verbatim from *Autobiography,* 10.
6. Verbatim from *Autobiography,* 50.

I had learnt EASE *and* POLITENESS IN SOCIAL INTERCOURSE[7]

As in great cities *men adopt the most ridiculous customs, for fear of appearing ridiculous,* I played, like others, my part in the motley mask of life.—[8]

An old philosophe, p. 50[9] more fameworthy than famous—the German Diogenes,[10] of Paris, Count Gustav von Schlaberndorf.— He was upwards of 60, lean and tall, with ragged hair, and a wornout dressing-gown, of indescribable color; a hermit of his charcoal-fire, which he scarcely ever quitted . . . . —[11] just escaped the guillotine—preserved in his little room (or rooms) as much coolness and self-possession in his views of the men and the events going on[12] around him, as if centuries lay between him & them—*Without seeking influence* he had obtained it, like Socrates, by instructive conversation, and a profound knowledge of men & things[?].[13]

Z 3

Yet I had become by this time too thoroughly Europeanized to relish the life of Rousseau's homme naturel[14]

"I understood neither the stones under my feet, nor the stars over my head, nor the commonest flower that blossomed in forest or meadow."[15]

"It was now I learnt how much more a teacher can learn of children than children can learn of a teacher.—[16]

It was early my endeavor to prevent any taste or predilection from becoming a psssion with me.—[17]/

Zschokke evidently, (with great natural goodness as a substratum) modeled his life, on principle, after the philosophy of Polonius' advice to his son, in Hamlet.—[18]

7. Verbatim from ibid.
8. Verbatim from ibid.
9. Written above "philosopher"
10. Deleted: "Co"
11. Verbatim from *Autobiography,* 50.
12. Inserted above "ar" in "aroused"
13. Preceding fifty-seven words based on *Autobiography,* 50.
14. Verbatim from ibid., 55.
15. Verbatim from ibid., 58.
16. Paraphrase of ibid.
17. Verbatim from ibid. Followed by line across leaf.
18. Inscribed in heavier writing. Followed by line to right margin.

Rei nec ke.

Manuscript in Rutgers. Inscribed in pencil, except where noted, on pink wove wrapper, 9¾" x 5⅝", the verso of "Letters of Junius." Hanging indentation. From Carlyle's essay, "German Literature of the Fourteenth and Fifteenth Centuries," *Critical and Miscellaneous Essays,* II (Centenary Edition), 328. The paper suggests a date of 1856. (Gene Edward Veith, Jr.)

Reī nec ke, a celebrated short[1] German epic poem in high repute in the latter part of the middle ages (passions, guised as animals.)/
Niebelungen Leid, (German)

1. Inserted in black ink above "G" in "German"

Hans Sachs.

Manuscript in NYPL (Berg). Inscribed in pencil on white wove butcher paper faded brownish, approx. 1¾" x 5¾", all corners trimmed. Paper identical to "Ferdusi, and the primeval" and "Author of the Neibelungen Leid," both of which are also notes from Carlyle. These notes on Hans Sachs (1494–1576) are taken directly from Carlyle's essay, "State of German Literature," *Critical and Miscellaneous Essays,* I (Centenary Edition), 32*n*. Written in 1856. (Gene Edward Veith, Jr.)

Hans Sachs 1494 to about[1] 1570 [:][2] by trade a shoemaker—one of the Master-singers in Nurenberg—from 1494 onward some 80 years—contemporary of Luther—wrote 6048 poems (208 of them tragedies and comedies)

1. "about" in a smaller hand above "70" in "1570" , probably added.

2. Brace. Preceding dates written beside and over an [*illeg.*] erasure. Following text written on six lines to the right of the brace.

Richter.

Manuscript in Duke (33, #19). Inscribed on pink wove paper, approx. 8⅞″ x 5 15/16″ in black pencil. Stovall describes it as a digest of data from Carlyle's "Jean Paul Friedrick Richter" (1827) and "Jean Paul Friedrich Richter Again" (1830). "The last paragraph on Richter and one or two words in an earlier paragraph are not in Carlyle's essays . . ." (*AL,* 26 [1954], 334). The comment on Carlyle and the German style is certainly WW's. Phrases that seem especially close to Carlyle are here noted. It is worth observing that WW did not agree with Carlyle's high opinion of Richter. See also "George Walker" and "Employments." The date, as the paper indicates, is 1856. First printed as two MSS in *N&F,* 110–111 (Pt. III, #s 89, 90; *CW,* IX, 121–123).

Richter

born 1763 aged
died 1825 62[1]

(Jean Paul) Friedrich Richter

Born 1763 at Wonsiedel[2] near Baireuth, (Germany) rather poor the earlier years, father a subordinate clergyman—went to the university—his father died—he was hard up for many years afterward.—Resolved to make his living by writing books—his first work being finished—no publisher—tried some time—at last found one in Berlin—unnoticed by the reviews, except one, and that gave a scornful notice.—Richter still holds his purpose—writes another work, "Selections from the papers of the Devil," ransacked high and low for a publisher, but found none—until some years afterward— Stood out in costume, wore his shirt open at the neck, &c—horrified all the "magisters"[3]—held out in costume seven years, and then returned to orthodoxy—

Living in the most scanty manner for some ten years, in 1793, when 30 years old, he began to be known and his works marketable, "the Invisible Lodge," "Hesperus" &c. about that time. (novels.)—The Reviews acknowledged him, and he went on writing, and receiving good returns.—He wrote many many works, (some sixty or more vols. I believe) He married 1798, a good wife of rather upper

1. Dates written in right corner. Two lines deleted: "you will see many good writers That"
2. Deleted: "in" ; inserted above: "near"
3. Carlyle uses *"magister"* in his account of Richter's dress in "Jean Paul Friedrich Richter Again," *Critical and Miscellaneous Essays* (London, 1847), II, 110.

grade. Had a pension from a princely prelate,[4] in 1802 and continued for life.—His eldest son died 1821—

[2] (Richter continued)[5]

Was writing on a favorite theme, Immortality,—[6] (had been quite blind some years,) when, 14th November, 1825, he died.—

Richter seems to have been a thoroughly irregular genius, according to the laws and models. He was gay, sparkling, a rattler, profound,—one of those that to new readers do not please, but once falling in with him, and reading his books, it is amply made up.—He seems to have "believed in Christ," and the orthodox tenets.—[7]

His person was huge, queer, irregular.—[8]

He is witty, very—yet a certain true pathos pervades even his comedy.—

I should say that he was unnatural, and lurid, judged by the calm and wholesome models.—He is full of love, and appears to be the originator of much of the soft and sentimental ways of the swarms of tale-writers of the last thirty years, in Britain[9] and America.—/

Carlyle certainly introduced the German style, writers, sentimentalism, transcendentalism, &c. &c. &c from 1826 to 1840—through the great Reviews and magazines—and through his own works and example.—[10]

4. Carlyle, ibid., 124 identifies him as a prince primate.
5. In a loop at top left.
6. Possibly from Carlyle's "Jean Paul Friedrich Richter," ibid., I, 10. Deleted: "when"
7. Deleted: "(Is this so?)" with hand underneath pointing to preceding statement.
8. Statement echoes Carlyle in "Jean Paul Friedrich Richter," ibid., 7.
9. "B" written over "in"
10. Paragraph printed as separate item in *N&F*.

Frederick Schlegel.

Manuscript in Duke (34, #21). Inscribed in black ink on Williamsburgh tax blank, 8⁹/₁₆" x 4⅝". WW may have read Schlegel's *Philosophy of History* (1829) or his *Lecture on the History of Literature* (1815), key works in the history of romanticism, but the passages noted have been identified by W.B. Fulghum, Jr. as coming from Joseph Gostwick's *German Literature* (1854), 279–280, on which WW drew heavily. See "The celebrated old German poem." Printed *N&F,* 109–110 (Pt. III, #88; *CW* IX, 120–121). The paper indicates a date in 1857.

Frederick Schlegel
1772–1829 (57)
(one of two celebrated literary brothers—the other named Augustus)[1]/

Had a strong predilection toward the wonderful and mysterious—1803, entered Roman Catholic Church.— Wrote "Philosophy of History,"—[2]most[3] valuable[4] tenet of which is,— *"the inexpediency of destroying old institutions before new ideas are prepared to develope themselves in consistency with the order of society."*—Lectures "(History of Literature" 1811–12) have chiefly extended his fame— *He*[5] *makes Literature the representative expression of all that is superior in a nation*— thus elevating it, especially poetry, far above the views of trivial and common place criticism, and regarding it as incorporating and being the highest product of human life and genius—He appreciates the great masters of all countries, and sets them off from crowds of temporary persons/
Prejudices[6]——But remember in[7] reading these Lectures, that Schlegel was full of the Prejudices of a zealous newly converted Roman Catholic.

1. Written in a column of seven lines at right edge
2. Following twenty-seven words from Gostwick.
3. Written over [*illeg.*]
4. Deleted: "idea" ; inserted above: "tenet"
5. Following forty-three words from Gostwick.
6. This pious warning is from Gostwick.
7. Fist pointed left at left edge; remaining text in hanging indentation.

Barthold Niebuhr.

Manuscript in Middlebury. Inscribed in black ink on white wove scrap, 4½" x 4¾". "German Literature" is Joseph Gostwick's *German Literature*. A clipping, Bucke's #504 (*No. Brit. Rev.,* American ed., x, 177–188 [February, 1849]), reviews several of Niebuhr's historical works. For Niebuhr see also "resumé — from Bunsen." See "The celebrated old German poem" for Gostwick. The date, from the writing and the reference to Gostwick, is probably in the late 1850s. First printed *N&F,* 107 (Pt. III, #78, *CW,* IX, 116).

Barthold Niebuhr [:][1] *1776*—1831—55 years

Born at Copenhagen—during youth visited London and Edinburgh—Was an occupant of political offices for the younger-manhood years of his life—but in 1823,—(aged 47) retired to Bonn, and became the great *Reformer of Roman History,* (and ancient History generally)—
Was much excited by the French Revolution of July, 1830— said to have hastened his death Jan 1831. —see page 249-50-51 "German Literature")

1. Name in larger script in left margin in front of a brace.

German Poet.

Manuscript in Texas (Hanley). Inscribed in black pencil and black ink ("Petäfy" entry) along right edge of business card of J. Jefferis and Son's "Fashionable Shoe Emporium," Camden. Along the opposite edge is a cancelled note: "Sidney Morse 25 Bromfield Boston." Giebel (1815–1884) was a lyric poet of the late nineteenth century. Ferdinand Freiligrath had written about WW in the Augsburg *Allgemeine Zeitung* in 1868 (See "Is Walt Whitman's Poetry Poetical?"). Petäfi's dates are 1823–1849. The source of WW's information is not known. Since Morse, the sculptor, visited WW in Camden, a date in the 1880s seems probable.

German poet Immanuel Geibel in Lubec next to Freiligrath Alexander Petäfy Hungary's greatest poet.

Louis 14th.

Manuscript in Duke (32, #11). Inscribed in black pencil on pink wove paper, approx. 9¾" x 6". Stovall (*AL*, 26, 343–364) suggests that his source is the reviews of Rachel's performances of *Athalie* at the Academy of Music (between September and November, 1855) or an article on Rachel which he clipped from *Putnam's Magazine*, 6 (September, 1855), 290 ff. (Bucke's #421) or an article "The Drama in France" in the same volume of *Putnam's Magazine* or conversations with William Swinton. According to Stovall, WW saw only the second act of *Athalie*. The paper indicates a date of late 1855. First printed *N&F*, 90–91 (Pt. III, #31; *CW*, IX, 82).

Louis 14th, born 1638—died 1715

Corneille[1] Louis 13th
Racine toward the last[2] of Louis 14th

Tragedies rigidly after the antique models—characters Greek or Roman—everything on stilts—all the talk in heroics.—/

I fancy the classical tragedies of Corneille, Racine, Voltaire, &c. must illustrate the vital difference between a native and normal growth (as the Greek tragedies themselves,) and all that comes from the mere study of that growth.—/

November[3] 1855. I saw Rachel in "Athalie," at the Academy of Music/

Myrrha, by Alfieri, the Italian—lurid passions—with long-winded dialogues between Myrrha and daughter mother[4] about nothing.—

1. Long space before next entry.
2. Preceding three words inserted in black ink in long space between "Racine" and "Louis"
3. Written over [*illeg.*]
4. Inserted: "mother" over "daughter"

Diderot.

Manuscript in Duke (32, #12). Inscribed in black pencil on white laid paper, approx. 5¼″ x 4¼″. Horizontal chain lines and conspicuous vertical lines in texture. Blue rules ⅜″ apart. On verso in ink: "Walter Whitman Classon Avenue near Myrtle Av Brooklyn" . In 1835 Walter Whitman, Sr. bought land at the corner of Classon and Myrtle Aves. in Brooklyn (Allen, 599), but in 1836 the family moved to the country. No other period of residence on Classon Ave. is known. If the writing is WW's, as it appears to be, no explanation can be offered. As Stovall points out (*AL,* 26, 357–358), the notes on Diderot were made in the 1850s and are drawn from Carlyle's *Critical and Miscellaneous Essays.* First printed *N&F,* 160 (Pt. IV, #22; *CW,* IX, 226). See also "Phrase — his biographer says."

Diderot (Dennis Diderot)
1713–1784 71 years)

His father a cutler, good man—mother also good
D educated well by the Jesuits
Came to Paris a young man — lived ten years a loafer, a rascal, a literary hack

Emerged by degrees—is the back-bone and brain of the French Encyclopoedia

(The Enc. was some years (12, 16, or 20) in being finished.)
Diderot was befriended by the Russian
Empress Catherine—she gave him
£3000

It is said of him that he had the
most encyclopoedical head ever in the world, and was a
most superb talker

Diderot with his *mouth of gold* —

Two Samples.

Manuscript in Duke (35, #27). Inscribed in pencil on white wove scrap. On verso is "Europe." The reference is to Voltaire's *Philosophical Dictionary,* ed. Abner Kneeland, 2 vols. in 1 (Boston, 1836), now in Yale. A pencil line is in the margin of the article "Character" and the heading is annotated "side head and set close." The article on "Great-Greatness" is similarly marked on pp. 403–4. Stovall (*Foreground,* 209) thinks these might have been meant for inclusion in WW's "fragment" on Voltaire in *Life Illustrated* (May 10, 1856) or for the Brooklyn *Daily Times.* See also "Voltaire's readable." First printed in *N&F,* 156 (Pt. IV, #13; *CW,* IX, 218).

TWO[1] SAMPLES of Voltaires writings.—

[2]Translated from his Philosophical Dictionary.]
(set what is marked on pages 173 and 174.)

translated[3] from the same
Great—Greatness.

1. Deleted: "Some" ; inserted above: "Two"
2. Brackets are WW's.
3. Capital "T" written over lower case.

J. J. Rousseau.

Manuscript in Duke (32, #14). Inscribed in faded black ink and black pencil (on verso) on white laid paper, approx. 8″ x 4½″. Vertical blue rules on recto and verso, ¼″ apart. Rules across leaf. Conspicuous vertical lines in texture. Numbered "3" in an unknown hand. Stovall (*Foreground,* 211) believes that WW's information was drawn from William Swinton's unsigned 1856 translation of the *Confessions*. The suspicion that Rousseau had committed suicide was not disproved until after WW's death. See also C. Carroll Hollis, "Whitman and William Swinton: A Co-operative Friendship," *AL,* 30 (1959), 428–429, and "The Social Contract." First printed in *N&F,* 90 (Pt. III, #30; *CW,* IX, 80–81). The date must be 1856.

J.J. Rousseau—Celtic, not Saxon[1]
Born 1712—Died 1778—
some say by suicide.—[2]
"Rousseau's Confessions"
translated N.Y. 1856.[3]/

An American poet may read Rousseau, but shall never imitate him.—He is a curious study, and will cause some contempt[4]

Born in Switzerland—parents decent substantial bourgeoisie/
—a sort of vagabond/
—copyist of music/

Lost his mother early—/

One brother—not much together/

Father a quiet, easy person.—/

Jean Jacques left home—lived with various persons—worked—was bashful—learned a little of everything—his "Confessions" are a singular opening up of

1. Three words circled at right.
2. Entry in hanging indentation.
3. Entry in hanging indentation.
4. At left, opposite two preceding entries, and set off by straight lines above, below and at right.

the trivial incidents, some quite disgusting, which find their tally in every man's life—[5]Madame de Warrens—over leaf[6]/

A sensitive, Frenchy, frivolous, keen, proud, unhappy, restless, contemplative nature

Note how "character" is built up, after all—from the beginning—/
—How the pompous "history" and "Biography" come down to just such as we are.

[2][7] After many wanderings, the last ten years of Rousseau's life, were in and around Paris.— He was very poor; he lived in a garret, and earned his food by coping music.— He was old, discouraged, not robust, not popular, not happy.—[8] What a ten years![9] and what an ending to them!— Six weeks before his death,[10] Rousseau was invited to a country mansion some[11] miles away.—[12] There he walked, meditated—thought who knows what? He spent in botanizing the[13] day before[14] the night of his death.—Did he,[15] or did he not, die of suicide?

5. Preceding entry in hanging indentation. Redundant dash before "Madame de Warrens" at beginning of new line omitted.

6. At right. Set off by half-circle. Nothing on verso.

7. Verso. Further entries in black pencil.

8. Deleted: "Six Thus ten years"

9. Deleted: "these must have been" ; inserted above: "and what an ending to them!"

10. Deleted: "he" ; inserted: "Rousseau" above the deletion and "was"

11. Deleted: "a few" ; inserted above: "some"

12. Preceding three words inserted above "ion" in "mansion" and "[*del.*] by" ; deleted: "he went.—The day of" ; inserted: "There he . . . botanizing" above the deletion and, on the next line, above "The day before and "[*del.*] his"

13. Uppercase "T" not deleted in MS.

14. Deleted: "his"

15. Deleted: "indeed" ; inserted: "or did he not"

Rousseau's Confessions.

Manuscript in Duke (32, #14). Inscribed in pencil on pink wove stock torn at lower right. See "J. J. Rousseau" and "The Social Contract." The date must be 1856.

Rousseau's Confessions—(Swinton's translation, fall of 1856)[1] in 1766, Rousseau, 54 years old, took refuge in Wooten, Staffordshire, England, and wrote this frivolous, chattering, repulsive, book, that still has a great lesson in its pages, and whose revelations one keeps reading somehow to the end.—

Rousseau born 1712 died a suicide[2] 17[78][3]
a Genevese (Swiss) a rover, vagabond,
copyist of music, never rich, exiled from Fran[ce] 40.[4]

[2][5] Remember in those days there were no journals—no "reviews," or masses of cheap literature demanded—

1. Deleted: "were"
2. Preceding two words inserted above "died 17[78]" . Leaf torn.
3. Leaf torn.
4. Leaf torn. "40" written below "France" may not be in WW's hand. An unidentified clipping associating the deaths of Rousseau and Voltaire is pasted on. Entry in hanging indentation.
5. Verso. Half erased above inscription is "finishing stroke George Steer's head" . Entry preceded by pointing hand.

The Social Contract.

Manuscript in Duke (32, #15). Inscribed in black ink on rectos of white wove paper, 9⅞" x 7¼". Blue rules ⅜" apart on rectos. Embossed with a crowned oval supported by rampant beasts, scroll beneath inscribed "London." This paper has not been found elsewhere in WW's manuscripts. The essay was first discussed by Bliss Perry in *Walt Whitman, His Life and Work* (NY, 1906), 52, 277–280. In "Whitman and William Swinton: A Co-operative Friendship," *AL,* 30 (1959), 431–432, C. Carroll Hollis identified William Swinton, WW's friend who had published a translation of *The Confessions,* as the source of WW's text, speculating, no doubt correctly, that Swinton made a viva-voce running translation. Swinton, however, is not the "French translator" who translated Victor Hugo's "Année Terrible" to WW in 1872. (See "Victor Hugo's Année Terrible.") For Swinton see "Rambles Among Words." Stovall (*Foreground,* 211–212) identifies Swinton's text as *Oeuvres de J. J. Rousseau,* 4 vols. (Paris, 1837), I, and identifies "Brissard" as G. Brizard, an editor of a thirty-eight volume edition of 1788 to 1793, who is cited in Swinton's text. Portions were first printed (somewhat freely) in Clifton Joseph Furness, "Walt Whitman's Politics," *Am Merc,* 16 (1929) as noted, and the complete text in *FC&I,* 33–41. The date is 1856.

The Social Contract, Or; Principles of Right.
Foederis Aequas
Dicamus leges   Virgil, Æneid, 11, 324

Preface, [1] to the First Edition

This little Treatise is extracted from a more extensive work, undertaken without consulting my resources, and long since abandoned.—The following comprises the greater part of the different fragments which had been written, and which seemed to me best worthy; all else destroyed.—

(1.) Montesquieu has only spoken of positive laws, leaving his splendid structure incomplete; but we must go to the very source of these laws, to trace the origin of this primitive implied or expressed Covenant which binds all societies together.—The *Contrat Social* has appeared; this forms the portico of the temple, and the first chapter of *L'Esprit des lois.*—We may say in truth of this author—"The Human Race had Lost its Title Deeds—Jean Jaques has found Them." (*Note by Brissard.*)

Rousseau has given the substance of his *Contrat Social* in the fifth book of

1. Deleted: "prefixed"

Emile, where traveling is discussed; and another abstract is given in Lettres de la Montagne, (letter Sixth)

Book First. 2[2]

I wish to inquire whether, taking men as they are, and laws as they may be made, some just rule of administration may not be established in the civil order.—In this research it will be my constant endeavor to ally that which the right permits,[3] with that which policy prescribes, that justice and interest may not be divided.—

I begin without expatiating.—I may be asked Who I am—a prince? a lawgiver?—No, neither; and therefore it is I write.—[4]

Chapter First,—Subject

Man is born free, yet he is everywhere in fetters.— He who fancies himself the master of others is only more enslaved than they.—Whence this anomaly?—I know not its cause.—What can legalize it?—I think I can answer. Did I only consider force, and the results arising from it, I should say:[5] So long as a nation is constrained to obey, and does obey, it[6] acts well; So soon as it is able to throw off the yoke, and does throw it off, it acts still better;— for[7] it regains its liberty by the same right which deprived it of liberty. For all this, social order is a sacred right upon which all others are based.— This right, however, originates not in nature, but is founded on covenants.— Now to investigate those covenants.

Chapter 2d. (3

The first Societies.

Family organization is the oldest society and the only natural one.— Yet children only remain subject to the father, while they need his care.[8] Afterward both father and children resume their independence; each is free from the other.— If they still remain united it is because they voluntarily elect to do so.— This common liberty is a consequence of the nature of man.— His first law is that of watching over his own preservation.— Subsequently, the chief is the symbol of the father,—the people, of the children[9]; and all being born free and equal, none can alienate their liberty except for their own interests.— The sole difference is,

2. WW's foliation.
3. "it's" in "permits" written over [*illeg.*].
4. Deleted: "Born a citizen of a free state, and member of its sovreignty,"
5. Comma deleted before colon.
6. Deleted: "does" ; inserted: "acts" above "s" in "does" and into right margin.
7. Deleted: ", as"
8. Deleted: "Then" ; inserted: "Afterward" above "en" in deleted "then" and "bo" in "both"
9. Deleted: ",—" ; written over: ";"

that in the family the love of the father for the children compensates him for the cares he bestows, (orig.? [10]—Is it not also that the like care was aforetime bestowed upon him—and now he only pays?)[11]—while, in the State the Ruler is compensated by the honor and profit of ruling[12].—

Grotius denies that all human rights ? [13] can be established in favor of the governed, citing slavery as an example.— His constant manner of reasoning is to establish the *right by the deed*.—(1)[14] A more logical method may be used—but less favorable to tyrants.—[15]/

(1.) The ablest researches into public rights often simply consist of the history of past abuses, and we bewilder ourselves to no purpose when we take the pains to study them deeply.—(*Traite des Interest, France;* Marquis Argenson.)—This is precisely what Grotius has done.—

4

It is doubtful, according to Grotius, whether the human race belongs to a hundred men, or these hundred men belong to the human race;[16] but he seems inclined to the first opinion.—This is also the sentiment of Hobbes.—See the human species thus divided into herds of cattle, each having its chief, who guards but to devour it.—As a shepherd is by nature superior to his flock, so the human shepherds.—Thus reasoned the Emperor Caligula, according to Philon, proving plausibly enough that the kings were gods, or the people beasts.—

The philosophy of Caligula is revived in that of Hobbes and Grotius.—Aristotle had said, before them all, that men are not equal by nature, but that some were born for slavery, and some for dominion.—Aristotle was right, but he mistook the effect for the cause. Every man that is born in slavery is born for slavery; nothing is more certain.—Slaves lose everything in their fetters; even to the desire of quitting them; they love their servitude, as the companions of Ulysses loved their brutishness. If there are slaves by nature, it is because there have been slaves against nature.—Force made the first slavery; cowardice has perpetuated it.

I have said nothing of King Adam, or the Emperor Noah, the father of the three great monarchs who divided the universe, like the children of Saturn, whom we seem to recognize in them.—

5th

Chapter 3d

The Right of the Strongest

The strongest man can never be strong enough to be always master, unless he

10. Written above "—Is it"
11. Parenthetical entry set off from body of text in three lines at right of center.
12. Deleted: "?—" ; inserted above: ".—"
13. Question mark above "rights"
14. Numeral written over dash.
15. In a smaller hand at right.
16. Deleted: "and" ; inserted above: "but"

transforms force into right, and obedience into duty.—From this arises the right of the strongest, a right which is seemingly claimed in irony, but really laid down as a principle.—But will they not define this word for us?—Force is a physical power; I cannot see what morality can result from its effects.—To yield to force is an act of necessity, not will.— At the most it is an act of prudence. In what sense can this be a duty?

Let us assume this pretended right for a moment.— Nothing but inexplicable nonsense results from it; as the effect changes with the cause, and every force which surmounts the first one, succeeds in right.— So long as we can disobey successfully, we do so lawfully; and, if the strongest is in the right, the only point is to prove who may be the strongest. Of what avail is a right which perishes when force ceases?—If we must obey by force, of what need is duty?

"Submit yourselves to the higher powers." If this means, yield to force, the precept is a good one, but superfluous.— I answer that it will never be violated.— All power comes

6

from God, but all sickness comes from Him also.—Are we therefore to conclude that we are forbidden to call the physician?—When a robber surprises me in a forest, I must surrender my purse to force,—but when I can regain it, am I obliged by conscience to give it to him?

We admit then,[17] that force does not constitute right, and that we are only obliged to obey the legitimate powers.— My first question returns.

Chapter 4th.

Since no man possesses a natural authority over his fellows, and since force does not produce any right, covenants therefore remain as the basis of all legitimate authority among men.

"If a private citizen," says Grotius, "has a right[18] to alienate and[19] cede himself as a slave to a master, why have not a whole nation an equal right?" There are equivocal words here, but we will confine ourselves to *alienate*—that is *to give,* or *sell.*— X X X X[20]

But if each individual could alienate himself, he could not alienate his children, and theirs, and theirs.— (that's the strongest point.)[21]

X X X X X X X

(This chapter is to prove that the *right* of Slavery, either through cession, victory, sparing life, or what not, is *null.*—)— He says "The words *Slavery* and *right* are contradictory,[22] each excludes the other."[23]

17. Inserted: "then," above wordspace between "admit that"
18. Written over [*illeg.*]
19. Preceding two words inserted above "to cede"
20. On the line with the end of the paragraph.
21. Parenthetical entry is slightly below and to the right.
22. A dash deleted.
23. Entry beginning "He says," written to right of center in three lines.

7

Chapter Fifth

We must always refer to a first Convention.— Should I grant all the positions which I have just refuted, the advocates of despotism would not be benefited thereby—there will ever be a wide difference between subduing a multitude, and governing a nation. Uncivilized[24] enslaved men and their masters, I do not regard as chief and nation—the interest of one being opposed to that of the other, there is no commonwealth.

X X X X

Chapter Sixth

The Social Compact.

I will suppose that men have reached that crisis where the difficulties that threaten their preservation in a state of nature, exceed their resources in that state. They perish then unless they improve that state. Now men cannot create new forces, but they can unite and direct those which already exist—they can associate, under a representative head, or[25] several heads.—

This union involves all,—yet how can each pledge his strength and liberty, without injuring his interests? X X X

Given: To find a system of association which shall defend and protect with the whole common force the person and property of each associate, and by which every member, while uniting with all, shall be subject only to himself, thus remaining as free as before the union.—This is the organic problem, the solution of which is given by the Social[26] Contract.—

8

X X X

The[27] articles of this Contract are so precisely worded that they cannot be modified.—When analyzed, they reduce themselves to a single point, *The entire alienation of each associate member, with all his rights, to the whole community.*
(?)[28]

X X X X

Chapter Sixth

The Sovereign power

Orig. W.W.[29] (In short, the whole of this *Contrat Social,* goes to prove, (1760?[30]–'70?[31]) that[32] the true government, and of course[33] the only one for men of sense,

24. Deleted: "men"
25. Deleted: "something like"
26. Deleted: "Compact" ; inserted following: "Contract"
27. False start at beginning of line: "These"
28. Preceded by hand pointing upward.
29. Written in indentation space.
30. Question mark above date.
31. Question mark above date.
32. Deleted: "go"
33. Preceding three words inserted above "the only"

is that of[34] *a compact* where laws are administered for justice, equal rights, and *inherent liberty* — as opposed to all the continental European, (Especialy French) ideas of Government ———

Chap. 8th

—This transition from the state of nature to the civil state, produces a remarkable change in man by substituting in his conduct justice for instinct—((Orig W.W.[35] —What is it then, but instinct,?—cultivated instinct?[36] and by giving morality to his actions—It is first at this point that, the voice of duty succeeding to physical impulse, and right to appetite, the man who until now had regarded no being but himself, is[37] brought to act upon other principles, and consult his reason before listening to his inclinations.

9

Although in this state he yields some of his natural advantages, he gains others, more important—and his faculties exercise and develope themselves, his ideas become enlarged, his sentiments ennobled, and his whole being is elevated to such a degree, that although abuses of this new condition may often degrade him beneath the state which he has quitted, he should unceasingly bless the happy moment which rescued him from it,—and which, from a stupid and insignificant animal, created an intelligent being and a man!

Let us reduce this balance of advantages to terms easy of comparison.[38] Man's *loss* by the social contract is his natural liberty, and an unlimited right to all that he may have the power to wrest or acquire—His *gain* is civil liberty, and protection in the ownership of what he earns or possesses.—

X X X

([39] We may also add, as gain, *moral liberty* which alone renders man truly master of himself—for *obedience to lower appetites* is *slavery*[40]

10

Chapter Ninth

Real Estate.

orig W.W.[41] (Where Rousseau is yet undeveloped is, in not realizing that the *individual* man or woman is the head and ideal, and the State, City, Government, or what not, is a servant, subordinate, —with nothing sacred about it—

34. Preceding two words inserted above *"a"*

35. Written above "What is"

36. Preceding ten words and double parenthesis inserted to right of center of leaf in three lines. Text from "Orig. W.W." to this point printed by Furness, "Walt Whitman's Politics," 465.

37. Deleted: "forced to"

38. Upper part of colon deleted.

39. Single parenthesis to left of entire entry.

40. Below this entry hand pointing upwards. Preceding two paragraphs printed in Furness, "Walt Whitman's Politics," *Am Merc* (1929), 465.

5. Preceding three words inserted above "my first"

nothing in a Judge or Court either—But all sacredness is in the individual, and, the other[42] at most, is but a reflection of the individual's.)[43]

X X

**Every man has a natural right to all that is necessary to him (*orig W.W.* yes but he must go out, where no one has planted stakes before him.—Also, all wealth, however large is inviolable, being the result of previous??—and because society and individual interests are more benefitted by leaving it inviolable than by taking any from excessive wealth and giving it to —whom?—to[44] the poor[45]

(Singularly[46] some of the most important provisions of the specific laws of the Public Lands of the United States are taken word for word, and idea for idea, from Rousseau's "Contract."[47]

11

I shall terminate this[48] book by a remark upon which every social system should be based—namely—That instead of destroying natural equality, the social compact, on the contrary, substitutes a civil and legitimate equality for the physical inequality that nature has caused among men,—and That, however unequal they may be in respect to strength or genius, all become equalized by strength, and by right.—

Note.—Under bad governments, this equality is but seeming and illusory, serving only to maintain the poor in their misery and the rich in their usurpations.— In this case the laws are always advantageous to the possessors, and injurious to non-possessors.—from which it follows that the social state can only be beneficial to men when all possess some, but none too much, property.—

orig.([49]—Or rather when all have opened to them an equal right to the avenues and means of[50] reaching property.[51]

42. Preceding two words inserted above "nd" in "and" and "at"
43. Printed in Furness, "Walt Whitman's Politics," ibid., 465.
44. Preceding two words inserted to left in pencil.
45. Preceding passage, beginning *"orig W.W."* inserted down the right edge of the leaf behind a series of large single parentheses.
46. Passage beginning "(Singularly," written behind large single parenthesis opposite preceding passage at left side of leaf.
47. Printed in "Walt Whitman's Politics," ibid., 466.
48. Deleted: "by"
49. Large single parenthesis.
50. Deleted: "posses"
51. Passage in hanging indentation.

Lafontaine.

Manuscript in Duke (32, #13). Inscribed in black pencil on white wove scrap, approx. 8¼" x 5¼". Left edge bears signs of earlier mounting; instructions for mounting on verso. On bottom half of leaf is pasted a headnote on Buffon from Charles Knight's, *Half Hours with the Best Authors,* I, 155. Knight is also possibly the source of WW's information on La Fontaine. The date is probably in the late 1850s. Printed in *N&F,* 104 (III, #73; *CW,* IX, 109).

Lafontaine, born about 1621
lived 73 years— 1694)
was of good family, inherited some property,—wrote fables in verse—somewhat like Æsop's—also wrote poems & plays—lived 20 years supported by a noble lady in her house—was intimate with (? Racine, Boileau, Bossuet, Moliere).—

"With the Fever."

Manuscript in LC (#79, sheet #747). Inscribed in black ink across scrap of white laid paper ca. 4¾" x 8¼". Blue lines ca. 5/16" apart. The quotation is from Matthew Arnold's "Joubert." WW may have found it, unsigned, in *Living Age,* LXXX (March 5, 1864), 470, under the title "Joubert; or, a French Coleridge." The writing suggests a date in the 1860s. Joubert is also mentioned in "Emerson Idaho—(Capt. Mullen)."

"with the fever of the senses, the delirium of the passions, the weakness of the spirit; with the storms of the passing time, & with the great scourges of human life—hunger, thirst, dishonor, diseases, death—authors may, as long as they like, go on making novels which shall harrow our hearts; but the Soul says all the while, "You hurt me."

Joubert, a modern French
writer (died 1824)

[*Illeg.*] Voltaire's Readable.

Manuscript in LC (#79, #734). Inscribed in black ink on irregular white wove scrap. Writing in purple crayon on verso is in another hand. WW was possibly using an edition other than the 1836 *Philosophical Dictionary* ("Two samples"), for in that edition the article is on p. 255–256. See also "Religions—Gods." The writing appears to be late, certainly not pre-1860.

[*Illeg.*] Voltaire's readable [*illeg.*] —of the settlement of Philadelphia, and of the Quakers, (ante 1776) see *Philosophical Dictionary*
pp. 197,–8.

Victor Hugo's Annee.

Manuscript in Virginia (Barrett). Inscribed in black pencil on three irregular scraps of white wove paper. The poems referred to are: [*1–2*] "Prologue"; [*3*] "Sedan," "A l'Allemagne," "A la France," "A Petite Jeanne." All are in the first twenty-odd pages of the Pléiade edition of Hugo's *Poésies*. Since the entire *Année Terrible* runs to almost two hundred pages in this edition, it is unlikely that Mr. Aubin translated it entirely. Whoever he was, Mr. Aubin was keeping up to date, for the book had been published in Paris as recently as April. See Traubel, II, 361, and V, 127. First printed in part in *WWD*. This was written in October, 1872.

Victor Hugo's *Annee Terrible* (Mr. Aubin) As translated to me by Mr. Aubin Oct. '72/ first the Prologue— —the splendid portraitures of the People & the mob.

[2]*Prologue*

A whole world, if it is wrong, does not outweigh one just man

Distinction between the *People* & *the Mob* Magnificent/

It is not *incense* that has broken the nose of the Sphynx/

—it is the bosom made vulgar by the belly

—the grand armor "old iron"

[3][1] *Sedan*

(the Close where the sword of France representing all the great heroic characters, and all the famous victories—(mentioned by name)—is "by the hand of a bandit" ignominiously surrendere/

To Germany—To France (my mother)/

To little Jane one year old (most beautiful)

1. An illegible mark in upper left corner may be "4."

Phrase.

Manuscript not found. Text from *N&F,* 161 (Pt. IV, #24; *CW,* IX, 228–229). See "Diderot (Dennis Diderot)."

Phrase—his biographer says of Diderot (1713–1784)—"all the virtues which do not require a great suite of ideas were his."

Boccacio.

Manuscript in Virginia (Barrett). Inscribed in black pencil on faded tan wove paper similar to that of "Dante," approx. 1⅜" x 5⅞". "Boccacio" is written to the left of the rest of the text and an erroneous "c" in the third syllable is deleted. The MS may once have been part of a larger MS. See "Ferdusi." Stovall, *AL,* 26 (1954), 61, says it is based on *Westminster Review* 51 (July, 1849), 186ff. First printed *N&F,* 167 (Pt. III, #51; *CW,* X, 14) as part of a jumble of notes. The date is possibly as early as 1849.

Boccacio Contemporary of Chaucer—Petrarch—"Next to Dante Boccacio was the greatest contributor to the formation of the Italian language—To the former it was indebted for nerve & dignity,—to the latter for elegance wit & ease.

—The Story of Dantes.

Manuscript in Duke (35, #27). Inscribed in black pencil on faded brown laid paper, approx. 5¹⁵/₁₆″ x 3⁹/₁₆″. Horizontal rules ⅜″ apart. The names are in column. See "Spring of '59." First printed *N&F* 165 (Pt. III, #43; *CW,* X, 11.) The date is certainly before 1860, possibly as early as 1849.

—the story of Dantes "Journey through Hell."

—The three great narrative poets of Italy—(great Italian poetic constellation) Dante born[:] 1265 died Pulci born[:] 1431 died Biordo[:] born 1434 Ariosto,[:] born 1474 Tasso,[:] born 1544

Dante.

Manuscript in Virginia (Barrett). Inscribed in black pencil on faded tan wove scrap, 1″ x 5⅞″. "Dante" is to the left of the rest of the text and separated from it by a short vertical line. The MS was possibly once part of a larger MS. See "Ferdusi." Stovall, *AL,* 26, 360–361, says the quotation is from the *Westminster Review* (American Edition), 51 (July, 1849), 186–188. Assuming that WW was using a current issue (which might not be the case), he was aware of Dante a decade before he read the *Inferno*. See "Spring of '59." First printed *N&F,* 167 (Pt. III, #51; *CW,* X, 14) in a jumble of short notes. The date may be 1849.

Dante see page 186—about 2/5 from the beginning of this book "Master of heaven, of purgatory, and of paradise—owning them by right of genius—he could bestow situation upon friend or foe, in any of them."

Spring of '59.

Manuscript in Duke (24, #25). Inscribed in black pencil and black ink on white wove paper, approx. 8″ x 6¼″. Embossed stamp of Owen & Hurlburt, So. Lee, Mass. in upper right corner. (Cf. "What name"). The translation of the *Inferno* WW read was that of John Carlyle (1849).

WW's interest in Dante was moderate at best, and his reading apparently did not go beyond the *Inferno*. His references to Dante in published works are all commonplace allusions. His knowledge of Dante is surveyed in Joseph Chesley Matthew's "Walt Whitman's Reading of Dante," *Un Tex Stud Eng,* 19 (1933), 172–179. James Matlack Scovel, a Camden friend, gave the rather surprising reminiscence, in *National Magazine,* 20 (1904), 168–169, that "he was fond of Dante, and often quoted one of Dante's Canzones": "Ascended is our Beatrice to the highest heaven;/ To those realms where angels dwell in peace; And you her fair companions, and Love and me,/ She has left, Alas! behind./ It was not the frost of Winter, nor was it the heat of Summer that withered her;/ It was the power of her virtue, her humility and her truth/ That ascended into heaven, and moved the eternal Father/ To call her to Him, seeing that this miserable life was not worthy for anything so pure and so excellent." (*La Vita Nuova,* 32, 2d stanza of "Gli occhi dolenti per pietà del core"). See also "return my book," "These hospitals," "the RR we go on," "Ethnology," "The theory of the poem," "Is Walt Whitman's Poetry Poetical?," "No one of the Themes," "The Bible Shakspere," "the story of Dante's," "Boccacio," "Dante," and "Ferdusi." Dante is referred to as "poet of penalties—poet of hell" in "Pictures," which is before 1855, the most firm of the early dates. The date of this MS is 1859.

Spring of '59—read Dante's "Inferno"——[1]It is one of those works, (unlike the Homeric and Shaksperian.) that make an intense impression on the susceptibilities of an age, or two or three ages of the peculiar temper fitted (by previous training and surrounding influences)[2] to absorb it, and be mastered by its strength.— But[3] as what it grows out of, and needs presently[4] for its understanding and love, has passed quite away, it has also passed away.— It rests entirely on the fame it achieved under circumstances fitted to it.—

The points of the "Inferno," (I am giving[5] my first impressions,) are *hasting on,* great vigor, a lean and muscular ruggedness,[6] no superfluous flesh[7]; and the

1. Redundant dash not printed.
2. Parenthesized words inserted above "temper fitted . . . to absorb"
3. Deleted: "it" ; inserted above: "as"
4. Inserted above "eds" in "needs" and "for"
5. Preceding three words inserted above "my first"
6. Parenthesis deleted.
7. Parenthesis deleted.

fascination there always is in a well told[8] tragedy, no matter how painful[2] or repulsive.— It signifies in its way[9] that melancholy and imperious[10] part of humanity, or its elements, out of which the whole structure of the[11] stern and vindictive Jehovahn theology has arisen—from the times of the primitive Jews down—[12] vengeance,[13] gloating in the agony of sinners, bad men, enemies to be punished, and the usual distinctions of good and evil.—

It is a short poem.— Dante's whole works appear to lie in a very moderate compass.— It seems strange that he should stand as the highest type of Italian imaginative art execution in literture—[14]so gaunt, so haggard and un-rich,[15] unjoyous.— But the real[16] Italian art-execution[17] flourishes of course in other fields—in music, for instance, peerless[18] in the whole earth[19] teaching[20] high over the heads of all lands, all times.[21] [3] Mark, the simplicity of Dante—like the Bible's—different from the tangled[22] and florid Shakespeare.— Some of his idioms must[23] in Italian cut like a knife.—[24] He narrates like some[25] short-worded superb illiterat, an old farmer, or some New England blue-light minister, or[26] common person interested in telling his or her story[27]—makes the impression of[28] *bona-fide* in all that he says, as if it were certainly so.— I do not wonder that the middle ages[29] thought he indeed[30] had really[31] descended into Hell and[32] seen what he

8. Preceding two words inserted above wordspace between "a" and "tra" in "tragedy"

9. Deleted: "a" ; inserted above: "that"

10. Deleted: "temperament" ; inserted: "part of humanity, or its elements," above the deletion and "out of" and "wh" in "which"

11. Deleted: "angry" ; inserted above: "stern"

12. Preceding eight words and dashes inserted above "ahn" in "Jehovahn" and "theology has arisen—". Redundant dash before "vengeance" not shown.

13. Deleted: "bad men,"

14. Word and dash inserted above "ve" in "imaginative"

15. Word and comma inserted above "and" and "un" in "un-joyous"

16. Deleted: "big"

17. Deleted: "is" ; inserted: "flourishes" above deletion and "of"

18. Deleted: "over" ; inserted above: "in"

19. Deleted: "and then"

20. Deleted: "all" ; inserted above: "high"

21. As far as we know, the only Italian music with which WW could have been familiar with was the bel canto opera of the generation just preceding his. Deleted: ".—" after "lands"

22. Deleted: "web" ; inserted above: "tangled"

23. Deleted: "be charming"

24. Preceding four words and end punctuation inserted above "ian.—" in "Italian.—" and "He" and "nar" in "narrates" . Redundant end punctuation not deleted, not printed.

25. Deleted: "talkative" ; inserted: "short-worded superb" above deletion and "illit" in "illiterate"

26. Preceding five words and comma inserted above "some common person" and "inter" in "interested"

27. Deleted: "; yet is not garrulous"

28. Deleted: "believing" ; inserted: "*bona-fide* in" above the deletion and "all"

29. Deleted: "really"

30. Inserted above "he had" and "de" in "descended"

31. Inserted above wordspace between "had descended"

32. Deleted: "saw" ; inserted above: "seen"

described.—[33] [*4*] Mark, I say,[34] his economy of words—perhaps[35] no other writer ever[36] equal to him.— One simple trail of idea, epical, makes the poem—all else resolutely ignored.[37] This[38] alone shows the master.[39] In this respect is the most perfect in all literature.[40] A great study for diffuse moderns.—

Dante's other principal work, the Paradiso, I have not read. In it, I believe, Beatrice, a pure and beautiful woman—[41] conducts him through heaven—as Virgil has conducted him through Hell. Probably he does not succeed so well in giving heavenly pictures.—[42]

¶ What is more effective, conforming[43] to the vulgar and extreme coarsely[44] rank pattern of Hell, than the tableaux in the "Ninth Circle," where two brothers that have hated and murdered each other are made to continually "butt" each other by their heads, steeped in mud,[45] ice, and filth?—

33. Deleted: "(How much is Milton indebted to Dante? How much is Swedenborg indebted?)"

34. Preceding two words and comma inserted above "his"

35. "— perhaps" inserted in ink above "no other" . Redundant dash not deleted, not printed.

36. "ever" inserted in ink above "eq" in "equal"

37. Deleted in ink: "It is beautiful"

38. Inserted in pencil above deleted "It"

39. Preceding four words and period inserted in ink above "is beautiful"

40. Sentence inserted in pencil on two lines above "A great study"

41. Preceding five words and dash inserted above "Beatrice . . . conducts"

42. Paragraph sign inserted in ink.

43. Inserted: "conforming" above "ive" in "effective" ; deleted: "after" ; inserted and deleted above: "out of" ; inserted: "to" under "[*del.*] out" and above "[*del.*] after"

44. Preceding four words inserted above the entries in *n*43 and "vulgar and" and "ra" in "rank"

45. Deleted: "ice" ; inserted below: "ice"

Tasso. Petrarch.

Manuscript not found. Text from *N&F,* 167 (Pt. IV, #51; *CW,* X, 14). Tasso is also mentioned in "Ferdusi." No date can be determined, but it is probably before 1860. First printed in *N&F* as part of a jumble of notes.

Tasso. Petrarch.

Torquato Tasso.

Manuscript in Duke (34, #23). Inscribed in black pencil on blue wove paper, approx. 6¾" x 3¾". Blue rules ⅜" apart on both sides. Written in hanging indentation except as noted. Stovall, *AL,* 26 (352) says that the notes correspond exactly with J. H. Wiffen, *The Life of Torquato Tasso* (NY, 1859). Printed *N&F,* 130–132 (Pt. III, #173; *CW,* IX, 163–166). The source and the writing suggest that WW wrote this in 1859 or 1860.

Torquato
Tasso
1544—1595——(51 years)

Born at Sorrento, near Naples.

Father a poet, and educated gentleman (Bernardo Tasso.)

Mother died at his 16th or 17th year.—

Torquato studied—moved among the nobility, the courts, the learned, &c

Wrote the poem "Rinaldo" in his 18th year—in 10 months.—rec'd through Italy with great applause.

At the age of 21, went to Ferrara, as a gentleman of the household of the Cardinal d'Este.

The two ladies, "the Princesses," sisters of the Cardinal d'Este, Lecretia aged 31 Leonora, 30. soon married to Prince D'Urbino.— With these "Tassino" was a favorite.—

(The father Bernardo died 1569, aged 76 "after a life marked by many vicssitudes and sorrows, but cheered throughout by a literary enjoyment, and a truly Christian philosophy.—"

In 1570 Tasso "attended his lord the Cardinal to the court of France."

Tasso made application some time after to be received into the service of Alphonso, Duk d'Urbino, Lucretia's husband[1] and succeeded.— He was assigned a pension of 1500 crowns of gold a month.—

(Taso 2)

He soon after worked faithfully and at leisure on the "Jerusalem."

But first finished and published his pastoral poem of "Aminta"—rec'd thro' Italy with great applause.—

Completed the Jerusalem in 1575 (ag 31)—He submitted this poem to the judgment of a number of his friends —"a step which in the sequel involved

1. Preceding two words inserted above "Urbino" in "Duk d'Urbino" and "and" and "suc" in "succeeded"

him in the greatest difficulties, not less from the diversity of opinions than from the ascetic severity of some of his censors, who professed to see, in his charming fictions, something profane and seductive," &c &c

The "Jerusalem" underwent several revisions, two grand ones, in particular—one of the censors read it not as a critic, but as an "inquisator"

(Jealousies, absurd criticisms, heart sickness, &c. &c)

Tasso goes to Rome.—But soon returns to Ferrara.)

Has "an interview with one of the Duke's greatest enemies.")

(Italian suspicion and treachery—fears, doubts, and cross-purposes.)

Several troubled years—the Jerusalem printed

Tasso had not long returned from Ferrara, ere his melancholy, induced originally on his ardent temperament by the severity of his critics, and the persecutions of his enemies, returned upon him more deeply than ever.—[2]

(Tasso 3)

He had "symptoms of that mental disorder which was soon to affect his reason."

He disturbed himself with hundreds of fantastic fears.—

"At length one evening in June 1577 (ag 33) in the chamber of the Duchess d'Urbino he ran after one of her servants with a drawn dagger."

The Duke now issued orders to have Tasso confined in his chamber.

(More fears groundless alarms, dread of losing the favor of the Duke.)

Tasso takes flight clandestinely from Ferrara leaving his MSS. &c

From this period a wanderer from Court to Court in Italy, a prey to sorrow and morbid heart

Goes to Sorrento, to his sister— Goes to Rome—at last returns to Ferrara, under a cool permission from the Duke

But leaves Ferrara again soon—wanders—wanders—wanders—at last bringing up again at Ferrara—during a marriage festival of the court—is neglected—in a fit of invective gives loose to the keenest invectives against the House of Este— The Duke is apprized of them, and Tasso, and Tasso is arrested and taken to the hospital of St. Anne, an asylum for lunatics & paupers.

(Tasso 4)

This was in 1579—years passed—sick, declining, sometimes sane, sometimes crazed—[3] *over seven years passed* in this prison—he was liberated in 1586—

—Again he travels up and down Italy— /

The last twenty years of his life seem to have passed very unhappily, wan-

2. Paragraph with standard indentation.

3. Deleted: "over [*illeg.*]"

dering, insane, (just conscious enough of it, to make it doubly poignant),—either persecuted, or, which is always[4] worse, supposing himself to be persecuted.—[5]

Personally, Tasso was of lofty stature, fair complexion, (eventually pale,) head large, beard brown, eyes large, (their look generally directed toward the heavens.)—of attractive appearance—born a gentleman in an age when the term had all its high distinction.[6]

4. Inserted above "wor" in "worse"

5. Paragraph with standard indentation.

6. Preceding eleven words inserted on two lines following "gentleman" . Paragraph with standard indentation.

The Amadis of Gaul.

Manuscript in LC (#115). Inscribed in black ink with occasional black and blue pencil on homemade white wove notebook, 6½" x 4⅛". Apparently no leaves were lost when the notebook was disassembled and mounted. WW's information is from George Ticknor's *History of Spanish Literature,* I (NY, 1849, 1854, 1853) as noted. He also drew on Ticknor for his notes on Cervantes ("Cervantes"). He probably took both sets of notes during his intensive period of self-education after 1855.

[*1355R*] Literature Romance of the 15th & 16th centuries[1]

The Amadis of Gaul

(he is called "the child of the sea"[2]

The representative romance, and type-book[3] of fiction and sentiment, in Spain, France, England, Italy, &c. &c. during the later part of the 15th 14—1500[4] and the whole of the 15—1600—centuries—with its progeny of Amadises, continuations &c.—translated into all languages—and re-edited, digested &c.[5]

also

The Palmerins.

(viz the Palmerin of Oliva the Palmerin of England, &c. &c. which closely followed on the heels of the Amadises[6]

[*1356R; 1355V blank*] 15—1600—1700[7]/

The Amadis de Gaul (all the Amadises,") and The *"Palmerins"*

—the above the types of the The Spanish Chivalry

Romances—and indeed of all Europe, and of England—commencing in the 15th century—the 16th crowded with them, and all their influence on taste and manners—and more or less carried into the 17th—/

Spenser's "Faery Queen" is the Daughter of them[8]

1. Scrawled in blue crayon.
2. Inserted in black pencil. The epithet is from Ticknor, I, 227.
3. Cf. Ticknor, I, 221: "poetical head and type . . ."
4. Inserted above in black pencil.
5. Hanging indentation.
6. Hanging indentation.
7. Inserted at top of page at the right in blue pencil.
8. In black pencil. Pointing hand at left.

[*1357R; 1356V blank*] Southey's works on[9] "Cid," London publisher (Ticknor[10]/ Southey's translation "Amadis de Gaul" Lond. pub. 1803.[11]/

"Amadis de Gaul,"

the father, type, and pioneer, (followed by numberless followers,) was a Portuguese fiction, (novel of those days) produced before the year 1400, MS. copies of course[12] George Vasco de Lobeira—the original Portuguese version lost—A Spanish one remaining—printed 1519— Many editions—translated into Italian, French, &c. and many, many editions

[*1358R; 1357V blank*][13] The Story[14]

Time.—No period of time is assigned to the events—which, however, begin to occur soon after the Christian era

The *Place* also, is unsettled

The main thing is the *purpose* of the story, (like directly or indirectly[15] all the romances, ballads, &c. of those ages.) which is to set forth the character of a *perfect knight,* founded on the virtues of courage and chastity.

[*1359R; 1358V blank*] Amadis is the illegitimate son of a king—exposed by his mother on the sea, found by a Scottish knight. —when grown, falls in love in Scotland with a peerless lady—Has a half brother, Galaor,—and they two, as wandering knights, meet with all sorts of adventures in England, France, Germany, Turkey, &c. and in unknown regions, with enchantments, magicians, giants, &c.—with numerous combats, some of them[16] with incredible accompanants— [*1360R; 1367V blank*] ending at last in the marriage of Amadis and his lady, (Oriana,) and all the enchantments &c being dissolved/

Ticknor says:

The Amadis is admitted, by general consent, to be the best of all the old[17] romances of Chivalry—it is true to the exaggerations of sentiment and all the manners and "spirit of knighthood."/[18]

in the book "Amadis" is called the "Child of the sea."

9. Preceding two words inserted above "Southey's" and "C" in "Cid"

10. In blue pencil in upper right corner.

11. Robert Southey (1774–1843), *Chronicle of the Cid* (London: Longman, Hurst, Rees, and Orme, 1808); first American edition, 1846. Southey also translated *Palmerin of England* (1807).

12. Preceding five words inserted on three lines to right of "1400."

13. Deleted: "—was the type romance of the [*del.*] 14th, 15th, and 16th centuries"

14. From Ticknor, I, 221–225.

15. Preceding three words inserted above in blue pencil above "all the romances"

16. Deleted: "of"

17. Inserted: "old" above wordspace between "the romances"

18. Cf. Ticknor, I, 226. The first half of the sentence is Ticknor's, the second ("it is true to . . .") is WW's.

[*1361R; 1360V blank*] The 'Amadis",[19] with all its offspring "disappeared before the avenging satire of Cervantes."[20]/

We are to remember,[21] as to that time, (1500) "romantic fiction, the only form of elegant literature which modern times have added to the marvellous inventions of Greek genius, was then fresh."[22]

—During the two centuries of its greatest popularity, it was more read in Spain than any other book./

It is, to modern taste, however, (of course),[23] tedious and somewhat ridiculous—with its repetitions.

[*1362R; 1361V blank*] The characters in Don Quixote, allude to it, (the curate, the barber, and the housekeeper, in the expurgation of the library,)/[24]

Montalvo,[25] who translated it, in Spanish, wrote also a continuation[26] on his own hook—"The adventures of Esplandian, son of Amadis and Oriana—but it is without spirit. It went through many editions however—the oldest one known, is dated 1526—[27] This continuation was again followed by others— and they by others—some [*1363R; 1362V blank*] giving the adventures of the *grandson* of "Amadis"—some of his *nephew*—all popular—all going through many editions[28]

Collection and Digest.

The various "Amadises" all being translated, as they came out, into French, and being printed in France,—at last a certain Sieur Duverdier collected them all, and digested them into a consecutive story, which he published in seven large volumes "And so ends the history of the Portuguese type of "Amadis of Gaul," as it was originally presented in Spanish translations*[*1364V;*[29] *1364R blank*]* a fiction which considering the passionate admiration it so long excited and the influence it has exercised upon the poetry and romance of modern Europe, is a phenomenon without parallel in literary history."[30]

[*1364V*] Of these romances of which the "Amadis" and the "Palmerin" are types.[31]

"the earliest of them were familiarly known in Spain during the 15th cen-

19. Deleted: "then"
20. Ticknor, I, 229.
21. Deleted: "that at" ; inserted: "as to" above "[*del.*] at"
22. Cf. Ticknor, I, 229. WW omits "recent and" before "fresh."
23. Deleted: "somewhat"
24. Cf. Ticknor, I, 230.
25. Garcia Ordonez de Montalvo's version was produced between 1492 and 1504 Ticknor, I, 223).
26. Deleted: "(1526)"
27. Cf. Ticknor, I, 231–233.
28. Cf. Ticknor, I, 233–234.
29. When it was mounted, leaf [*1364*] was reversed. In the original notebook the inscription was on the recto. This passage is written on the lower part of the page and is here inserted following WW's asterisks.
30. Loose quotation from Ticknor, I, 234.
31. Cf. Ticknor, I, 235–238.

tury—the 16th is thronged with them—and far into the 17th they are still much read"— They exceed seventy in number—these romances— all in folio—some in two or more vols.-

The common people, reading or hearing, no doubt took the narratives for *real occurrences.*[32]

[*1365R*] *The Palmerins*

Closely on the heels of the "Amadis" followed the adventures of "Palmerin of Oliva," also a Portuguese original—a warlike knight-adventurer, who gets to be Emperor of Constantinople.—

Then "the Palmerin of England," —the characters, Palmerin, the faithful knight, and Florian, the free gallant—

Thre were other parts, or "books," all only second in popularity to the "Amadises"—

(16th century 1500—to 1600) they flourished)

32. Cf. Ticknor, I, 249–251.

Cervantes.

Manuscript in Virginia (Barrett). Inscribed in black ink in homemade self-covered notebook, 6⅜″ x 4″. Paper is white wove with a "parchment" texture. Cover pasted at spine; only [2–8] bound by string. As Stovall points out (*Foreground,* 180) the notes are from George Ticknor, *History of Spanish Literature,* II (NY, 1849, 1854, 1853), 52–119. Verbatim passages or close resemblances are noted. There is no evidence that he read *Don Quixote*. He probably read Ticknor during his intensive period of self-education after 1855. For more on the Cid see "81 Clerman." First printed *N&F,* 83–84, (Pt. III, #21; *CW,* IX, 64–69).

Cervantes, (1547 . . . . 1616 . . . contemporary with Shakspeare) and *Don Quixote*.[1]

X X X "bear in mind that this delightful romance was not the result of a youthful exuberance of feeling, and a happy external condition, nor composed in Cervantes' best years, when his spirits were light and his hopes high;—but that—with all its unquenchable and irresistible humor, with its bright[2] views of the world, and its cheerful trust in goodness and virtue—it was written in his old age, at the conclusion of a life whose every step had been marked by disheartening struggles and sore calamities; that he began it in prison and finished it when he felt the hand of death pressing cold and heavy on his heart."[3]

[*3; 2 blank*][4] Miguel de Cervantes Saavedra, —born about 20 miles from Madrid, 8th or 9th of October, 1547

Wrote verses while a youth—attended the theatrical[5] pieces of Lope de Rueda

1570—(23 years old,) serving at Rome in the household of a Cardinal

Whence he volunteers as a common soldier in an expedition sent by the Pope and the Venitians against the Turks——1570–75.—was in battles by sea and land.

1575–80 . . . . in 1575 was captured and carried to Algiers as prisoner—remained in durance as a slave 5 years.

[*5; 4 blank*][6] 1580—Is ransomed, and returns home—father dead—family poor.—

1. Centered as a heading; "Cervantes" and "Don Quixote" in larger script. Deleted: "and" "above contemporary".
2. Deleted: "trust in" ; inserted: "views of"
3. Almost verbatim from Ticknor, II, 119.
4. All entries on this page in hanging indentation.
5. "theatre" emended to "theatrical" ; inserted: "pieces" above "of"
6. All entries on this page in hanging indentation.

1581—joins the army again as a soldier—serves in Portugal—becomes familiar with Portuguese literature

1584—Is at home again in Madrid, and writes and publshed "Galatea," a prose pastoral.

1584—Marries—poor, but a lady. . . . . (remained united in marriage 30 years, and his widow, at her death, desired to be buried at his side.

Dramatic performances.—Now for several years writes plays for the theatre.

[*7; 6 blank*][7] 1584–5–6.—Does not seem to have gained much position or profit as a play-wright. Two of[8] these earlier plays are in existence yet—but resemble too much the "miracle-shows" of the times, for modern taste Cervantes remains poor—was maimed, from an old wound.

1588. Goes to Seville. Acts as agent to a government Commissary—and money collector, &c.

1588–98 . . In these employments, or the like, he travels Andalusia and Granada

Imprisoned. Was imprisoned as a defaulter—released in 1597.

[*9; 8 blank*][9] 1598–1603. We lose any exact trace of Cervantes . . . but in

1603. He is estalished at Valladolid. (the court is there under Philip 3d and his favorite, the Duke of Lerma.)

1604–5 . . *Don Quixote.* In 1605, the "First Part" of Don Quixote was printed at Madrid, (licensed 1604.) The received tradition in Spain is that Cervantes having been employed by the Prior of the Order of St. John in La Mancha to collect rents due the monastery in the village of Argamasilla—that he went there, and was persecuted and thrown into prison himself by the debtors—and that while there he started Don Quixote, and located the hero in La Mancha perhaps in revenge.

[*11; 10 blank*][10] The First Part of Don Quixote was received at once with great favor—a second edition was immediately called for.

1606. Follows the court back to Madrid.

1609. Joins the Brotherhood of the Holy Sacrament—a religious association.

(All this time, Lope de Vega, the poet, is the great literary idol of the age, in Spain.)

Cervantes was full of good nature—full of *cheerfulness, activity,* and *a happy tolerance* toward every thing and every body.

[*13; 12 blank*][11] 1613—publishes "Novelas Exemplaras" (Moral Tales.)—very good, since[12] very popular in Spain,—but not in other countries.

1614. "Journey to Parnassus," a satire poem

1615. From this time forward, writes plays (also *entremeses,* (interludes.)[13]

7. All entries on this page in hanging indentation.
8. Deleted: "his" ; inserted: "these earlier" above the deletion and "plays"
9. All entries on this page in hanging indentation.
10. All entries on this page in hanging indentation.
11. All entries on this page in hanging indentation.
12. Inserted to left and above "ve" in "very"
13. Preceding three words inserted on two lines above "es" in "writes" and "plays—" and "Eig" in "Eight"

—Eight plays for popular acceptation, and caliber —are inferior productions./

Don Quixote—Second Part.

1615—In this year also, appears the second Part of Don Quixote—dedicated to the Count de Lemos. —Cervantes in this dedication[14] alludes to his failing health, and anticipated death. This second part, written in very old age, is said to be better than the first.

[*15; 14 blank*][15] *Death.* 23d april 1616. at the age of 68 . . . was buried in the convent of the Nuns of the Trinity . . .[16] but a few years afterward this convent was removed to another part of the city and[17] what became of the ashes of the greatest genius of his country is from that time wholly unknown.

(1835—a bronze monument of Cervantes was raised in the Plaza del Estamento, Madrid.

1818—a medal in France, in a series, to commemorate geniuses.)[18]

Persiles and Sigismunda.

1617. Printed by Cervantes' widow. The story is a northern romance the hero the daughter of a king of Iceland—the story full of savage men and frozen islands—wild and strange adventures—then the scene changing to south of Europe

[*17; 16 blank*][19] *Don Quixote.* The object, besides writing a good and amusing story, was to foil the fanaticism for romances of Chivalry, of the Amadis de Gaul type, which then generally prevailed in Spain . . . (The esoteric meaning discovered by modern critics is mostly bosh.)

The effect. No romance of chivalry of the old pattern, appeared after the publication of the First Part of Don Quixote in 1605. The effect was perfect: from that time they have been rapidly disappearing

A bogus Second Part. a bogus second (1614) part to Don Quixote was sent out 1614[20] by Alonzo F. de Avellanada,—very inferior, and with insulting allusions to old Cervantes.

[*19; 18 blank*] Cervantes seems to have originally intended his hero to be a parody of the character of Amadis, but soon to have made him the independent creation he is.—very distant—a crazed, gaunt, dignified, knight— . . . with his round, selfish, amusing squire.[21] [*20 blank*]

14. Preceding three words inserted above "tes" in "Cervantes" and "alludes"
15. All entries on this page in hanging indentation.
16. Remainder of entry verbatim from Ticknor, II, 99.
17. Remainder of entry marked at left by a waved vertical line and pointing fist.
18. Parentheses indicate line around two entries.
19. All entries on this page in hanging indentation.
20. Inserted above "by"
21. Almost verbatim from Ticknor, II, 114.

(Passing Through the Town.

Manuscript in Duke (35, #27). Inscribed in black pencil on verso of bill blank of Rome and Milton, Book Card and Job Printers in Brooklyn with printed date "185-." Embossed stamp: "Congress" with Capitol in perspective. Fastened to pink wove paper with four blobs of sealing wax. For a much later reference to Johann Ludwig Runeberg (1804–1877), see *"At the Ferry houses."* Bucke dates this October, 1855. First printed *N&F,* 98 (Pt. 3, #53; *CW,* IX, 95–96.)

(passing through the town of Borgo in[1] old Finland, Russia,)

Runeberg, the favorite poet of the Fin—He is said to possess more than mediocre talent, and tunes his harp gracefully to granite, firs, and the rough music of the northern blasts—all of which the Finnish people love.

Of Finland the roads are good, the scenery wild, pleasing landscapes, of which granite boulders, hills, lakes, and pine trees are the principal features—prevented from appearing monotonous by the endless variety of their arrangement.—The country is rough—the people are rough also—but friendly and strong.

Correspondence N.Y. Tribune
Oct. 1855.

1. Preceding five words inserted above "rough" in "through" and "old" and "Fin" in "Finland"

Old Age.

Manuscript not found. Text from *N&F,* 158 (Pt. 4, #19; *CW,* IX, 223), where it is evidently part of a collection of notes brought together by Bucke. The others are identified as marginalia. The topic may be misleading as to the date, for WW admired old men throughout his career. Since it was a Bucke MS, the date is probably before 1860.

Old age of great masters — Pythagoras, Socrates, Plato, Demosthenes.

The Iliad The Bible.

Manuscript in Duke (34, #22). Inscribed in black ink on two scraps of blue Williamsburgh tax form, approx. 5″ x 4¼″, 8½″ x 4¼″, respectively, glued together. First printed *N&F,* 100 (Pt. III, #58; *CW,* IX, 100). As the paper indicates, the date must be after 1857.

The Iliad The Bible (? & The[1] Eschylean tragedies)[:] (as Prometheus) the principal Shaksperian tragedies as the Hamlet[2] [:] Are[3] not complete.— Each of these poems is but a portion of a poem— Each strictly considered[4] is but an episode;[5] neither of them is a filled up,[6] entirely perfected work of art.—Though what is supplied is admirable,[7] something far more is wanted[8] than all that is supplied.—The building is grandly planned, and what is done is done by great mastery; but the building is not even half done.—
[2] Of the Bible the parts do not have that[9] unquestionable, self-proved, identity that is necessary[10] Nor does Christ merge and make fruitful all the Syrian canticles that preceded him.—[11] The real owners and heirs of the Hebrew Bible, rejecting the New Testament, and what[12] it stands for, still wait for the climax of the poem.—[13] Taking it altogether, it is wonderful how such a contradictory repertoire[14] was brought together, and has[15] held[16] sway.—Or is this diversity the very reason it has held together?—Has there been something[17] to touch, or approach every phase[?] of human[18] want, developement, tenderness, fanaticism, &c?

1. Deleted: "Æneid" ; inserted: "Eschylean . . . Hamlet"
2. Preceding matter at left side of leaf with brace at right.
3. Deleted: "neither of them" ; inserted: "not" above deleted "er" in "neither" and "of"
4. Preceding two words inserted above "each is but"
5. Deleted: "not" ; inserted: "neither of them is" above the deletion and "a filled"
6. Deleted: "richly" ; inserted above: "entirely"
7. Preceding six words inserted above "art.—Something far more" ; uncorrected capital "S," following, not printed here.
8. Deleted: [*illeg.*]
9. Preceding two words inserted above "not" and "unq" in "unquestionable
10. Deleted: [*illeg.*] ; inserted and deleted on one line: "Neither is Christ a result of the"
11. Preceding sentence inserted on two lines.
12. Deleted: "it" ; inserted and deleted above: [*illeg.*]
13. Preceding eight words inserted on two lines above "stands for,"
14. Deleted: "could have held" ; inserted: "was [*del.*] brought" printed above the deleted phrase and "togeth" in "together"
15. Inserted above wordspace between "and held"
16. Deleted: "such"
17. Deleted: [*illeg.*]
18. Inserted above "want"

Oct & Nov. '57.

Manuscript in Virginia. Inscribed in black ink on blue wove Williamsburgh tax blank. (For another wove blank, see "Aesthetics—Art—Science." Stovall, (*AL,* 26 (1954), 346–347) says that most of the notes are based on his reading of *The Works of Virgil,* trans. Theodore Alois Buckley, (NY, 1857). First published *N&F,* 100 (Pt. III, #59; *CW,* IX, 100–101) The date must be 1857 or a little later.

Oct & Nov. '57

Reading Virgil's, Bucolics, Eclogues & the Æneid.

(The Æneid was one of the very first books (translated in English) printed after the invention of printing—It was printed before 1500 by Caxton)[1]
Virgil born 70 B.C.[2] died 19 B.C.[3] aged 51 Was of the patrician order—was well educated—naturally of elegant tastes, and poetical studies—had patrons among the leading Romans—/

Of the Æneid, it seems to me well enough, except for the fatal defect of being[4] an imitation, a second-hand article—Homer's Iliad being the model.— It is too plain an attempt to get up a case, by an expert hand, for Roman origin, and for the divine participation in old Italian affairs, just as much as in those of besieged Troy, & in[5] mythical Greece. The death of Turnus, at the conclusion, seems to me a total failure, as a piece of invention, description[6] &c.—

The Bucolics and Georgics are finely expressed—they are first rate.—

1. Written on four lines and enclosed in loop at top, right, and bottom at left of leaf opposite "Ecologues & the Æneid."
2. "B.C." written above the line.
3. "died 19 B.C." written below the line and below "born 70 B.C."
4. Inserted and deleted: "in a serious view" on two lines above "an imitation"
5. Preceding four words inserted above "mythical Greece"
6. Deleted: "and"

Memory.

Manuscript in Duke (35, #24). Inscribed in black ink and black pencil as noted on pink wove paper, 7⅞" x 5 15/16". Stovall, 175, *n*50, traces the contents to John and William Langhorne's edition of *Plutarch's Lives* (1770). The Langhorne *Plutarch* was reprinted by Harper in NY in 1844, but Stovall thinks that WW probably read the Cincinnati edition of 1854–1855. First printed *N&F,* 112–113 (Pt. III, #97 and #97; *CW,* IX, 126–127). As the paper indicates, the date is late 1855 or 1856.

MEMORY.—*Nothing makes this faculty so good, as the employment of it.*—Locke.—[1]/

Many trouble themselves about conforming to laws.—A great poet is followed by laws—they conform to him.[2]/

Plutarch[3]—born about[4] the year 50 a/c probably. died, it may be 125 a/c/

Notes of Life, books &c. translations when[5] appeared.—/

Plutarch's Lives[6]—Amiot's translation (French) 1558[7] in Greek text, at Paris,—1624[8] First English translation—during reign of Queen Elizabeth/Dryden, with many others in Co. also made a translation "a motley work."[9]/

Plutarch—born in Boeotia, in Greece,[10] about the year 50 of the Christian era

studied (like the general[11] Greek youth)—acquired a great art of memory—read all the books (MSS.) of his time—leaned toward the tenets of Pythagoras.—

1. Written with broader-nibbed pen.
2. Paragraph written in pencil.
3. Large printed script at center written heavily (with broader-nibbed pen?).
4. Inserted above "the"
5. Preceding two words inserted on two lines above "&c" and "ap" in "appeared"
6. Written heavily (with broader-nibbed pen) over [*illeg.*]
7. Loop at left and partly below.
8. Loop at left and partly below.
9. Large loop at left and below, extending from "Notes of Life. . . ."
10. Preceding four words inserted above "born about the" and "y" in "year"
11. Inserted above "Greek"

was of patrician family—supposed wealthy—had two brothers his associates in study and amusements—he always speaks of them with pleasure and affection—Probably traveled into Egypt—Certainly into Italy—studied Latin quite late in life—never made much progress/

Lectured in Rome—([12] *So Lectures, it seems, there were, even in those* days; quite like the modern fashion, they seem to have been.) Plutarch had a good reputation at Rome.—some say he was preceptor to the Emperor Trajan[13]/

Notes, in the time of Plutarch, were unknown in literary compositions—this accounts for his digressions and tedious episodes.—[14]

Late in life retired to Chæronea, a philosopher, priest.—/

Was married—had five children, four sons & a daughter had a good wife.[15]/

I suppose he attained a good old age—"a long life"/

Most of his writings, with Many Lives, are Lost—Those that remain being but a portion of what he wrote[16]

12. Large loop at left of following sentence, which is written on right half of leaf.
13. Sentence written on left half of leaf, opposite preceding, brought in on brace.
14. Hanging indentation.
15. Hanging indentation.
16. Hanging indentation.

Plato.

Manuscript in LC (Feinberg #704). Inscribed in black ink, black pencil, and blue crayon, as noted, on white wove paper folded horizontally and pasted together as a notebook, 8″ x 4⅝″. Vertical blue rules ½″ apart. Red-blue-red margin. Most of the short entries are in irregular indentation. In upper left corner of [*1*] is a pencilled "f" or "4" in an unidentified hand. The six-volume Bohn edition of Plato began to appear in England as early as 1848, but Vol. I was not published until 1854. WW was probably using a Harper reprint. There is no evidence that he read further in Plato, although Robert K. Martin in *The Homosexual Tradition in American Poetry* (Austin, 1979), 85, sees the influence of the "Symposium." The MS dates from 1859 or a little later.

[*1*] (1st Vol. Plato) [1]
PLATO,[2]
430–to 350 years B. C/
Bohn's edition —1858
translated by Henry Cary, A.M.

born at Athens, (or Ægina) 429 B.C died 348 [B.C] [3][:] aged 81./
was a pupil of Socrates (as young Plato in the hands of Socrates) [4] during the latter part of S's. life, (8 or 10 years)/
was a poet & traveler—
— [5] had a school, in Athens,[6] & was teacher,[7] traveled in Egypt/
real name *Aristocles* —the name Plato is said to come from his gymnastic teacher who gave it him from his broad breast & shoulders —Plato = platitude, broad

[*3; 2 blank*] *Plato* [8]
"never married—never mingled in public affairs—seems to have regarded the constitution & character of his native city with disfavor & almost despair."/
Plato is the reporter of Socrates (as the disciples [9] of Christ, in the New Testament.) —/

1. Blue crayon, loop around left, bottom right.
2. In large open capitals, approx ¾″ tall.
3. WW used ditto marks.
4. Parenthetical statement looks like a later insert between lines.
5. Deleted: "was"
6. Two words inserted above "ool" in "school" and "&"
7. Deleted: "in"
8. In large script about ¾″ tall.
9. Deleted "are the" ; inserted and deleted above: "were" ; inserted: "are"

He makes Socrates the defender & eulogist of the platonic love Phædrus,—and Lysis[10] —advocates it, plainly, but carries it into higher & purer regions/
There is a vein of too-fine-drawn argument in many of these dialogues—too much of mere verbal point & distinction—it is often quite a nuisance,[11] being carried on tediously and interminably.

[5; 4 *blank*] "The great business of the philosopher, therefore, is to emancipate himself, as far as possible, not only from the dominion of the animal appetites, but also from the illusions of sense—& to retire into that interior world of reflection in which his mind can commune with its kindred essences."
Art. Plato
Vol. 13— Appleton's
Encyc.[12]/

In Phaedrus

the admirable legend of god[13] Theuth and King[14] Thamus, in Egypt—on the effect of the invention of letters. —they favor not wisdom itself, but the appearance of wisdom /

In Phaedrus

Socrates is presented as making light of the written discourse in comparison with the speech of the live & learned speaker

[7; 6 *blank*] *Phâé-drus* [15] (Plato)

purports to be a dialogue between Socrates & Phædrus—the latter a young man, who, coming to Socrates, is full of a discourse by Lysias on *Love*—he reads it to S.—who finally proceeds to give a discourse on the same theme — —by love he evidently[16] means the passion inspired in[17] one man, by another man, more particularly a : beautiful youth. The[18] talk seems to hinge on the question whether such a youth should bestow his "favors" more profitably on a declared lover." or on one not specially so.
[9; 8][19] at §29 Socrates begins: (it is quite rhythmic, even in translation) His whole treatment assumes the illustration of Love, by the attachment a man has for another man, (a beautiful youth as aforementioned, more especially) —(it is astounding to modern ideas)—

10. Preceding three words inserted above "onic" in "Platonic" "love" and "adv" in "advocates"
11. Deleted: "& is"
12. Ripley, George and C.A. Dana, eds., *New American Encyclopedia,* (NY, 1858–1863), XIII, 602.
13. Inserted to the left.
14. Inserted above "d" in "and"
15. Page in pencil except for inked accent and hyphen in "Phâé-drus"
16. Inserted above "means"
17. Deleted: [*illeg.*]
18. Deleted: "have a"
19. Placed on [9] to which it is a note.

§54 — he makes an ingenious comparison—the gross & spiritual in a human being in love—80–81—They "lie down together" "kiss" & fondle each other &c &c

[*8*] See indeed as very significant[20] §§80–81–82–83–84/
Socrates has first a statement —which secondly he repels & repudiates makes "recantation"

[*10*] Socrates was *a poet* —while in prison, waiting for death, he[21] made a hymn to Apollo, & put in verse the Fables of Æsop.

[*11*] In "Lysis" (another piece or argument on Love)

— —"for from my childhood I happen to have had a desire for a certain thing—as another person may have had for something else; for one desires to possess horses, another dogs, another gold, & another honors; but I, for my part, am indifferent about these things—but have a fond desire for the possession of friends—& I had rather have a good friend—aye, by Jupiter! I should much prefer the possession of such an intimate, than the gold of Darius, or even Darius himself—so fond am I of intimate friends."

(Lysis is a beautiful youth whom[22] loves & pines for.)

[*12*] All the preceding refers to the 1st vol. Plto.

[*13–18 blank*]

20. Deleted: "verses" . Section symbols inserted in ink.

21. Deleted: [*illeg.*]

22. WW had trouble writing "Hippothales," deleted it, wrote it correctly following and then deleted the correction.

Aesthetics.

Manuscript in Virginia (Barrett). Inscribed in black ink with emendations in black ink and black pencil on Williamsburgh tax blank, torn along left edge. Stovall (*Foreground,* 176) says that this passage is from F.W. Schlegel's *Lectures on the History of Literature* (NY, 1841, 99f. or London [Bohn ed.], 1859, 82ff). WW may, as so often, have found the quotation in a magazine. See Stovall (*Foreground,* 170) and "Frederick Schlegel" for evidence of WW's interest in Schlegel. The paper suggests a date after 1857. First printed in *N&F,* 168 (Pt. IV, #59; *CW,* X, 16).

Æsthetics—Art—Science/

Plato treated philosophy as an *Art*—Aristotle as a *Science*/
That is [:][1] *Plato* was intuitious, and was calm, full of enjoyment, admiration, beauty—the pictorial—[2]was large, flowing, relied on the feelings,[3] and made swift and imperious conclusions—Often he was a mystic. Can only be understood from the same platform with himself.[4]
But [:][5] *Aristotle* was rather intellect, purer from the rest, keen, convinced by proof and argument,[6] inquiring into all things from a devouring[7] need of knowledge in itself. Aristotle[8] mediums between extremes, also experimental philosophy. (It seems to be the substratum on which are based[9] modern literature, education, and very largely modern character.)/

Then there is the Hebrew, rapt, spiritual,

1. Written on two lines to left of a brace before "Plato"
2. Preceding two words and dash inserted in pencil above "uty" in "beauty" and "—was"
3. Preceding four words and comma inserted in pencil above "wing" in "flowing" and "and made"
4. Sentence inserted in pencil in small writing on two lines above "*Aristotle* was rather"
5. "But" written to left of brace before "*Aristotle*"
6. Preceding five words and comma inserted in pencil above "keen, inquiring"
7. Deleted in ink: "want" ; inserted above: "need"
8. Deleted: "also represents" ; inserted in ink: succeeding seven words above "knowledge in itself. . . . (It"
9. Preceding two words inserted in ink above "ch" in "which" and "m" in "modern"

The Odyssey.

Manuscript not found. Text from facsimile in *CW,* V, facing p. 12. Also in *Complete Prose Works* (Boston: Small Maynard, 1898), facing p. 176. Stovall (*Foreground,* 175) believes that WW bought Grote's *History of Greece* "in 1852, or 1853 at the latest." MS in hanging indentation. The date is after 1853. The writing suggests a date before 1873.

The Odyssey is compact, tells a straight story, full of wonder, variation,—& ([1]we knowing nothing[2] of its predecessors) may be called the mother of the earlier, the middle age, & even[3] also the modern tale or romance/

It is of more absorbing interest than the Iliad—& as a mere work of construction, (good art,) it is superior.[4]

Still, the Iliad has grander passages.)/

Grote says "If it had happened that the Odyssey had been preserved to us alone, without the Iliad, I think the dispute respecting Homeric unity would never have been raised."[5]/

Grote p 204 vol. 2. seems to favor the theory that the Odyssey was not written by the same hand as the Iliad—but appeared during the same age.[6]/

"No didactic purpose is found in the Iliad or the Odyssey." I am not so sure about this Aristotle said the Iliad was for the purpose of presenting warlike types of character for the benefit of Greece.[7]

1. Deleted: "without" ; inserted above: "we"
2. Deleted: "any" ; inserted above "y" in "any" and in right margin: "nothing"
3. Inserted above "also"
4. Entry in hanging indentation.
5. Entry in hanging indentation. Rule across leaf.
6. Entry in hanging indentation. Rule across leaf.
7. Entry in hanging indentation. WW's response to the quotation is inserted above " 'Odyssey' " into the right margin and in two lines across the bottom of the leaf.

Pythagoras Was.

Manuscript in Duke (35, #26). Inscribed in black pencil and ink, as noted, on pink wove paper, 9¾″ x 5¾″. Square brackets printed here replace WW's ditto marks. Hanging indentation. Stovall (*AL,* 26, 346) has not found the source of the quotations (which appear to have been inserted later) but finds the source of WW's information in Grote's *History of Greece,* VIII, 323. WW bought Grote in 1852 or 1853 (see "The Odyssey"), but the paper indicates a date in 1855 or 1856. See "Even now Jasmund." First printed as two separate MSS: *N&F,* 164 (Pt. IV, #34; *CW,* X, 9), 99 (Pt. III; #57; *CW,* IX, 98–99).

Pythagoras was of beautiful large person, rich, dressed elegantly, practised athletics, exercised, bathed, used perfumes[1]
Homer, about 907 years B.C. Pythagoras [*about*] 600 [*years B.C.*] Trojan expedition 1136 years B.C. Troy taken 1127 [*years B.C.*] [*:*] the Iliad Phidias, the sculptor, born 488 B.C. Socrates from 469 B.C. to 399 B.C. Plato (*"broad"*)[2] 429[3]–347[4]
Sophocles, Eschuylus, Euripides, flourished just before the maturity of Socrates. Their best works have not come down to moderns.[5]

In *Eschuylus,* the figures are shadowy, vast, majestic, dreamy—. moving with haughty grandeur, strength, and will. "the high-wrought, tumpet-tongued eloquence of Eschuylus"[6] born 525 B.C. to 455[7]

In *Sophokles,* the diagloue and feelings are more like reality—the interest comes home nearer.—("the harmonious gracefulness of Sophokles tuning his love-labored song like the sweetest warbling from a sacred grove"[8] Great poetical beauty born 495 B.C. died very old[9]

1. Inserted on three lines in black ink at top of leaf in smaller hand.
2. Inserted in a space between "Plato" and "429"
3. Inserted and deleted: "about 350"
4. Preceding seven items in column.
5. Deleted: "—born 498 [*ins.*]B.C.—died very old" Entry in hanging indentation.
6. Quotation inserted.
7. In smaller hand between entries and above "the dialogue" . The entire entry about Eschylus is in hanging indentation.
8. Quotation inserted on two lines above "are more . . . interest"
9. "born . . . old in smaller hand between entries above "love and compassion" in next paragraph. The entire entry about Sophocles is in hanging indentation.

In Euripides love and compassion—scientific refinement—something like skepticism. ("the subtle[10] reasoning & melting pathos of Euripides,")[11] This writer was a hearer of Sokrates. born 480 B.C.—nineteen of his tragedies remain out of eighty or ninety.[12]——

Aristophanes, contemporary of Sokrates, whom he lampoons in "The Clouds."[13]

Aristotle born 384 B.C. at Stagira in Macedonia went early to Athens—studied under Plato—was afterwards tutor to Alexander the Great—returned to Athens, opened a gymnasium or school—left to escape a charge of atheism—poisoned himself.[14]/
Plutarch born a.d. 50, lived to old age/[15]

Zoroaster,—two centuries after Moses
Menu preceded both Zoroaster & Moses, 1700 B.C.
Confucius, (China) 500 B.C.
Menu (first then) Moses Zoroaster[16]
[*2*] All together Socrates Eschylus Sophocles Aristophanes Plato[17]

10. Deleted: "pathos and" ; inserted: "reasoning"
11. Quotation inserted above "ement" in "refinement" "—something like" and "skeptics" in "skepticism"
12. Date and number of tragedies on two lines in smaller hand between lines above "contemporary of Socrates, whom" . Entire entry about Euripides in hanging indentation.
13. Hanging indentation.
14. Hanging indentation.
15. In left margin opposite preceding with loop above, to right, below.
16. Three names in box in lower right corner; "first then" in brace following "menu"
17. Names in column.

Lucretius.

Manuscript in LC (#107). Homemade notebook of five leaves, 8″ x 5″, made of half-sheets of white laid paper. Blank leaves have been removed in mounting. Blue lines ⅝″ apart on one side only. MS shows three punched holes for string binding at the left. Hanging indentation as noted. Attorney General's letterhead on [*1217V*]. Inscription in black ink and black pencil as noted. The presence of the Attorney General's letterhead and the flowing handwriting indicate a date after July, 1866, when WW entered the Attorney General's department. The notebook was first printed by Jean Catel, "Un inédit de Walt Whitman," *Études Anglaises,* III (October, 1939), 359–360.

[*1213R,*[1] *V blank*] Lucretius.
De Rerum Natura
"*The Nature* of Things"[2]
Translation
Rev. J. S. Watson.—1851.[3]

[*1214R;*[4] *1213V blank*] *Lucretius* (Titus Lucretius Carus.) (Virgil comes immediately after him in point of time[5] De Rerum Natura (The Nature of Things.) Supposed to be Roman by birth. Born 95 B. C. Died 52 [*B. C.*][6] aged 43. (supposed to have died by his own hand.)

—expounds Epicurus—reason.—the reason why—the how—practical—materialistic—(seems to[7] confound spiritualism with superstition & credulity.)[8]

Reason—*stern, Explanatory Reason* the Natural Laws.—no gods or Mythologies—they are fancies of poets—[9]

[*1215R;*[10] *1214V blank*]—The work is largely[11] aimed at calming the fears of the

1. Text in black ink on unruled side of paper. Laid out like title page.
2. Preceding four words in black pencil.
3. London, 1851, in the Bohn Library, and often reprinted.
4. In black ink on unruled side of paper.
5. Statement written in four lines in upper left-hand corner enclosed in large parenthesis at left.
6. Two ditto marks in the original.
7. Deleted: "identify" ; inserted above in black pencil: "confound"
8. Hanging indentation.
9. Entry entirely indented.
10. In black pencil on ruled side of paper.
11. Deleted: "&"

Romans[12] against suffering after death—it seeks to convince the reader that death is[13] cessation, annihilation "an eternal sleep"—/

It teaches a good, mild, benevolent, contented, life./

The inference from the book is that the terrors of death,[14] & of what happened afterward, were great among the masses of the people—the priests kept up the delusion, for their own purposes, as always.

[*1216R;* [15] *1215V blank*] *Love—Desire.* &c latter part Book IV treats of amativeness, procreation, conception, &c.—describes the heat of the amorous appetite, &c[16]—tells the female[17] how to act to conceive the best—enters into minute details, &c.

—the lesson & general influence of this latter part of Book IV is however sane & good

[*1217V;* [18] *1216V, 1217R blank* [19]] *Six Books*

1st Book—Apostrophe to Venus as the reproductive power—invective against superstition [*?*]—"nothing can be produced from nothing."

2d Book—Atomic theory.

3 [Book][20]—Body & soul are one—the latter ceases with the former—the folly of fearing death

4th [Book][21] The senses, sleep &c—*Love*

5th [Book][22] the Origin of the World—the seasons—progress of man

6th—Extraordinary natural phenomena

12. Deleted: "at"
13. Deleted: "ann"
14. Deleted: "in them" ; inserted above: "& of . . . afterward,"
15. In black pencil on ruled side of paper.
16. Deleted: "enters"
17. Preceding two words inserted above "ls" in "tells" and "how"
18. In black ink on ruled side of paper. Entries in hanging indentation.
19. Attorney General's letterhead scribbled over in ink.
20. Ditto in original.
21. Ditto in original.
22. Ditto in original.

Aeschuylus.

Manuscript in NYPL (Berg). Inscribed in black ink on white wove paper, 5½″ x 3½″. Vertical blue rules on verso, 5/16″ apart. Entries in hanging indentation. George Grote's *History of Greece* was published in NY by Harper's from 1851 to 1859. Although WW admired it, as Stovall (*Foreground,* 175–176) points out, it is not clear how much of it he read. The citation of Vol. II is a mistake for Vol. I. C.C. Felton's *Greece, Ancient and Modern* was republished a number of times after its first edition in 1866. WW told Sydney Morse ("My Summer with Walt Whitman, 1887," *In Re,* 383–385) that he had got the book when he first went to Washington, but Stovall thinks he bought it not later than 1853. None of the cited passages indicate anything more than that WW was informing himself of facts. First printed *N&F,* 168 (Pt. IV, #58; *CW,* X, 16). The writing suggests a date after 1873.

Æschuylus —
  383—vol. II—
      Grote
   Felton—vol 1—207/
Sophocles—Grote "
      Felton vol 1—p. 218
            et seq./
Hesiod
  Felton—vol. 1—p. 134–5/
Tyrtaeus
  Felton—vol 1,
      p. 160/

See pp. 52–57.

Manuscript in Texas (Hanley). Inscribed in blue crayon on irregular white laid note-paper. Blue rules ⅜″ apart. "Alger's book" refers to W.R. Alger, *The Poetry of the East* (Boston, 1856), a copy of which was given WW by the author in Boston in 1860. WW noted on the flyleaf that he had read pp. 3–92 "over and over" (Traubel, "Notes on the Text of Leaves of Grass," *Conservator* [March, 1898]. Pp. 52–57 of Alger's book contain a general characterization of Persian poetry. The writing and crayon suggest a very late date.

See pp. 52–57 &c Alger's book

For the Notes.

Manuscript in Texas. Inscribed in black ink on white wove scrap, 3⁵/QY″ x 8″. According to Edward G. Bernard, "Some New Whitman Manuscript notes," *AL,* 8 (March, 1936), 61, the reference is to the second edition of the *Rubaiyat* (1868), stanza lxxii. In "Notes (Such as They Are) Founded on Elias Hicks" (1888), *Prose 92,* II, 639 WW quotes stanza LXXI (possibly from memory, since he misquotes the third line). Stanza LXXII reads:

> Heav'n but the Vision of fulfill'd Desire,
> And Hell the Shadow of a Soul on fire,
> Cast on the Darkness into which Ourselves,
> So late emerg'd from, shall so soon expire.

The "three other stanzas" have not been identified. First printed Bernard, *AL,* 8 (1936), 61.

for *the Notes*—¶ Then there are[1] *three* other stanzas
Heaven but the vision of fulfill'd Desire &c p 18

1. Deleted: "two" ; inserted above: "three"

X. English History.

Old Theory Started.

Text from *N&F,* 181–192 (Pt. V; *CW,* X, 39–60). Written, according to Bucke, on versos of extra fly-titles, of *LG* (1855). According to Stovall (*AL,* 26, 361–362) the notes are based on George L. Craik and Charles MacFarlane, *Pictorial History of England* (10 vols., London, 1840–1846), I, 1–138, but WW also drew on pp. 139–146 for the latter part of his notes. According to Stovall (ibid.) the note on the Phoenician alphabet is probably from Schele DeVere, *Outlines of Comparative Philology* (1853), which WW owned (" 'Even now Jasmund' "). WW's only identifiable use of his reading is from "I see where Druids walked . . ." in "Pictures" and then in "Salut au Monde!" (1856), sec. 6, l. 95, but he may have learned from it of metempsychosis. See notes on English history in "Autobiographical Notes," which is also early 1856. The date is late 1855 or early 1856. First printed *N&F.*

Old theory started or revived by Geoffrey ap Arthur (12th century): That the English part of the islands was "first" populated by a colony of the Trojans, guided, 100 B. C., by Brutus (whence Britains) a grandson of the great Æneus, more than 2776 B. A., 1000 years before the Christian era.

The Romans themselves pretended to be of Trojan descent—as Æneid.

Gogmagog—a giant before the Trojans—Trojans came 1000 B. C.

Albion, a giant also—son of Neptune.

Samothea (from Samothes, a King of England) a name of Britain after the Trojans.

The Triads, Welsh poetical histories, supposed to be written time of Edward I.

One theory is that (the islands being inhabited by Picts) they were visited and settled by Phœnicians—and that they were the same as the Celts—also that the Picts, or Caledonians, were the ancient Cimbri.

Positively.—The numerous inhabitants found in Samothea at the appearance of the Romans 50 years before Christ—were of Celtic origin. (The British coast is visible from France.)

A political friendliness existed then (50 B. C.) between Gallia and Samothea or Albion.

The names of the towns are Anglo-Saxon—but the hills, rivers, woods etc. are Celtic.

Everything reliable, of the greatest antiquity in Albion is Celtic.

Both Celts and Goths are branches of the same paternal stem—both are Caucasian or Japhetic.

One author (Whitaker 1773) says *Britain* means a separated people—he supposes Britain and France to have been at one time united by land.

Ireland, very anciently, with a highly civilized and renowned people.

Ireland had the name of *Scotia* in the 7th and 8th centuries and was eminent in scholarship and civilization.

Erin, Celtic name of Ireland—Hibernia another form.

Some writers consider the Celts identical with the Persians—Mr. O'Brien makes Ireland a colony of Persia, and the Irish tongue a Persian dialect.

Positive—the Irish tongue is Celtic.

Theory—that the Phœnicians were a branch of Persians.

Positive—from Spain the progenitors of the present population came to Ireland—whoever they were.

Ancient name of Scotland—Caledonia.

"The Scots," the name of the most noted of the Irish tribes.

Picts—they were not Celts but Teutons or Goths, north of Britain, Roman time, painted or tattoo'd people. Had a kingdom and king—till the middle of the 9th century along the east coast of Scotland.

Ossians poems—1762—James Macpherson.

Positive—Scottish Highlanders descend from Irish settlers there middle 3rd century.

Erse (Scottish dialect), Irish.

Celts—classical derivation from the Keles (Kelets) a horse—or *Kello,* to move about.

Down to 11th or 12th century by Scots was meant the Irish.

Quite positively, the "original" Scots of Scotland were Irish.

Scot-Scythian—a scattered or wandering people.

Supposed (quite plausibly) that the (Irish original) Scots were really a tribe of Scythians, a people from Germany, from the north of Europe, therefore of Teutonic blood and language. If this how can they be Celts?

Albin or Albion, an ancient name of the island of Great Britain, and that by which it was first known to the Greeks and Romans.

Ierne (Erin, Herne, Hibernia) the ancientest name of Ireland.

Welsh, Wales, consider themselves the hereditary representatives of the natives of Albion before the arrival of the Saxons and even before the Romans.

Cymry or Cymri one of the Welsh names.

Scythia, the north of modern Germany, and Denmark a peninsular of Jutland etc.

Arthur—the chivalrous Welsh (he is the one of the Round Table).

Pictorial History thinks the Welsh (Cymry) are the visible representatives of the Cymri of antiquity.

Migrations. That of the Celts, thirty-four hundred years before the American era (1600 B. C.) from Western Asia.—That of the Goths twenty-six hundred years before the American era from north-western Asia.—That of the Slavic races some centuries posterior to the Gothic migration.

Tartars, or Tatars, middle of Asia, toward the Pacific Mongol Tatars.

Phœnician alphabet is the prototype of all these of modern times (its after times).

55 B. C. Julius Cæsar having invaded and conquered Gaul (the present France, Belgium etc.) determined to cross to England. He did so, conquered them. They had helped the Gauls against Cæsar.

Nineteen hundred years ago Albion was a sort of "holy land," a great centre and stronghold of the Druids.

Cæsar landed on the coast of Dover, was met, fought, succeeded.

Cassivellanus—opponent of Cæsar—general of the British contributions —brave—patriotic.

Previous to and at the time of the Roman invasion the life, huts, villages, ways of Albic natives were very much like those of the Ceylonese,[1] thatched houses, some conical etc. Still, they seem to have made a pretty good fight—had war chariots—were certainly civilized enough to hold their own.

War chariots—these seem to have been great affairs—terrible—dreaded. They were peculiar to the Britons—some call this a link connecting them with Persia, an old place of such chariots.

Horses. The ancient Britons had horses—a small tough breed.

Throwing off the clothing when going to fight. All the Celts seem to have had a way of throwing off the clothing when going to fight—Goths too I think.

War Weapons—War British—axes, stones, lances, spears, clubs, cutlasses, heavy pointless swords—the metal used is nearly all copper hardened with tin.

Roman javelin—War Roman—Roman javelin (pilum) six feet long, terminating by a strong triangular point of steel, eighteen inches long.

Helmet etc. Open helmet, lofty crest—breast plate or coat of mail—greaves (plates bent or grooved to the shape of the legs) strong shield carried on the left arm—this shield or buckler, four feet high and two and a-half feet wide, framed with light but firm woods, covered with bull's hide and strongly guarded with knobs of iron or bronze.

Warlike facts of Romans—pages 34 and 35 Pict. Hist. Eng.

For 100 years after the departure of Cæsar Britain was left uninvaded by any foreign soldiery—internally there were dissensions and wars among the tribes and kings.

Cæsar did not establish government. Ninety-seven years after Cæsar's departure the Emperor Claudius determined to subjugate and establish government in Britain—making it a Roman province.

A. D. 43 Britons had a great defeat on the banks of the Severn.

Caractacus—British hero of the second Roman invasion.

Claudius himself came to the assistance of his generals to subjugate Britain, returned to Rome after six months absence and was given a triumph.

Massilia—viz., Marseilles.

1. (Bucke's note?): "I.e., of course, the Ceylonese in the 19th century."

Propraetor—proprietor. Ostorius, the Roman propraetor, had many fights—was a cautious and shrewd man.

Silures, inhabitants of South Wales.

(Amid all these things Caractacus.)

The final battle. Caractacus gathered his forces, (in North Wales?) in Shropshire—and here was fought the final battle with Ostorius.

Caractacus was taken prisoner soon after, carried to Rome, preserved an undaunted demeanor—his final destiny is unknown.

Dauntlessness of Britons. For twenty years the Britons still resisted, harassing the Romans. Subjugated at length and Roman rule established.

Anglesey (ancient name Mona) "groves of Mona."

Romans wished to destroy the Druidical institutions—the Druids had taken refuge in Anglesey island—the battle—fierceness of the religious excitement.

Romans victorious—destroying the Druids.

Boadicea—widow of the king of a British tribe the Iceni—her wrongs—dignity—energy of character—became the head of a combination against the Roman invaders.

Native British rising under Boadicea. The Romans were forced to retreat from London—the British entered it and slaughtered and ravaged, burnt etc. A pitched battle was forthcoming. Boadicea mounted on a chariot, her long yellow hair loose, her two daughters with [her][2] drove through the British ranks and harangued. British were defeated with great loss. Boadicea poisoned herself.

Yet still the British continued more or less rebellious.

Cnæus Julius Agricola now appeared in Roman command. (Tacitus was his son-in-law.) He was a great ruler (perhaps thanks to Tacitus).

Agricola endeavored to improve the British and tame them, governing them wisely.

A. D. 83—Agricola makes conquest of most parts of the island, goes to Scotland.

Galgacus—the Scotch leader at this time—Scotch defeated.

A. D. 120—Hadrian, the emperor, visits Britain. 138—Antoninus Pius. 183—Commodus emperor. 207—Emperor Severus, old, landed in Britain (an iron-hearted and iron-framed old man)

Caracalla, son of Severus, departs from Britain. After that a 70 years blank in British history.

Caracalla made the people of the provinces free citizens of the Roman empire.

70 years quiet.

A. D. 288—Roman reign of Diocletian and Maximian—the Scandinavian and Saxon pirates begin to ravage the coasts of Britain and Gaul. "Old pirates of the Baltic."

Carausius was appointed admiral to destroy the pirates—was charged with

2. Bucke's insertion.

collusion—Roman message to put him to death—he set up for himself—gathered the British about him. The joint Emperors of Rome were fain to purchase peace by conceding him the Government of Britain and of the adjoining coast of Gaul with the title of Emperor.

Under Carausius Britain figures first as a naval power.

297—Carausius was murdered by Allectus, who succeeded him, and reigned as Emperor three years.

Saxons appear now to be more or less at home in England.

A. D. 296—On the resignation of the Roman Emperors Britain fell by succession to Constantius Chlorus. 306—He died at York (Eboracum).

Constantine (afterwards called The Great) then began his reign at York.

Now Britain seems to have enjoyed tranquility till 337.

Roman Government removed from Rome to Constantinople. Roman power decaying.

Franks, Saxons, Picts, Scots etc. harass England. Romans had various luck in repelling these thieves and pirates.

London, also named Augusta.

A. D. 382—Maximus set up to be independent Emperor in Britain, had varied success, was at last defeated and put to death by Theodosius The Great—(This monarch reunited the east and west empires).

395—Theodosius died. He divided by his will the empire he had previously united. All this while the enemies harassed England.

403—The Roman decadence seem to have been been quite complete. No unanimity, no head, in Britain.

403—Alaric the Goth ravaging Italy on his way to Rome.

Now the standing soldiery (Romans and others I suppose) in Britain chose one, two, three Emperors—two deposing and put to death directly the third—"Constantine" had a longer time but fell at last.

420—Under Honorius, after many futile attempts, the Roman rule over Britain finally fell—the governors etc. departed after not quite 300 years.

After 420—dark for the historian in Britain for some years. It appears that the municipal governments of cities etc. were overthrown by military chieftains of Roman character principally.

"Kings and kinglets of the earth"—now many, many kinglings—"the miserable weakness of Britain on the breaking up of the Roman government" causes "mad disunion," "horrid crisis."

Coracles (small British boats, for one person) shoals of these.

Thousands of Roman citizens no doubt remained after the departure of the government.

411—Petitions of the Britons to Ætius, thrice consul,—"The barbarians chase us into the sea—the sea throws us back upon the barbarians,"—(no defence rendered by the Romans).

Religious dissensions also. The Britons consumed their time in sectarian disputes.

449—Vortigern, head of the British as against the Roman party, invites the "hardy freebooters of the Baltic"—the Saxons.

Hengist and Horsa now (perhaps the standards). It appears to have been on the deck of their marauding vessels the Saxons received the invitation.

Druidism seems to have originated in Britain—Anglesey (Mona) was the "holy land." The Druids were judges, arbitrators etc. They had more or less learning—wrote in Greek? etc.

Doctrine of Metempsychosis—the spirit at death passes into some other body.

Wicker-work frames, filled with living persons, fired, sacrificed to the gods.

Deities—Mercury, Teutates, Taut, Thoth, Mars, Apollo, Bel, Jupiter (Jove) Minerva. Mercury is probably the same as Bhuda, also Woden.

Gauls supposed themselves descended from Pluto.

They reckoned time by *nights,* not days.

Drui (Greek, an oak, a tree) Dryades, wood deities.

(Mercury figures more largely as a leading deity under various names, through all ancient religions, than I supposed.)

"Cromlech"—the Druidical sacrificial stone—literally, the stone to bow at or worship at.

New year commenced 10th March.

Three orders, the Druids, Vates and Bards. The Bards sung the brave deeds of illustrious men—sometimes composed entreaties, invectives etc. and and chanted them to the accompaniment of an instrument resembling the Greek lyre.

"Vates" is frequently used for "poet"—The British Vates were priests and physiologists.

Faidh (modern Irish—"Prophet.")

Druids lived together in communities or brotherhoods.

Kings were sometimes Druids.

(Tiberius or Claudius issued decrees—Claudius 100 A. D., for the extinction of Druidism.)

Three Druidical precepts—to worship the gods, to do no evil, and to behave courageously.

Ancientest Druidical worship—appears to have been of the sun and other heavenly luminaries—and of fire. Water was also worshipped. The serpent was an emblem of use among them also.

Pythagoras is supposed to have introduced into the Greek metaphysics the idea of the metempsychosis.

Probably both the Druids and Pythagoras drew their philosophy, numbers etc. etc. from the same source (from the Indus or the Nile?). An oriental origin to all.

The Germans, Goths etc. had no Druids.

Middle of the 5th century—Druidism in Ireland fell under the attacks of St. Patrick.

Rich pagan temples were during the Roman occupancy built in all the cities and large neighborhoods of Britain, to the deities.

A. D. 209—"Even those places in Britain hitherto inaccessible to the Roman arms, have been subdued by the gospel of Christ." Tertullian.

286—St. Alban, the first British Christian martyr, perished (at this time Christianity had numerous followers in Britain).

314—Christian bishops go from Britain to the great church councils. Arianism was greatly in Britain.

Pelagius, a British monk of the 5th century, who denied original sin, and maintained the merit of good works.

Before the Roman conquest Britain must have been known to the Phœnicians or Tyrians. It was divided into many tribes or nations. On the coast were comparatively new-comers, "Belgians" superior, having their own appearance, laws etc. etc.

"Brigantes" were the leading tribe.

Females ruled indifferently with men, in the supreme power.

Comprehensiveness of the education of a Roman, for leading public office, or eligibility to it—instances of the same man being juris consult, general, public professor of law, pontifex maximus, consul, dictator,—(war, politics, metaphysics, sciences, actual knowledge of the *present* of the earth). Courage, sternness, a hardened tough body—a ready tongue.

Defence of Rome and Romans, pp. 79 and 80, Vol. I. Pict. Hist.

Rome pursued a generous policy toward subjugated nations—confirmed their municipia, who were charged with their own affairs, viz., religion, administration of municipal revenues, police, certain judicial function.—Some were advanced to the full dignity of the Freedom of *Roman* citizens.

In Britain, under the Romans, there were magnificent public buildings, theatres, baths, palaces, roads, populous and orderly cities, laws, trades, manufactures, fine wares, travel etc. etc.

Architecture as cultivated by the ancients, spoke not merely to the eye—it spoke far more to the mind.

Pandect, a treatise that comprehends the whole of any science (the digest of the laws of Justinian)—Justinian A. D. 527–565

Tarshish—(probably a general appellation for the countries lying beyond the Pillars of Hercules).

Ezekiel (Bible) six centuries before Christ.

Tin used by Phœnicians (supposed from Britain) 1500 B. C.

Bronze—Copper and tin.

Brass—Copper and zinc.

Himilco, the Carthegenian navigator, 1000 B. C. Supposed to have voyaged to Britain.

Palmyra (Tadmor of the desert). Supposed to have been founded by Solomon 1000 B. C.

Coracle. Small boat, formed of ozier twigs, covered with hide.

Lead. Britain has always produced more lead than all the rest of Europe.

Linen. The manufacture of cloth, (linen), etc. colored various hues, was prevalent in Britain as in Gaul, previous to the Romans.

(The shelfish "mussel" not "muscle").

Ships.—Vessels "ships" (doubtless small and rude enough) carried on commerce in Britain from shore to shore, at the Roman times.

Money.—They had money, in rings, or three-quarter rings.

Weights.—It is quite settled that our modern "Troy Weight" and others, are of antiquity long before any reliable dates of Greece, Rome, or any other ancient history.

Tax money—paid to Romans by the inhabitant of Britain—"poll money," "corn money," "sheep money" etc.

Justinian A. D. 527–565.

Vineyards existed in old Britain.

Agriculture was encouraged and improved in Britain by the Romans.

Gael—Gaul—the Scottish Highlanders.

The Druids "were not merely their priests, but their lawyers, their physicians, their teachers of youth, their moral and natural philosophers, their astronomers, mathematicians, architects, poets, and their historians."

They did not *share* their knowledge with the people (do any priests?) — their power depended on its exclusiveness.

Chief Druid obtained his place by election.

Reading and Writing—The Druids had—used a written language—Greek letters, it is supposed—though not the Greek language.

Eloquence was certainly sedulously cultivated by the Britons, Irish, Gauls—indeed by the Celts generally.

"Displays of oratory in all their public proceedings. Harangues by Galgacus, Boadicea and other chiefs."

Druids of Mona, with frenzied appeals and invocations.

The common mother tongue of Englishmen and Americans, uniting the two nations by "a tie lighter than air yet stronger than iron" (Burke).

The Gauls represented their Hercules Ogmius (God of Eloquence) as an old man surrounded by a great number of people, attached to him in willing subjection by slender chains reaching from his tongue to their ears.

"Poetry and its then inseparable accompaniment, music, were doubtless also cultivated by the British and Gallic Druids" or that part of them called the Bards. "Hymners" Strabo calls them.

Mistleto and Vervain—were the vegetables venerated and used in medicaments—as talismans etc.

Druidical religion *full of minute formalities*—are modern religions any different? I see where Druids walked the groves of Anglesey—I see in their hands the mistletoe and Vervain[3]

O'Brien's "Round Towers of Ireland" assigns the creation thereof to an an-

3. Bucke's note: "This line first written: 'I see the Druids in the groves of Anglesey — I see the sprigs of mistletoe and vervain.'—*Then changed to above*. As first used in 1856 edition it stands: 'I see where Druids walked the groves of Mona, I see the mistletoe and vervain.' The line was not changed after that except to covert 'walked' into 'walk'd.' "

terior order of priests, of the Buddhist faith, who far exceeded the Druids in astronomy and learning.

Astronomy was a branch [of learning][4] of much importance among the Druids —for festivals etc.—certain times of the moon, constellations etc. being important.

"The national religion has been in almost all cases, the principal cement, of the national civilization."

(*Don't be too severe on old religious delusions—or modern ones either.*)

When the Romans ruled, the Britons adopted largely the Latin language and applied the youth to Latin literature and art.

Schools (Roman) were established in all British towns.

Juvenal. End of 1st and beginning of 20th century.

Thule (?) was the most northern land known to the ancients (Romans and Greeks).

Manners and customs

Aboriginal Britons before Cæsar—houses contained rude, plain furniture —tables—stools—beds etc.

Cannibalism is attributed to them.

Personal appearance. Large limbs, and great muscular strength.

Warlike British weapons—page 121, Vol. I., Pict. Hist.

Marriage—"matrimonial clubs"—wives in common. Women were honored and respected.

Not savage neither civilized. But partaking in parts of both, was the condition (summed up) of the aboriginal Britons, before Cæsar. They probably had wide diversities of condition both from individual to individual, and from tribe to tribe.

From the arrival [of the][5] Saxons 449 A. D. to that of the Normans 1066 A. D.

Saxon—some say from—Seax, the short Baltic sword—others say from (and this most likely) Sakai-suna, or descendants of the Sakai, or Saceae, a tribe of Scythians, who were making their way toward Europe as early as the age of Cyrus.

"Saxons"—name applied to different tribes. They were all of the pure Teutonic or Gothic blood. All their kings claimed descent from Woden or Odin.

Vortigern, smitten with Romena, daughter of Hengist, at a feast—"Dear King—your health" (Wassail).

Saxons settled plentifully—chastised the northern Scots and Picts—soon quarrels arose—Britons revolted from any obedience to them—Britons and Romish remnants made common cause.

The two centuries after the Saxons' arrival are dark and perplexing historically.

Feast of Reconciliation—Saxons "unsheath your swords"—Britons slain.

Eric son of Hengist, King of Kent.

4. Bucke's insertion.
5. Bucke's insertion.

A. D. 477—Ella the Saxon, with his three sons, and a large force landed in Sussex—fought—succeeded—King of "the South Saxons."

Cerdric (Wessex)—King of West Saxons.

527—Ercenwine [?][6] landing, succeeding, north of the Thames, founded Essex—King of the "East Saxons."

Suffolk—from South folk.

Norfolk—from North folk.

470—Gaul was overrun by the Visigoths. 12,000 British left Cornwall to take part in this war (!).

Heptarchy—the seven separate and independent States or Kingdoms of the Anglo-Saxons. Saxons mixed interpenetratingly with the British, the Roman residuum, and all "Rustics."

A. D. 647—The Resistants—the people of Strathclyde and Cumbria—their disposition fierce and warlike—retreated fought courageously—defeat followed them—submitted (A. D. 647) to the Anglo-Saxons "who by this time may be called the English." "In this rapid sketch—Saxon conquest—which seems in amount to have occupied nearly 200 years."

"Arthur" Pict. Hist. thinks a mythical personage. He seems to have been an obstinate and bold resistant of the Saxons.

"Bretwalda"—Lord Paramount "Wielder" of Brit. (the seven States Saxon).

510—Ella, Sussex (South Saxons).

568—Calwin, King of Wessex, stepped into the Sussex dignity too.

Ethelbert, fourth King of Kent.

"For long before the Anglo Saxons subdued the Britons they made fierce war upon one another."

593—Ethelbert became Bretwalda.

Christianity—Ethelbert converted, with all his Court, by Augustine and forty Italian monks, sent into Britain by Gregory the Great. He had espoused a Christian wife before (which accounts for it).

Ethelbert's close connection with the Christians and civilized nations of the continent, and his frequent having to do with churchmen proved beneficial to England.

Laws. In the code of laws Ethelbert published before his death—indebted to the suggestions and science of foreigners—although the code has more the spirit of the old German lawgivers, than of Justinian and the Roman juris consults. This code was not octroyed as from an absolute sovereign (a quality to which none of the Saxon princes ever attained), but was enacted by Ethelbert with the consent of the States—formed the first code of written laws promulgated by any of the northern conquerors.

616—Death of Ethelbert, who seems to have been a thoughtful and superior prince.

616—Eadbald, son of Ethelbert, enamored of his stepmother, broke with the

6. Bucke's insertion.

Christians and returned to the old Teutonic idolatry. The whole Kentish people set up again the rude Scandinavian altars.

The priest Laurentius persuaded Eadbald to come back again to Christianity, and the people, en masse, obsequiously followed.

617—Bretwalda passed to Redwald, the Angle (the first three Bretwaldas had been Jutes). Redwald was a "kind of Christian."

621—Edwin the fifth Bretwalda—Northumbrian—converted fully—his people followed. In writing to him (625 the Pope styles Edwin "Rex Anglorum"—King of the Angles.

633—Penda the Saxon prince of Mercia rebelled.

Henry VII.

Manuscript in LC (#118). Inscribed in black pencil on rectos only in a white wove homemade notebook bound at side, 9⅜″ x 5⁹/₁₆″. Hanging indentations. The reference to "H. of E." is probably to Craik and Macfarlane, *Pictorial History of England,* which WW had used in "Old theory started." The date is late 1855 or early 1856.

[*1364R*] Henry VII, died 1509 in 53d year of his age—reigned 24 years—Succeeded by[1]
Henry VIII, then (1509) 18 years of age—Queen Catherine, (8 yr's older)—wars in France— Scotland—Flodden Field—Wolsey, who, "for more than 20 yrs was more King of Eng. than Henry himself" (Francis I, king all through[2] of France)—"field of the cloth of gold"—(Time 1520)—events, events, events, /[3]
The volcanoes of brutal passion—for 25 years England bending, cringing & cowardly, more like some Oriental despotism than the sturdy race we are fond of thinking her—the horrible human-burnings—the axe of the headsman—the tragedies of the Tower—the occasional popular[4] revolts—[5]
1529 trial of Queen Catherine fall of Wolsey—Anne Boleyn made 1533[6] queen—*the Reformation* 1536 death of Q. Catherine—(her daughter Mary)—1536 Anne Boleyn arrested for adultery—her trial—execution—Jane Seymour—Suppression of the monasteries and convents—confiscation—Oct. 1537 Jane Seymour gave birth to a son (Edward VI)[7] & died—1539–40—Anne of Cleves—'41 Catherine Howard[8]

[*1375R*] '42—Catherine Howard executed—Cranmer—Cromwell—Cardinal Beaton—Catherine Parr—burnings, martyrdoms &c 1547—Death of Henry VIII, aged 55 yrs 7 mos—reigned nearly 38 years—[9]
Edward VI. Son of Henry VIII & Jane Seymour 1574—had entered on his 10th

1. Entry in hanging indentation.
2. Preceding two words inserted above "of" and "Fran" in "France"
3. Entry on hanging indentation.
4. Inserted.
5. Entry written vertically on five lines in left margin. Inserted here for lack of any other indication by WW.
6. Inserted above "que" in "queen"
7. Inserted above "son &"
8. Block paragraph.
9. Block paragraph. After a space of several lines, deleted: "Queen Mary—daughter of Henry & Catherine of 1547"

year—protestant interest—Earl of Hertford—a rebellion, (Ket's) 1553—Edward VI dies—in 16th year of age[10]

Queen Mary, aged 38 or 7[11] 1553—Lady Jane Grey—arrest of Cranmer—1554[12] marriage with Philip of Spain (a widower) aged about 30 Son of Charles V[13]—Catholic cause ahead—Earl of Devon—1554 Sir Thos. Wyatt's rebellion—arrest twice[14] of Elizabeth & Devon—Eliz. committed to the Tower, as prisoner—Exc. of Jane Grey—Throgmorton's case—"several times Elizabeth fancied that her last hour had come"—liberated—Philip,—"no one loved him, but "Mary"[15]—suppositious pregnancy—burnings at the stake—[16]
[*1376R*] Cranmer, Ridley & Latimer all burnt at the stake 1556—Philip comes & goes—scenes of the trial and death of Cranmer—(nearly 300 (55 women) 4 children[17] were burnt to death for trivial doctrinal opinions in Mary's reign)—Elizabeth conforms, ostensibly—An ecclesiastical commission established in England, really, in effect, the Spanish Inquisition (p. 510 vol. 2. H. of E.) (on the continent still worse, not hundreds but thousands, many thousands were burnt, slain, massacred, beheaded on the scaffold,[18] in the Netherlands, France, Germany & Spain, these years) 1555. Emperor Charles V, Philip's father, 55 yr's old, resigned to Philip, & retires—Pope Paul IV fierce & bigoted[19]—the Duke of[20] Alva March 1557 Philip visits England, enters London in State—in July departs, & never afterward returns—1558 the Duke of Guise *takes Calais, for the French*—marriage 1558[21] of Mary Stuart and the Dauphin Francis—& 1558 Death of Mary, aged nearly 44 years—reigned 5⅓d years (see pp. 517, 18, vol. 2. H. of E. for character)

10. Entry in hanging indentation.
11. Preceding four words inserted above "ry" in "Mary" and "1553"
12. Inserted on a separate line above "marri" in "marriage"
13. Preceding nine words inserted: "a widower" inserted above "of Spain" ; "aged about 30" inserted below "of Spain" ; "Son of Charles V" inserted on next line above "—Catholic"
14. Inserted above "est" in "arrest" and "of"
15. Preceding six words inserted above "p" in "Philip" and "suppositious" and "pregn" in "pregnancy"
16. Entry in hanging indentation.
17. Preceding four words inserted above and below "nearly 300 were"
18. Preceding four words inserted above "in the Netherlands"
19. Preceding three words inserted above "and IV—"
20. Deleted: "Ald"
21. "1558" inserted above "of"

Queen Mary.

Manuscript in LC (#60, sheet #269). Inscribed in black ink and black pencil on white laid paper, 3⅜" x 4¾". One of a number of notes for an essay or lecture on sixteenth-century history, chiefly English, arising from WW's reading of Tennyson's *Queen Mary* in 1875. See "16th Century—Queen Mary " The date is 1875.

Queen Mary.

16th century——it was the Century of Luther[1] Calvin (died 1564) & before its close of[2] Galileo, (born 1564 Shakspere [3](born 1564) Peasants' war in Germany, (1522) Age of the opening[4] of America, & first voyages & settlements

1. Inserted above "died 1564"
2. Preceding five words inserted in pencil above "Galileo, (born 1564)"
3. Deleted: "e" in "Shake"
4. Deleted: "&"

Henry 8 th.

Manuscript in LC (#60, sheet #271). Inscribed in black ink on soft gray paper, approx. 8″ x 4¾″. Traces of glue at left edge. One of a number of notes for an essay or lecture on sixteenth-century history, mostly English, arising from his reading of Tennyson's *Queen Mary* (1875). See "16th Century—Queen Mary." The date is 1875.

Henry *8th*—[1]then his son Edward 6th then his (Henry 8th's) daughter, Queen Mary (bloody Mary) who reigns 5 or 6 years viz: 1553 to 1588 then Henry 8th other daughter Queen Elizabeth (Lady Jane Grey & her husband beheaded on Feb 12—1554)[2] (Lady Jane Grey was daughter of the Duke of Suffolk—the Duke was beheaded 12 days after her execution)[3]/ It was a fierce contest which should carry the day, (the throne) —Catholic's or Protestants—& also personal ambition was [*illeg.*][4]

1. In upper right corner: "t"
2. Inserted in loop in margin. Entry to this point randomly lineated and indented.
3. Preceding entry in hanging indentation.
4. Paper torn. Preceding entry in hanging indentation.

(Q. Mary) The 16th.

Manuscript in LC (#60, sheet #272). Inscribed in black ink on white wove paper, 9⅜" x 5½". Hanging indentation. Numbered in wrong order by LC. One of a number of notes for an essay or lecture on sixteenth-century history, mostly English, arising from WW's reading of Tennyson's *Queen Mary* in 1875. See "16th Century—Queen Mary." The date is 1875.

[273] (Q. Mary)[1]

The 16th Century, *the struggle of the Protestant Reformation,* entwining Kings & Kingdoms,—aye,[2] a continent—& all the interests of life, politics & morals,[3] (The breaking up of the monasteries in England 1537) in its folds, and blending in its throes[4]

1526—first English version of[5] New Testament printed—but interdicted[6] by the King

Luther—1517—

The Popes bull against him [:][7] 1520

the Diet at Worms, order'd by Charles V. Emp. Germany

(1521—Henry 8th writes a book against Luther, defending the Pope) —for this the Pope gave him the title "Defender of the Faith," which the British sovereigns bear to this day!)[8]

1531—The English Catholic Clergy indicted &c. by Henry 8th—he begins breaking down the Papal & Catholic power

[272] 1536—Coverdale's Bible for popular use

1539 Cranmers or *The Great Bible* illustration,[9] or frontispiece by Hans Holbein

now—"the war of the Reformation"

Henry 8th's reign was only anti-Catholic—*not* Protestant however, by any means—

Edward 6th's reign commenced something more like Protestantism—P. makes substantial headway

Mary's reign reverses this—soon she begins stern, violent, wholesale measures for Catholicism

1. In upper right corner.
2. Inserted above "a"
3. Entry in hanging indentation to this point, after which indentation is at random.
4. Remaining entries are separate items, usually in hanging indentation.
5. Deleted: "Bible" ; inserted: "New Testament" above "of" and the deletion and "pr" in "printed"
6. Deleted: "from the popular use"
7. Brace.
8. Large single parenthesis at right of entire entry.
9. Written over "illustrated"

Richard 2d.

Manuscript in LC (#60, sheet #274). Inscribed in black ink, red pencil, and black pencil on white wove paper, 9⅜″ x 5⅜″. One of a number of notes for an essay or lecture on sixteenth-century history, chiefly English, arising from WW's reading of Tennyson's *Queen Mary* in 1875. See "Sixteenth Century—Queen Mary." The date is 1875.

[*Illeg.*][1] }[2] Richard 2d

1399 to 1413 } Henry 4th

1413 to 1422 } Henry 5th H. of Monmouth } King from 24 to 34th year—*died in or near Paris* *1413–1422*

L[3] 1422 Henry VI. son of Henry V. & Catherine of France, infant 9 mo's old

1461[4] Edward IV.—York

L 1470[5] Henry VI briefly restored, (previous 5 years prisoner in the Tower)

Y[6] 1471 Edward IV again, till

1483. Edward V, or rather

" Richard 3d reigned 2 yr's & 2 mo's[7]

1485 Henry VII Shakspeare's

to 1509[8] Earl of Richmond

1. Deleted at top of page: "for there is in the Intellect of man, the ages, a last eternal, appellat court, or judgment" . The dates are probably Richard II's regnal dates, 1377–1399.
2. Brace.
3. That is, Lancaster
4. "6" written over "5"
5. "0" written over "1"
6. That is, York
7. Preceding six reigns noted in red pencil.
8. Preceding two words in black pencil.

Of the 16th Century.

Manuscript in LC (#60, sheet #265). Inscribed in black ink on white wove paper, 8⅜" x 5". One of a number of notes on sixteenth-century history, especially English, arising from WW's reading of Tennyson's *Queen Mary* in 1875. See "16th Century—Queen Mary." The date is 1875.

Of the 16th Century in Europe, (crowded as it[1] was with great events,) perhaps the most important,[2] in itself and in giving a tinge more or less to[3] every thing else, large or small, was the conflict[4] between Roman Catholicism & Protestantism. For three quarters of the Century[5] it involved all the hot passions & strongest obstinacy, and[6] mutuality of cruelty, to say nothing of convictions,[7] not only of[8] potentates and councils and parliaments, but the masses of the people; our own Slavery contest, culminating in the war of 1861–'65, affords some analogies to it, and we[9] are now accustomed to think[10] that war furious and cruel & uncompromising enough; but it was innocence itself to the general[11] horrors & blood and flames and scaffolds of[12] the long continued struggle alluded to[13] in Europe. Historically and every way of first-class interest,[14] the Protestant contest is markedly so

1. Deleted: "is" ; inserted above: "was"
2. Deleted: "and" ; inserted: "in itself and in" above "t" in "important" and the deletion and "giving"
3. Deleted: "all other [*illeg.*]" ; inserted above: "every thing else, large or small,"
4. Deleted: "of"
5. Preceding six words inserted above "It involved" ; "It" not reduced in MS.
6. "and" inserted over "stin" in "obstinancy" ; inserted and deleted: [*illeg.*] following "[*ins.*] and" ; inserted: "mutuality of cruelty" above "to say nothing of"
7. Deleted: "of [*illeg.*]"
8. Deleted: "rulers and"
9. Deleted: "thought may" ; inserted above: "are [*ins.*] now accustomed to"
10. Deleted: "it" ; inserted: "that war" above deletion and "furi" in "furious"
11. Inserted above "hor" in "horrors"
12. Deleted: "that" ; inserted: "the long continued" above the deletion and "stuggle"
13. Preceding two words inserted above "in" and "Eu" in "Europe"
14. Deleted: "it" ; inserted: "[*illeg. del.*] the Protestant contest" above "is markedly so"

Wolsey.

Manuscript in LC (#60, sheet #268). Inscribed in black ink on white laid scrap, 3⅜" x 4¾". One of a number of lecture or essay notes on sixteenth-century history, mostly English, arising from WW's reading of Tennyson's *Queen Mary* in 1875. See "16th Century—Queen Mary." The date is 1875.

Wolsey, the most gorgeous & puissant of prelates
Luther comes in about 1518 or '20 (just begins) (in 1517, aged 34. Prof. of Philosophy at Uni. of Wittemburg, he came out, in that city, against the sale of "indulgences" by the Pope's agent.)

Era of Queen Mary.

Manuscript in LC (#60, sheet #263). Inscribed in black ink and black pencil on white wove paper. 9⅜" x 5½". One of a number of lecture or essay notes on sixteenth-century history, chiefly English, arising from WW's reading of Tennyson's *Queen Mary* in 1875. With these notes is one leaf [270R and V] in another hand. If it is W. D. O'Connor's, they must be earlier than 1872, when he and WW quarrelled. The recto discusses an unidentified book, *The Religion of Republicanism,* which O'Connor thinks WW should read; the verso seems to list the contents of Vols. 2, 4, 6 of Giuseppe Mazzini's *Life and Writings* (London, 1864–1870). See "Sixteenth Century—Queen Mary." The date is 1875.

Era of
Queen Mary,
part of[1] the *16th Century,* (say about from 1520? to Mary's death, 1558) Elizabeth begins[2] 1558—reigns 45 yrs—dies aged 70[3]
The 16th Century in English history[4] fill'd mostly[5] with the long sovereignty of Henry 8th and his second[6] daughter Elizabeth, has the intercalation[7] between them, of the short reigns of his boy-son Edward 6th, and of his[8] first daughter, Queen Mary.[9]
Though Feudalism still maintain'd its state, modern Democracy either had birth though unsuspected,[10] or took its embryonic condition. The importance of the discovery of America began to be realized.[11] The English language assumed the state in which we now have it.

1. Preceding two words inserted above "the"
2. Inserted above "eth" in "Elizabeth"
3. Entry randomly lineated and indented.
4. Deleted: [*illeg.*] ; inserted and deleted above deletion: [*illeg.*] ; inserted: "fill'd" following second deletion.
5. Deleted: "between" ; inserted: "with the long [*del.*] reign sovereignty" above "[*del.*] between" and "of Henry 8th"
6. Inserted above "his"
7. Deleted: "s of his first daughters" ; inserted: "between them" above "of his"
8. Deleted: "second" ; inserted above: "first"
9. Paragraph in hanging indentation.
10. Preceding two words inserted in pencil above "birth or took"
11. Preceding sentence inserted above "condition. . . . language"

(Queen Mary. of England.

Manuscript in LC (#60, #267). Inscribed in black ink on white laid paper, 3⅜" x 4¾". One of a number of notes for an essay or lecture on sixteenth-century history, chiefly English, arising from his reading of Tennyson's *Queen Mary* in 1875. See "Sixteenth Century—Queen Mary." The date is 1875.

(Queen Mary.

of England—English
history—

remembering what we are rather apt to forget, that there were great oceans of life, business, humanity,[1] in Asia and Africa, & in unrecorded parts of Europe, far

transcending the narrow circle
of England—

1. Deleted: "Far transcending those"

XI. World History.

Resume—(From Bunsen).

Manuscript in Duke (38, #32). Inscribed in black ink on pink wove paper, 6⅜" x 5⅛". Once pasted to white paper on left edge. Stovall (*AL,* 26, 338) identifies the source in Bunsen as C. K. J. Bunsen, *Outlines of the Philosophy of Universal History, Applied to Language and Religion,* (tr. 1854), I, 231. For Bunsen see also "Bunsen—the native name." The paper indicates a date in 1855 or 1856. First printed in *N&F,* 77 (Pt. III, #4; *CW,* IX, 52) as part of one of Bucke's synthesized MSS.

resume—(from Bunsen)

—Thus there in Assyria, (as in Egypt,) they had a written language, numerals,[1] weights, tables, calculations,[2] financial mediums, and dispatches—they had an appropriate religion, poetry, history, amusements, /[3]
(*Bunsen p 231*) "The inscriptions on the rocks on the road, on the west side of the Sinaitic peninsula, to Mount Sinai, had already occupied the attention of Cosmos Indicopleustes,[4] in the earlier part of the sixth century.— ([5] After many suggestions from others, different ages, Niebuhr divined their contents, and scorned the idea of anything but greetings and memorials of travelers in different ages.)[6]

1. Deleted: "cal" "calcul"
2. Deleted: "the"
3. Perhaps this short line was meant to be above the next entry, matching the line below.
4. Cosmas Indicopleustes of Alexandria, merchant, traveller, monk of Mt. Athos, *Topographia Christiana,* ca. 548.
5. Deleted: "Niebuhr" before "after" ; "after" capitalized.
6. See "Barthold Niebuhr."

(Bunsen).

Manuscript in Duke (38, #32). Inscribed in black ink with one black pencil query on pink wove paper, approx. 6⅜″ x 5¼″. First five entries in hanging indentation. Stovall, *AL,* 26, 338, notes a source in C. K. J. Bunsen's *Outlines of the Philosophy of Universal Histories, Applied to Language and Religion,* I (1854). For other notes on Egyptian and Near Eastern history see "memorials." The paper indicates a date in 1857 or shortly thereafter. First printed in *N&F,* 77 (Pt III, #4; *CW,* IX, 51–52).

(Bunsen)[1]

The native name of Egypt is *Khami,* (black) /

The Semitic and Iranian families are primitively connected with each other. ?(Are they not the same?)[2] /

Ancient Chaldee (Babylon and Assyria i.e. Nineveh[3] cuneiform inscriptions[4] /

Aramæan (from Aram) a name which applies equally to Mesopotamia & Syria /

(' "Chaldean Christians" in Kurdistan called Nestorians.')/

In Egypt and in Assyria, and doubtless in other ancient[5] nations, there were separate castes in language, as in men—there was one written[6] language for religion, one perhaps[7] for the nobility, and without doubt one for the common mass of people.

1. Curved line below and on either side.
2. Query in black pencil.
3. Followed by a brace.
4. Deleted: "languages" ; inserted and deleted above: [*illeg.*] ; inserted below: "nations"
5. Inserted above "one" and "lan" in "languages"
6. "perhaps" inserted above "com" in "common"
7. Inserted above wordspace between "one for" : "perhaps"

Still More Is Due.

Manuscript in LC (Feinberg #705). Inscribed in black ink on soft yellow wove paper, 5¾" x 4¼". Cf. "Probably the best education." The paper may be the yellow end paper noted in a 2nd. issue of *LG* 1855 by Furness in the Facsimile Text Society reprint. Bowers also reports yellow wrapper stock. The writing also seems to be of the 1850s.

Still more[1] is due those episodes of France—[2] ? plutonic among lands,[3] more dreadful than any[4] yet indispensable, they,[5] another larger, latest among the few moral strata,[6] enfolding[7] the[8] globe, is theirs.— They are not inviting— They are not good—they[9] lie gashed, streaming with blood.— but,[10] examining them, we know the future will not have credentials,[11] more to be envied, than,[12] sole among men, different, colossal, those dread deeds will present for the race of France!

1. Opening passage deleted: "Farther yet from [*illeg.*] born American" ; inserted: "Still more" above "arther" in "[*del.*] Farther" and "[*del.*] yet"

2. Deleted: "cruel [*ins. above* cruel]/ sole" ; inserted: "? plutonic" above "among"

3. Deleted: "different from all'

4. Deleted: "more colossal" ; inserted above: "yet indispensable"

5. Deleted: "sole among [*two words ins.*] have all the sense of another new" ; inserted: "another" above "[*del.*] sense"

6. Deleted: "necessary"

7. Deleted: "their"

8. Deleted: "beautiful, this venerable globe ; inserted: "globe is theirs.—" above "deletion."

9. Deleted: "[*illeg.*] gashed, covered" ; inserted: "[*illeg. del.*] lie" above illegible deletion and "gashed" on next line above "[*del.*] gashed,"

10. Deleted: [*illeg.*] ; following nine words inserted above the deletion and "credentials"

11. Deleted: "and I doubt if ever the [*illeg.*]"

12. Deleted: "[*illeg.*] dread deeds [*illeg.*] them [*illeg.*]" ; following nine words inserted above "[*del.*] [*illeg.*] them" . . . present for"

Lycurgus.

Manuscript not found. Text from *N&F,* 168 (Pt. IV, #61; *CW,* X, 17).

Lycurgus—some short time after Solomon—that is about 900 years before Christ.
Demosthenes—aged 27 533 years before Christ.
Cicero—born 104 years before Christ.

Scythia.

Manuscript in Trent. Inscribed in black pencil on blue Williamsburgh tax blank. All rules across leaf. Printed in *N&F,* 78 (Pt. III, #7; *CW,* IX, 53–54). The date is between 1857 and 1860.

Scythia (as used by the Greeks)—the Northern part of Europe & Asia[1]—the people thereof "Kelts" viz (woods-men[2] (these were descendamts from the same ancestors as the Greeks & Romans themselves.)—another name of the above the "Umbri"/

The Celtic, Teutonic & Gothic races are all of Japhetic stock[3]/

Sarmatia ancient Russia & Poland[4]/

?"the Teutonic Races, originally from Persia"
—"Then the inhabitants of India, and the descendants of the Keltic and Teutonic nations, are all of one family, and must all have migrated from one country,[5]
—Whether that country was Persia, or Cashmir, or a country farther east, is not easily determined—but it seems that, accordingly, the white man of Europe and the tawny man of India have a common ancestry.

1. Stovall, *AL,* 26, 339, traces this back directly or indirectly to Herodotus, Book IV.
2. According to Stovall probably from a dictionary.
3. "The notes on the origins of the Celtic and Germanic races are probably from" C. K. J. Bunsen, *Outlines of the Philosophy of Universal History,* 2 vols. (tr. 1854), I, pp. 130–131 (Stovall).
4. From the Geographical Table, *Tacitus,* ed. Arthur Murphy (Philadelphia, 1836), p. 707 (Stovall).
5. Deleted: "the separation of the nations of the"

Tacitus.

Manuscript in NYPL (Berg). Inscribed in black pencil on scrap of blue Williamsburgh tax blank, approx. 2 15/16" x 4½". Stovall (*AL,* 26, 355) says it is from Arthur Murphy's translation of *The Historical Annals of Cornelius Tacitus,* which had gone through at least two American editions by 1831. For another reference to Tacitus, see "Old theory started." First printed in *N&F,* 154 (Pt. IV, #5; *CW,* IX, 214). The paper suggests a date of 1857 or shortly thereafter.

Tacitus—of the Germans

(? Scythians).

"In ancient songs they celebrate *Tuisto,* a god sprung from the earth, and his son Mannus, the origin & Founder of their nation. To Mannus they assign three sons"

Immortality Was Realized.

Manuscript in Middlebury. Inscribed in black pencil on white wove paper, 8⅝″ x 5½″. The theme of the second paragraph is developed more fully in "The most immense part." The date is between 1855 and 1860. First printed (except for last word) as part of *N&F,* 100–101 (Pt. III, #60; *CW,* IX, 101–103).

Immortality was realized—[1]the influence of the thought of it, entering into the positive acts of the[2] citizens every day;—[3] living sending[4] yet[5] its tangible bequest to modern ages it looks with calm[6] and rugged quaintness to day[7] from the slopes of the pyramids.—[8] Personal qualities were accepted and obeyed:—[9] (When are they not accepted and obeyed?—) Through them[10]? Sesostris more than three thousand years ago[11] ruled Egypt for[12] more than three score years.—He was six feet ten inches high and nobly proportioned and supple.—He was considerate of the common people?—[13] He conquered Asia and Europe honoring most those[14] that resisted him most.— He was a rugged,[15] wholesome[16] and masculine person, and in the list of Egyptian greatness[17] comes first[18] after Osiris.—[19]

Not only Assyria and Egypt— not only Phœnicia and Lydia and Persia

1. Deleted: "it" ; inserted: "the influence . . . of it" on two lines above "[*del.*] it" and "entering"
2. Deleted: "people" ; inserted above: "citizen"
3. Deleted: "It"
4. Inserted; inserted and deleted: [*illeg.*] above "living yet"
5. Deleted: [*illeg.*]; inserted above: "its tangible bequest to modern ages"
6. Deleted: "features"
7. Preceding two words inserted above "ss" in "quaintness"
8. Sentence begins in middle of line; in left margin opposite is "out" with line descending to the end of the paragraph. Possibly WW felt that the passage was a digression.
9. Deleted: "as"
10. Preceding two words inserted above "? Sesostris"
11. Inserted above wordspace between "years ruled"
12. Deleted: "sixty years" ; inserted above: "more than"
13. Sentence inserted above "supple . . . Asia"
14. Deleted: "people"
15. Deleted: "and"
16. Deleted: "and [*illeg.*]"
17. Preceding four words inserted above "and comes first" and the illegible deletion in *n* 18.
18. Deleted: "[*illeg.*] It"
19. Stovall, *AL,* 26, 347 points out the source of WW's information about Sesostris in Sir John Gardner Wilkinson's *Manners and Customs of the Ancient Egyptians* (1836–1840), I. See "mamorials" for further notes on Egypt.

and Media—and India[20]—had their literature, growing out of the nature and circumstances and governments[21] and enjoyments of the people, with more or less[22] specimens, of course long since lost[23] of the grandest and most perfect [2][24] forms of expression—but the men and women of[25] other nations other empires and states, other mighty and populous cities, contemporary with them in other parts of the world, or ages[26] antecedent of them,[27] it may be in distant regions of the eastern[28] hemisphere,[29] or it may be in North or South America, had their loves and passions and prides and aspirations also typified and put in shape and held in compositions.—[30] Language was systematized and passed on from[31] one generation to another[32] in methods[33] answering to what was needed.— These[34] unknown empires and cities,[35] and their literature existed just as certainly as[36] the known ones, and[37] perhaps in greater vigor and fluency than the known ones. Travelers in every age and in all parts of the world[38] come upon their dumb and puzzling relics.—

—Hindostan

20. Preceding two words inserted above "a— in "Media—"
21. Preceding two words inserted above "ces" in "circumstances" and "and"
22. Preceding three words inserted above "with" and "spe" in "specimens"
23. Preceding three words inserted above "of the" and "gr" in "grandest"
24. Deleted: "composition" ; inserted above: "expression"
25. Preceding five words inserted above "other nations"
26. Inserted above "an" in "antecedent"
27. Deleted: "perhaps" ; inserted above: "it may be"
28. Deleted: "continent"
29. Deleted: "perhaps" ; inserted above: "or it may be in"
30. Preceding two words inserted above "d" in "held" and "— Language"
31. Deleted: [*illeg.*].
32. Preceding seven words and deletion inserted above "in methods . . . was"
33. Deleted: "fit for" ; inserted above: "answering to"
34. Deleted: "other nations"
35. Deleted: "are unknown by name or date yet they certainly existed." ; inserted: "and their literature existed just as certainly" above "cities" and the deletion.
36. From *N&F;* not visible on photocopy.
37. Deleted: "and with" , "with more likely a date yet they certainly existed" ; inserted: "perhaps greater vigor and fluency than the known ones."
38. Preceding seven words inserted above "age come upon"

The Most Immense Part.

Manuscript of first part in Duke (3, #1). Manuscript of latter part not found. Text from *N&F,* 76–77 (Pt. III, #4; *CW,* IX, 50–51). MS inscribed in black ink on six scraps of white wove paper with embossed stamp surrounded by scroll work marked "Superfine" on scrap 1. On verso of scraps 1, 2, and 3 are cancelled draft lines for "S of M", secs. 6, 7, 27, 28. Scraps 5, 6 have cancelled pagination, "203" on 5 and "143" on 6, both at upper right. The text contains phrases later used in "Unnamed Lands" (1860), but was evidently conceived as an essay rather than as a poetical draft and does not develop the theme of the poem. The same ideas are touched on in "Immortality was realized." Stovall (*Foreground,* 163–164) proposes the prefaces to C. K. J. Bunsen's *Egypt's Place in Universal History* (5 vols., 1845–1867), vols. I and II, as a source. The writing is the smoother style of the 1860s, but considering the verso of the MS and the thought of the essay, the date WW wrote this can be set only between 1855 and 1860.

The[1] most immense[2] part of Ancient History is altogether unknown.—[3] There were busy, populous,[4] and powerful nations,[5] on all the continents of the earth, at intervals[6] Through the stretch of time[7] years ago down to[8] previous to twenty six[9] hundred years ago,[10] there were busy populous and powerful nations on all the continents of the earth.—[11] Signs and materials of them remain.—[12]

Previous to ten thousand years ago, there were surely empires,[13] cities,[14] states[15] and pastoral tribes and uncivilized hordes upon the earth[16]

their[17] literature, government, religions, social customs, and general civiliza-

1. Preceded by deleted: "It is doubtless the case The"
2. Deleted: "share"
3. Deleted: "Powerful" ; inserted: "There were" above dash; "busy [*del.*] and" above "l" in "powerful" and "pop" in "populations" . Beginning of second scrap.
4. Deleted: "and" ; inserted: "and powerful" above the deletion and "nat" in "nations"
5. Deleted: "existed,"
6. Deleted: "of time" ; since "through" is raised to uppercase, WW probably intended to end the sentence.
7. Deleted: "from ten thousand"
8. Deleted: "the historical records which give us begin to glimmer" ; inserted: "previous to" above "glimmer"
9. Deleted: "or twenty-seven"
10. Deleted: "—"
11. Deleted: "and doubtless for the certain signs and certain" ; "signs" raised to uppercase.
12. End of second scrap.
13. Deleted: "and cities" ; comma probably inserted.
14. Deleted: "and"
15. Deleted and inserted: "and"
16. Preceding three words in black pencil.
17. Preceding "Of" deleted.

tion,[18] precise mention[19]—silence;—for[20] no one can now tell even the names of those nations.—[21] They had, in their own way, something corresponding to all[22] the essentials of[23] a modern political[24] power.—[25] Their[26] agriculture factories and handiwork, houses and modes of domestic[27] life, their forms of worship and[28] what they thought of[29] death and the soul,[30] how they were ruled, their trade or want of trade, their traditions and[31] dress,[32]—the physiology of these various and separated[33] races—which of them[34] were [35]of fine person[36] and[37] style, warm hearted and clean, heroic simple,[38] and of a beautiful candor and dignity—what sort of marriage—[39] what[40] condition of schools and[41] art and medicine and the laying out of cities,—and what about liberty[42] and slavery[43] among them, and public benevolence—[44]

Sublime characters[45] lived and died, and we do not know when and where—full as[46] sublime as any that are now[47] celebrated over the[48] world.—[49] Beautiful

18. Deleted: "little"
19. Deleted: "[*illeg.*] to be made" ; inserted: "—silence; —" above illegible deletion and "[*del.*] be"
20. Deleted: "we"
21. Deleted: "[*illeg.*] But they had But" ; inserted and deleted: "These unknown people" above "[*del.*] they had" ; inserted: "They had in their own way [*del.*] what [*ins. above deletion*] something corresponding to" above "[*del.*] But" and "all" and "[*del.*] those" and " [*ins.*] the essentials of"
22. Deleted: "those" ; inserted: "the" in wordspace following.
23. Deleted: "first class"
24. Deleted: partially: "power" . Not printed.
25. Deleted: "these now unknown peoples, with"
26. Raised to uppercase.
27. Inserted above "of life"
28. Preceding five words inserted above "what they" and "thou" in "thought"
29. Deleted: "God" ; inserted above: "death"
30. Deleted: "their forms of worship" . See "Unnamed Lands" 1860, l. 7, for use of preceding eight words.
31. Inserted above wordspace between "traditions" and "dress"
32. Deleted; "[*illeg.*] their" ; inserted; "the" above "[*del.*] their"
33. Deleted: [*illeg.*] ; inserted below: "races"
34. Preceding nine words inserted above "[*del.*] their" "physiology" "and deletion. Deleted: "whether they"
35. Deleted: "personally"
36. Final "s" deleted.
37. Deleted: "dem"
38. Preceding two words inserted above ", and of"
39. See "Unnamed Lands," l. 6, for preceding four words.
40. Deleted: "sort" ; inserted above: "conditions"
41. Deleted "arts and conditions"
42. Deleted and reinserted above; "liberty" . See "Unnamed Lands," l. 7.
43. Deleted and reinserted above "slaves"
44. End of scrap four. Deleted at beginning of next paragraph: "What great" ; inserted following: "Sublime"
45. Deleted: "have"
46. Deleted: "great" ; inserted above: "subline"
47. Deleted: "so well remembered"
48. Deleted: "earth"
49. Deleted: "Grea"

poems,[50] essays of philosophy, witty replies, excellent histories,[51] works of art and ornament,[52]

Do you suppose that[53] History is complete when[54] the best writers and get all they can[55] of the few[56] communities that are known, and arrange[57] them clearly in books?[58]

and war and justice, and who were witty and wise, and who were brutish and undeveloped, and who were accomplished and elegant and rich—all these are to be thought about as facts. No dates, no statistics not a mark nor a figure that is demonstrably so.

Upon America stood many of these vast nations and upon Asia, Africa and Europe. In the trance of the healthy brain of man. Time, the passage of many thousands of years, the total vacuity of our letters about them, their places blank upon the map, not a mark nor a figure that is demonstrably so. With all this they lived as surely as we do now. They lived upon America and upon Asia, Africa and Europe. In the trance of the healthy brain of man these unknown peoples show afar off dim and filmy in their outlines. Some grand and elaborated, some with graceful faces learned and calm, some naked and savage,[59] some like huge collections of meaningless insects, some engaged in the chase living for generations in the woods and unfenced fields.

Nobody can possess a fair idea of the earth without letting his or her mind walk perfectly easy and loose over the past. A few definite points mark deeds and national eras, lists of titles and battles and the like make up very little of the movement of humanity and events at any time. The best and most important part of history cannot be told. It eludes being examined or printed. It is above even dates and reliable information. It is surer and more reliable, because by far the greatest part of the old statistics of history are only approaches to the truth and are often discrepant and suspicious.

50. Deleted: "work"
51. Deleted: "[*illeg.*]
52. End of scrap five.
53. Deleted: "when"
54. Deleted: "the" ; inserted: "the best writers and [*del.*] digesters get all they can"
55. Deleted: "records"
56. Deleted: "nations"
57. Deleted: "d"
58. End of MS text; *N&F* text follows.
59. See "Unnamed Lands," l. 14, for preceding four words.

Assyria & Egypt.

Manuscript in Duke (37, #29). Inscribed in black pencil on white laid paper, 6⁵⁄₁₆″ x 4⅜″. Faint blue rules ⁵⁄₁₆″ apart. Embossed "So Lee, Mass" in small capitals in upper right corner. Similar embossing is found on "Spring of '59" and "Edmund Spenser." The subject matter is related to "memorials." "those stages," "Egypt (and probably," "Egyptian religion." Stovall, *AL,* 27, 347 suggests that WW had been reading C. K. J. Bunsen or Sir John Gardiner Wilkinson on Egypt. For Wilkinson see "memorials." For Bunsen see "resume—from Bunsen." The paper, writing and contents suggest a date just before 1860. First printed *N&F,* 101–102 (Pt. III, #62; *CW,* IX, 104) in one of Bucke's synthesized MSS with "Egypt (and probably)". The MSS does not support his arrangement.

Assyria & Egypt

Greeks[1][:] illustrating the aesthetic and intellectual developements of our race, in fluency, poems, the beautiful, in theory and action,[2] in[3] friendship, architecture, manners[4] philosophy, and much else.

Romans[5][:]—the physical, that which makes a[6] commanding and mighty race,[7]—that which gives[8] perfection to invasions war, conquest,[9] audacity amplitude, victory, the majesty & discriminations[10] of law, the dignity[11] in attitude, or[12] speech, and the like

?India[13] (Where does India come in? Before? see preceding leaf)[14]
Hebrews[15][:] the spiritual element, the indefinite, the immortal, sublimity,[16] the

1. In left margin followed by irregular vertical line.
2. Preceding four words inserted above "beautiful,"
3. Inserted.
4. Deleted: "and so on"
5. In left margin followed by irregular vertical line.
6. Inserted in wordspace between "makes" "commanding"
7. "race" inserted in space in right margin. Deleted: "mastership, rudeness"
8. Deleted: "a great"
9. Preceding eight words inserted.
10. Preceding two words inserted above "majesty of"
11. "ty" written over "fied" . Deleted: "of" ; inserted above: "in"
12. Inserted.
13. In left margin without brace or vertical line.
14. This leaf has not been found.
15. In left margin followed by short vertical line.
16. Inserted above "rtal" in "immortal"

realm[17] to which the material tends, the realm of shadows, meditation, the influence of the stars in solitude at night, the sublime[18] idea of a coming[19] man or saviour, a perfect individual

[2][20] More or less,[21] undoubtedly in Hindostan, Egypt, Assyria, Persia[22] China, Phœnicia, and other[23] elder lands,[24] preceded the Greeks, Romans, and Hebrews— But what preceded these latter,[25] is hard to tell except[26] by the process of reasoning from effects to causes—[27]

17. Deleted: "of that"
18. Inserted in black ink above "the idea"
19. Deleted: [*illeg.*]
20. Pasted on [*1*] at left edge.
21. Deleted: "in India" ; inserted: "undoubtedly in Hindustan" above "less" and "[*del.*] "India" and "Egypt"
22. Inserted above "China"
23. Deleted: "lands"
24. Deleted: "Doubtless much"
25. Inserted above "these"
26. Deleted: "from"
27. Deleted: "Egypt, Assyria, India, Phoenicia, China"

The Mouldering Bones.

Manuscript in LC (#70, sheet #369). Inscribed in black ink on white wove scrap, 6⅝″ x 5⅜″. No date can be assigned. It seems totally unrelated to the tramp and strike MSS with which it is filed.

The mouldering bones and dry skeleton, or part[1] of the skeleton,[2] are all that is presented us as[3] Past History.— But that is not Past History. The Past! The peoples of a hundred, or a thousand, or ten or twenty thousand—yea of fifty or a hundred thousand—years ago— They too lived, in blooming flesh, with sparkling eyes and speaking lips—knew love, ambition, war, perhaps even[4] science the[5] sane as we do now

1. Emended from plural.
2. Deleted: "that is"
3. Deleted: "the"
4. Preceding two words inserted above "war, science"
5. Clearly "they" in MS.

XII. United States Geography.

The Ruins.

Manuscript in Virginia. Inscribed in black ink on pink paper, possibly wrapper stock for *LG* (1855). First printed in *N&F,* 77 (Pt. III; #5; *CW,* IX, 52). The paper suggests a date of 1856.

The Ruins in North America—the copper mines of Lake Superior which have evidently been worked many centuries since, (probably[1] more than a thousand years ago—perhaps, two or three thousand,)—the mounds in the valley of the Mississippi—the vast ruins of Central America, Mexico and South America—grand temples, walls, &c; now overgrown with old trees—[2]all prove beyond cavil the existence, ages since, in the Western World, of powerful, populous, and probably civilized nations, whose names, histories, and even traditions, had[3] been lost long before the discoveries of Columbus and Vespucius.

1. "ly" written over "le"
2. Preceding nine words inserted in two lines above "th" in "South" and "America—all"
3. Deleted: "long"

Maine.

Manuscript in LC (Feinberg #839). Inscribed in black pencil and black ink (as noted) on the verso of blue Williamsburgh tax blanks and soft pink paper, probably wrapper stock from *LG* (1855). Written in short entries which are here divided by spacing. Since the order of the MSS in the folder was unsystematic and there is no evidence that it was WW's, they are here arranged in as close to a geographic order as possible. WW seems to have been reading and quoting from a geography book, but it is noteworthy that his notes occasionally become rhythmic [*4, 6, 10–13*], and at one point he proposes a "song" [*11*]. The mere lists often suggest his catalog style. The notes were possibly made over a relatively short period, for pink paper is associated with late 1855 and the Williamsburgh tax forms are from early 1857 or later.

[*1*] Maine[1] [:] Fish—codfish herring mackarel salmon lumber [:][2] White pine red oak Hemlock spruce beech maple ash Lumbering—[3] limestone[4] (burned for lime plentiful[5] staples—boards, staves, wood, fish, beef, lime, ice Shipping ([6]Is a great ship-building state—the first in the Union—builds one third of all the U.S. ship building/

Merrimac state[7] New Hampshire "granite state"[8] [:][9] the white pine sometimes 200 ft high, and 6 ft in diameter/ Granite is found in all parts of the state/ apples, pears, plums, cherries,/ cotton factories/ maize,[10] wheat, rye, cattle,

[2] Vermont[11] [:] —mainly grazing springs and brooks are numerous/ wool is a staple-product/ Maple sugar is "numerous"[12]/

1. Principal items to right of brace or vertical line; specific items (codfish, herring, etc.) to right of principal items.
2. Small brace.
3. Brought up from bottom on line.
4. A fist opposite this word to left of brace.
5. Deleted: "timber" ; inserted above: "staples"
6. Fist opposite this word inside the brace.
7. At left edge inside line curved above and below
8. Below "New Hampshire" at left edge.
9. Brace on vertical line. Items grouped in column.
10. Deleted: "India" before "Maize"
11. At left edge. Items grouped in column to right of brace or irregular vertical line.
12. Double line across leaf.

Massachusetts[13] [:] Massachusetts Bay—historical —Commerce[14] "The commerce of Massachusetts, the factories, the perfect cultivation of the land—the[15] schools, the benevolent institutions, the curious inventions[16] Massachusetts[17] aesthetic ennuyeed, with always concealed fires—[18] unpersuadable,[19] unmasterable, the originatress[20] of The States, a[21] divine title, well-deserved,[22]

[*3*] —How would it do to change the names of New Jersey, Rhode Island, New Hampshire?/

The State of Narragansett Bay[23] [:] the sea air, the[24] cool summer, commerce extensive —the cotton, woolen, iron & lace manufactures—/[25]

Connecticut[26] [:] large manufactures of clocks, cotton goods, and gutta-percha,/ shad fishery (of Connecticut river is quite large/

Middle States [:][27] New York, Pennsylvania, New Jersey, Delaware, & Maryland[28]

Alleghany Mts Cattskills/ Valley of the Mohawk. Great lakes & small lakes,/ Susquehannah river/ Animals—bear, wolf, moose, (in the north)/ Minerals—iron, coal, & marble—/ Wheat[29]—apples, peaches, pears & grapes/ "The vast and numerous mines— the exhaustless stores of iron and coal."

[*4*][30] The[31] maize fields of the earth—the tall, gracefull[32] long-leafed maize—slender, bright-green—with tassels—with beautiful ears, each[33] folded in its husks—the beautiful maize!

13. At left edge. Items in column to right of brace or irregular vertical line.
14. "C" written over "T"
15. Deleted: "inventions"
16. Block paragraph.
17. Original first word deleted: "The"
18. Preceding five words and dash inserted above "unpersuadable and "[*del.*] the" and "originatress"
19. Deleted: "the" ; inserted: "unmasterable, the" above "originatress"
20. "ress" over [*illeg.*] ending in "originatress"
21. Deleted: "an a"
22. Deleted: quotation mark or dash.
23. At left edge; description of state to right of vertical line.
24. Inserted and deleted: "uniform climate"
25. Double line across leaf.
26. At left edge; the two descriptive entries in column to the right of a vertical line.
27. Brace.
28. Following items in column at right of the brace.
29. Deleted: "and" ; dash inserted above.
30. Irregular pink paper scrap, approx. 5" x 3¾".
31. Deleted: "measureless"
32. Preceding two words inserted above "long-"
33. Inserted above "fold" in "folded"

[5] Empire State/

the 12,000 public[34] schools—/[35] Salt, 6,000,000 bushels annually in Onondaga Salt Springs the great railroads and canals[36]—the[37] Mannahatta— the population and wealth— —the superb scenery— the interior lakes—.[38]/

[6] *The Empire State*

(put this name instead of New York)[39] The population, Wealth & commerce/ Mts, the Mohegan Mt's (also the Katskills) *River—the Hudson,* "the wild-fowl and fish of Paumanok"/ "Mannahatta Bay"/ the falls of Niagara, — The amplitude,[40] ease, and perfect proportions of the scenery—[41] the broad[42] stream inland seas pouring over the ledge, and[43] striking a hundred and sixty feet below,/ The railroads—/ The Mannahatta (that's it *the* Mannahatta)[44]—the nest—hemmed—the egg in the nest of the beautiful bays—my city—ma femme—O never forgotten by me[45]

[7] The Sea-side State, (New Jersey, fruit, vegetables—[46] the falls of the Passaic—fisheries/

Pennsylvania—

—valley of the Sus

—the Susquehannah river —Alleghany Mts—in the forests the wild catalpa, and the laurel-tree —*staples*—wheat & maize the great mines of iron & coal "the Keystone State"

[8][47] *Principal products*

Delaware— wheat (The Wheat of Delaware and Maryland

[9] Delaware

—the Cypress Swamp—staple—Wheat (flour)/

34. Deleted: "sho" ; inserted following: "schools—"
35. Heading, item about schools, and line in black ink.
36. Preceding two words and dash inserted above "ads" in "railroads" and "the" and "hu" in "[*del.*] hundreds"
37. Deleted: "hundreds"
38. Preceding seventeen words in pencil with hanging indentation.
39. Preceding seven words to right of heading with loop above and below. Following entries in column.
40. Deleted: "and"
41. Preceding nine words brought up from below on an arrow.
42. Deleted: "river" ; inserted: "stream [*del.*] of [*del.*] the inland seas" above "broad . . . pouring"
43. Deleted: "falling down a one" ; inserted: "striking a" above "[*del.*] falling down"
44. Parenthetical text written at the right of leaf with loop to the left and below.
45. Hanging indentation.
46. Deleted: "Passaic"
47. On scrap, approx. 2¼" x 4⅞".

Maryland

—river the[48] Patuxent (100 miles Bay—the Chesapeake Bay —the western portion of Maryland, 2000 feet above the sea, forms[49] an elevated table land—the other portion is lower warmer,[50] & moister —Manufactures of cotton, woolen[51] glass, paper—& copper and iron rolling mills/

[*10*] Southern states

Animals,[52] the alligator, rattlesnake, &[53] moccasin-snake— the Humming birds, the turkey-buzzard/ the yellow-pine (producing tar pitch[54] & turpentine [*the*][55] live oak [*the*] cypress (magnolia (orange [*the*] graceful palmetto, lemon fig [*the*] scented bay tree Staples—cotton, sugar, rice, & tobacca —fruits—oranges lemons & figs —the sweet potato and the yam[56]/ Rivers Roanoke length 500 miles Savannah 600 Altamaha 500 Alabama 500 (the sluggish rivers, flowing over the sands or through swamps)[57] warm land,—sunny land, the fiery land, the rich-blooded land,[58] quick-mettled land,[59] my land—land of impulse and of love

[*11*] ?[60] Song[61]

Dear to me the sunny land, sweet land, the silvery land, my land,[62] the fiery land, quick-mettled land, luscious and generous land,[63] rich-blooded land, land of impulse and of love [*12*][64] silvery land, sweet land,[65]—wild, generous land—land of luscious fruits [*13*][66] The[67] luxuriant forests,[68] charged with misleto—the odor,[69] density, gloom,—the[70] awful natural stillness,[71]

48. Deleted: "Potomac"; "Patuxent" written below, followed by "(100 miles" on same line.
49. Deleted: "p"
50. Inserted above "&"
51. Inserted in right margin.
52. Preceding "the" written over with "A" in "Animals"
53. Deleted: "the"
54. Inserted above "&" "turp" in "turpentine"
55. WW's dittos here and following.
56. Preceding dash and six words possibly inserted later.
57. Preceding ten words in four lines with rules above below and at right to left of "Altahama" and "Alabama"
58. Deleted: "hot"
59. Preceding two words inserted.
60. Irregular scrap of pink paper, approx. 5″ x 4⅝″.
61. "?Song" at left margin. Deleted: "Always the South, the" ; inserted above: "Dear to me the"
62. Deleted: "wild generous" ; inserted: "the fiery" above.
63. Preceding four words inserted above "ed" in "mettled" and "land"
64. Scrap 2⅞ x 4½″. Hanging indentation.
65. Deleted: "gen"
66. Irregular scrap, approx. 2½″ x 4⅝″. Hanging indentation.
67. Deleted: "rich"
68. Deleted: "overhung" ; inserted above: "charged"
69. Inserted above "de" in "density"
70. Inserted above "aw" in "awful"
71. Deleted: "—[*illeg.*]"

[*14*][72] an entirely new system, theory & *practice* of education, viz: to Do that which will *teach to think* every one for himself—giving facts, data/

The honey and beeswax of Missouri, Kentucky and Tennessee,[73]

The rice of South Carolina[74] — The wool of Ohio and of the Empire State, — The tobacco of Virginia and Maryland[75]

The cotton of[76] Alabama, Mississippi,[77] Georgia, South Carolina and Texas, — The sugar of Louisiana.[78]

[*15*][79] Virginia

The subterranean caves—the sulphur springs with their medicinal waters/ Animals—deer, opossum, raccoon[80] —the mocking-bird, and the wild turkey/ Minerals[81] Iron, coal & limestone/ The[82] Capitol on Shockoe hill (Richmond Va. a picturesque, commanding hill, & the building looking down, as it were, over the town and upon James river)[83]/

[*16*] Virginia

Salt—(3,000,000 bushels made annually)[*:*][84]—the Blue Mountains (260 miles long— Otter Peaks—4260 ft high/ River—the Potomac—500 miles the Great Kanawha — The wild passage of the[85] The river Potomack—the wild passage through the mountains—the water dashed from rock to rock[86] The[87] great chasm spanned by natural rock, sixty feet across—the stream flowing under[88] [*17*][89] — the sugar-maple—in western Virginia/

The[90] plenteous area —[91] The three millions of square miles — the diverse spread[92]

72. Irregular pink paper, approx. 8¼″ x 5″.
73. Hanging indentation.
74. Deleted: "and Georgia"
75. Hanging indentation.
76. Inserted and deleted: "Georgia" above "Alab" in "Alabama"
77. Deleted: "South Carolina" ; inserted above: "Georgia, South Carolina"
78. Hanging indentation.
79. Entries in hanging indentation.
80. Inserted above "ssum" in "opposum"
81. Deleted: "limestone and" ; "I" inserted over lowercase.
82. Deleted: "Cap"
83. Deleted: beginning of new paragraph, "the"
84. Brace to left of names of mountain ranges.
85. Deleted: "P"
86. "The river Potomack . . ." in hanging indentation.
87. Deleted: "rocky bridge"
88. Entry in hanging indentation.
89. Scrap, 5⅞″ x 4½″.
90. Deleted: "territory" ; inserted: "plenteous" above "ritory" in "territory" and "are" , "in" , "area"
91. Preceding three words and deletion all inserted above "the three" and "mil" in "millions"
92. Hanging indentation.

The valley of the Mississippi—the[93] slope[94] to the Eastern Sea[95]—that to the Western Sea—that to the great[96] Gulf./

[*18*][97] (N. Carolina

The Great Dismal Swamp northeast part of N. Carolina, extending into Virginia—10 x 30 miles full of pine, juniper & cypress trees with white & red oak in the drier parts[98] Lumbering is carried on to a great extent—the yellow pine, so esteemed for its beauty and durability (it is what I see for spars &c, in the spar-yards—the men cutting with axes & adz.[99]

[*19*] North Carolina

—[1]The coast with rude sea-headlands—The gold mines—The valuable forests[2] The[3] mountains,[4] the Bald Peak, the Smoky Peak, and the Pilot Peak/ Pamlico Sound — (it must be something like the L. I. South Bay)[5] It communicates with the sea by inlets—Okracoke inlet is the principal one[6]/ The forests of pitch pine (the tar, turpentine & lumber of this tree make one half the exports of the state) Soil—generally sandy

[*20*][7] Model

North Carolina, with rude sea-headlands— [*illeg.*]

[*21*] South Carolina

Rivers—the Great Pedee— the Santee the Edisto

trees—the Palmetto—40 feet high (the "cabbage Palm) —the laurel with large white blossoms —cotton, rice,[8] hemp, indigo — the[9] sand-hills of the middle-country, like agitated[10] waves—the pleasant table-lands beyond

93. Deleted: "Atlantic slope"
94. Deleted: "of"
95. Capitalized over lowercase.
96. Deleted: "South"
97. Scrap, 6″ x 4⅝″. Heading at left in loop.
98. Hanging indentation.
99. Hanging indentation.
1. Deleted: "its" ; inserted above: "The coast with
2. Deleted: "Mts"
3. Deleted: "peaks of"
4. Deleted: "peaks" ; inserted "s" on "mountains"
5. Hanging indentation.
6. Hanging indentation.
7. Scrap, approx. 2³/₁₆″ x 4½″.
8. Preceding two words inserted on two lines above dash originally written before "hemp"
9. Deleted: "sand waving"
10. Inserted.

[22][11] Georgia

Rivers[12] — The Savannah, (its[13] Eastern boundary) —the rafts on the rivers —the island-studded coast —Nicojack Cave, with the huge mouth, and the flat floor laved by water, and the high roof of limestone —the pine-barrens/

Alabama

Rivers the[14] Tombigbee Coosa Staple—Cotton

[23][15] Georgia

Cotton and rice. —(*staples*) the olive, the orange, indigo[16]/ (in the woods) Oak, pine, hickory, cedar/ (animals) deer, wild turkeys, (the alligator)

[24] Florida

Rivers Apalachicola—(flows S into G of M. the springs—"the transparent lakes"—the Okeechobee the everglades "the Wakulla Fountain[17] bubbling up pure & cold trees the palm, the[18] live-oak, the papaw, the titi with blossoms the parrots in the woods/ the hummock land/ the yellow pine &[19] live-oak of Florida[20]

[25] Mississippi

Staple—Cotton/

Louisiana

sugar-cane —the coast—the levee of the[21] Crescent City/

Texas

Cotton, sugar,[22] maize, wheat & wool Rivers — the Sabine — nav. 300 miles —the Colorado—the Brazos —the rich soil and pleasant climate —the herds of buffaloes and wild horses on the prairies. —

[26][23] Tennesse[24]

The cattle and wool of Tennessee —Tobacco is a leading article "Old Tennessee" —T is the oldest of the Western States, —settled first 1754/

11. Scrap, 6⅝" x 4½".
12. Inserted above dash originally written before "The"
13. Deleted: "north" in the insert above.
14. Deleted: "Mobile"
15. Irregular scrap, approx. 2¾" x 4½".
16. Deleted: "cotton"
17. "F" over lowercase.
18. Inserted above wordspace before "live-oak"
19. Preceding three words inserted above "live-oak"
20. New entry "the" deleted.
21. Deleted: "city"
22. Deleted: "corn" ; inserted above: "maize"
23. Scrap, 5" x 4½".
24. Loop below word.

In Kentucky salt-works, (quite extensive) Kentucky—the rich garden in the centre—

[27] Arkansas

Rivers—the White river the Arkansas river 1200 m —the beautiful valleys of the Arkansas and the Washita/a great deal of this state is prairies— — "bottom lands, heavily timbered with — the otter, beaver, & raccoon —the sleeping lakes and stagnant bayous —the dead level/

in South generally

the orange, lemon, fig, peach, grapes, berries, pomegranate, dates, pears[25] — sweet potato/ ginseng, blood-root, snake-root

[28][26] The[27] Rio Grande with its tributaries, the Colorado[28] with its,[29] and the Brazas and Sabine with theirs,

[29][30] the thirteen thousand towns, cities, and villages[31]

25. Preceding three words inserted above "s" in "grapes" and "berries,—" and "swe" in "sweet"

26. Irregular pink scrap, approx. 2½″ x 5″.

27. Deleted: "Red River and" ; inserted above: "Rio Grande with"

28. Deleted: "and" ; inserted above: "with"

29. Deleted: "tributaries and"

30. Irregular pink scrap, approx. 2⅜″ x 5″.

31. A long division problem: 30,000,000 divided by 13,000. Answer: 2300.

The Beef, Wheat and Lumber.

Manuscript not found. Text from *N&F,* 169 (Pt. IV, #69; *CW,* X, 19). In *CW,* Burke printed only three dots.

The beef, wheat and lumber of Chicago, the copper of Wisconsin—the region of Green Bay. The railroads with their hundreds of lines and interlines, over the prairies and up into the pineries and mines, the myriad rivers—the great inland lakes . . . . . .

Editorial for Insertion.

Manuscript not found. Text from *N&F,* 165 (Pt. IV, #40; *CW,* X, 11). See "The New Inland America" and "here are vast," which are on the versos of a draft of an article, "The Opera," which appeared in *Life Illustrated,* November 10, 1855 (See "A VISIT TO THE OPERA.") The tone of these instructions suggests that WW was in control of editorial policy; he began editing the *Brooklyn Times* in February, 1857. Neither the "Editorial" nor the "article" alluded to is listed in William White, *Walt Whitman's Journalism,* 32–61.

Editorial for insertion same day with the article, "The New Inland America."
American Expansion and Settlement Inland.

The New Inland America.

Manuscript in LC (#47, #127V). Inscribed in black ink on tattered white laid scrap, approx. 8½" x 6⅜", heavy chain lines 1¼", vertical hair lines. The verso of a draft for an article, "The Opera," which appeared in *Life Illustrated* (November 10, 1855). (See "A VISIT TO THE OPERA."). This proposed editorial, perhaps for the *Brooklyn Times,* which WW began editing in February 1857, is not listed in William White, *Walt Whitman's Journalism,* 32–61. See "Editorial for insertion," which alludes directly to this fragment.

The[1] New Inland[2] America

Progress Southwestward—new accessions—new adjustments/

Is not the America West side[3] *of the Mississippi destined to preponderate over the East side?*

1. Deleted: "A" ; inserted above: "The"
2. Inserted above "Am" in "America"
3. Inserted above "of"

Here Are Vast Mountains.

Manuscript in LC (#47, sheet #125V). Inscribed on verso of draft for "The Opera." See "A VISIT TO THE OPERA." Probably part of the projected article "The New Inland America "

here are vast mountains spread over the surface, like crowded flakes of cloud in the [*illeg.*][1] salt lakes, barren[2] with shores corpse-white.—steppes—plateaus—but[3]

1. Inserted: "salt lakes . . . white."
2. Deleted: "and" ; inserted: "with shores corpse" on a line above "barren with"
3. Preceding three words written under "vast" . The lines intertwine so that the order of inscription is uncertain. Entire entry written sideways on length of leaf.

(Emory) Whatever Population.

Manuscript in LC (#76, sheet #585). Inscribed in black ink on a scrap of blue Williamsburgh election form. "Emory" is W.H. Emory (1811–1887), cartographer and soldier. He was graduated from West Point in 1831 and commissioned in the Topographical Corps. He accompanied Kearney on the expedition from Ft. Leavenworth to Southern California in 1847 and compiled *Notes of a Military Reconnoissance from Fort Leavenworth to San Diego in California, including Parts of the Arkansas, Del Norte and Gila Rivers. Made in 1847–1848* (Washington, 1848) (30th Congress, 1st Session, Senate Executive Documents No. 7). He also served as cartographer for the boundary dispute. He retired as a brigadier general in 1876. WW does not quote Emory, but the information here and elsewhere (except possibly the height of the mezquite tree) is to be found there. The date is possibly between 1857 and 1859.

(Emory)

Whatever population may now or hereafter occupy the mountain system must depend on grazing, and on [*illeg.*] cultivation of the grape. Also, something great is to be expected of the mines.—

Southern California, the whole of the upper vally of the Gila, and the upper valley of the del Norte, as far down as the Presidio del Norte, are finely adapted for wine-making.—[1]

Cotton and corn grow with luxuriance where the soil[2] can be irrigated./

chapparal (clusters of mezquite trees—they grow from 10–15 ft. high—are very tough and gnarled, and full of thorns.)
arroyos,[3] (deep gullies)

1. Deleted: "cotton"
2. Deleted: "is" ; inserted: "can be" above "[*del.*] is" and "irr" in "irrigated"
3. "Arroyos" inserted above "arroyos" and deleted.

New American Pictures.

Manuscript in LC (#76, sheet #580). Inscribed in black ink on verso of blue Williamsburgh tax form dated by hand 1854. At lower left is a series of sums in the millions. the addition is incorrect. It is, first of all, difficult to imagine how WW got hold of someone else's tax bill. This aside, 1854 need not be the date of WW's note for, according to Bowers's theory that he found a large supply of obsolete Williamsburgh forms when he took over the *Times,* he used them for several years. The date is therefore probably after 1857.

New
American Pictures

Coast Range (or Cordilleras)[1]—(in California (California is evidently a land of Mountain ranges,)/

Wasatch[2] Mountains—(in Utah Humboldt Mts (Utah) (Mountains spread over the surface like crowded flakes of clouds in the heavens,)/

Wind River Mts. (toward Nebraska and Oregon,)[3]/

Cascade Mts.—[4]

Our[5] inland empire at the South-West

—the trunk of the

1. Parenthetical phrase inserted above "Range—"
2. Inserted above false start: "Wahsa"
3. WW's geographical knowledge was better than this suggests. G.K. Warren's "Map of the Territory of the United States" (1857) in Wheat, *Mapping The American West,* IV (1960), 84, shows them as contiguous.
4. Deleted: "Our"
5. Deleted: "new"

Vast National Tracts.

Manuscript in LC (#76, sheet #s 581, 582). Inscribed in black ink on verso of fragment of used Williamsburgh tax form dated in ink 1854. Page [2] (581) is on verso of an undated election form. In any case the date is after 1854.

Vast national tracts, (large enough for many[1] a swarming inland empire,) are yet entirely unpenetrated,[2]—their resources and riches[3] unknown.—/

This[4] wide-spread region is full of mountains.— Nature has struck out from here smoothness and monotony, and piled ridge upon ridge, chain upon chain, scattering them with prodigal profusion, colossal[5].— It is[6] the America of Titanic forms.— Yet there are intervals, the pastoral character is there too;[7] of vast[8] wonderful plains, hundred and[9] almost thousands of miles in extent.— [2] (on the same plains.) occasionally[10] sand-dunes, encircling what might at first be supposed to be dried up lakes./[11]

The real "plains"

(as in the papers
"News from the Plains")

The term *plains* is applied to the extensive[12] inclined surface reaching from the base of the Rocky Mts. to the shores of the Gulf of Mexico, and to the Valley of the Mississippi, and form[13] perhaps the greatest feature in Western Geography. Except on the borders of the streams which traverse the plains in their course to the valley of the Mississippi, scarcely any thing exists

1. Deleted: "great" ; inserted above: "a"
2. Deleted: "marke—none having bra"
3. Inserted in right margin: "and riches"
4. Deleted: "vast" ; inserted and deleted above: "wide" ; inserted: "wide-spread" above "[*del.*] wide" and "region"
5. Inserted above ".—" which was originally written after "profusion"
6. Deleted: "indeed"
7. Preceding six words inserted above "Yet there are intervals,"
8. Inserted above "w" in "wonderful"
9. Deleted: "even" ; inserted above: "almost"
10. Inserted above "sand-"
11. Rule across page.
12. Deleted: [*illeg.*]
13. Deleted: "a" ; inserted: "perhaps the greatest" above wordspace between "form feature" and "feature"

New Mexico.

Manuscript in LC (#76, sheet #583). Inscribed in black ink on scrap of blue Williamsburgh tax blank. Emory is not WW's source. The date is 1857 or later.

New Mexico

Rio Grande runs through this territory—the total length of the river being 2000 miles.—[1]This territory too, like Utah,[2] has salt water lakes, which furnish the population with salt—caravans[3] travel with it as an article of trade.—[4] All this part of the world is to be remarked as unsurpassed[5] upon earth in its sanitary fitness for human occupancy.—Those subtle atmospheric influences—[6]that curious[7] something[8] in the chemical, geological, hydrographic, and meteorologic[9] attributes of a country, which give[10] virtue to the blood, and vigor,[11] clearness, and security therefrom to the whole physique.—

1. Deleted: "It" ; inserted: "This territory"
2. Preceding two words inserted above.
3. Deleted: [*illeg.*]
4. Deleted: "(one of the greatest countries"
5. Deleted: "for heal" ; inserted above: "upon earth in [*del.*] the its sanitary [*del.*] perfection [*ins.*] fitness for human occupancy.—"
6. Deleted: "those"
7. Deleted: "interplay of cause and effect between the natural conditions around it and"
8. Deleted: "that" ; inserted above: "in the chemical . . . which"
9. Deleted: [*illeg.*]
10. Deleted: "n"
11. Deleted: "and clearness" ; inserted above: "clearness and security"

Nov. '57—Talks with Mrs. Farnham.

Manuscript in LC (#76, sheet #584). Inscribed in black ink on blue laid paper, 7¹/₁₆" x 6¼". Mrs. Eliza Farnham (1815–1864) was a well-known traveller and social reformer. From 1844 to 1848 she was matron at Sing Sing, where she instituted reforms in the treatment of prisoners. In 1846 WW recommended in the *Eagle* her *Life in Prairie Land* (she had lived six years in Illinois) as a school book. She lived in California from 1849 to 1856, returned to NY, and published her *California, Indoors and Out* (1856). Her enthusiasm for California was boundless. She studied medicine for two years and organized a group of women to emigrate there with her. In 1859 WW reviewed her *My Early Days* in the Brooklyn *Times*. In 1864 she published *Woman and Her Era*. WW first met her at the Price's in 1856 and, on being introduced, said he had heard of her often from friends at Sing Sing. In 1862 he mentions her being back in NYC ("return my book"). Mr. Burns has not been identified. The date is 1857.

Nov. 57—Talks with Mrs. Farnham—and with Mr. Burns about California.—Every thing seems to be generated and grow on a *larger scale*—fruits, vegetables for[1] cooking, trees, &c.—[2] Humanity[3] is also freer and grander—the children[4] seem cast on a[5] fuller pattern, grow[6] better, breathe more air, make more blood, are sounder, every way a superior type. The passions are also stronger,[7] the soul more clarified and apparent;—life seems more intense and determined;—there is more individuality and character[8]/
immense cloud-piercing Mountains long stretching—Prairies 4000 ft—Waterfalls/ the tulé grass—the canõn the ranch—[9] the adobé hut—the gulch—the vaquero—

1. Deleted: "the"
2. Deleted: "The"
3. Inserted: "ity" ; deleted: "growth" ; "humanity" capitalized.
4. Deleted: "are larger and more"
5. Deleted: "larger"; inserted: "fuller"
6. Deleted: "larger" ; inserted: "better"
7. Deleted: "every thing"
8. Rule across leaf.
9. Two words and dash inserted above "the"

New Mexico.

Manuscript in LC (#76, sheet #586). Inscribed in black ink on blue Williamsburgh election form. All entries except the last are in some kind of hanging indentation. The publishing house, Harper and Row, suggests that the reference to Harper's Gazetteer may be to *McCulloch's Universal Gazetteer* published by Harper in 1847. The date is after 1857.

New Mexico (Harper's Gazetteer)

Religion Catholic/

Agriculture Largely growing wheat, maize,[1]—neat cattle—horses, mules and sheep/
Climate temperate, constant and healthy—in parts, as on the mountains, severe winters, with great falls of snow.—/
Pueblos,[2] the villages of Christianized[3] native mexicans/

—Race of the serape, (colored blankets, worn by men, common orders)
the reboso, ([4]small shawl worn on the head by women,) the cigarito, the fandango, and the game of monte.—[5]/

Santa Fe, situated at the base of a spur of the Rocky Mountains, and 15 miles east of the Rio Grande del Norte, on a small branch of it. Two[6] printing offices, 7000 population, and sundry churches (all Roman Catholic)

1. Inserted and deleted: [*illeg.*]
2. False start; "Pub" deleted before word.
3. Deleted: "aborigines"
4. Deleted: [*illeg.*]
5. Rule across leaf.
6. Inserted and deleted: [*illeg.*].

In the Region.

Manuscript in LC (#76, sheet #587). Inscribed in black ink on a scrap of Williamsburgh tax form dated 1854 in ink and fragment of election form pasted together. The date is 1857 or later.

In[1] the region of these mountains there are many detached valleys and basins affording facilities for irrigation, and having a rich soil, where the cereals, the vine, and all the plants which conduce to the comfort of man, are produced luxuriantly;—but they form more[2] the exception[3] than the general,—and are separated by[4] unproductive hills, or arid plains.—[5]

(one of the features)

Between the ridges of mountains, the traveler occasionally encounters vast plains, which when the sun is high,[6] furnish the phenomena of the mirage, presenting the appearance of the sea.—

(animals on these plains)

filled with antelopes, prairie-dogs, and rabbits.—the grass, the nutritious[7] gramma[8] grass)

1. Deleted: "these [*illeg.*]"
2. Inserted above "the"
3. Deleted: "rather"
4. Deleted: "the"
5. End of tax form.
6. Deleted: "produce"
7. Inserted above "e" in "the" and "gram" in "gramma"
8. Emory (see "[Emory] Whatever population") spells the word, "grama"

Rio Grande del Norte.

Manuscript in LC (#76, sheet #588). Inscribed in black ink on blue Williamsburgh election form. WW is drawing on Emory's *Report on the United States and Mexican Boundary Survey* (1857) for his account of the navigational difficulties (78) and the description of El Paso as a "garden-spot" (89). The date must be 1857 or later.

Rio Grande del Norte, or Rio Bravo del Norte (indifferently) running a course of 2000 miles[1]/ Steamboats may ascend 700 miles—but the upper portions of the river have so many shallows, rocks, and sand-bars, that navigation is impossible.[2]/ In New Mexico—*silver mines*[3]/
(Lieut Emory says) The grama (or mezquite) is incomparably the most nutritious grass known[4]/
Lieut. Emory gives discouraging accounts of the soil, as being productive only through systematic irrigation./ El Paso it seems (the town) is one of the garden-spots of N. A.[5]/ The air is DRY—THIS IS UNIVERSAL[6]

1. Hanging indentation.
2. Rule across leaf. Block paragraph.
3. Rule across leaf.
4. Hanging indentation. Rule across leaf.
5. Hanging indentation.
6. Pointing fist at left . under "the air"

N.W. Texas, Utah, New Mexico.

Manuscript in LC (#76, #589). Inscribed in black ink on scrap of blue Williamsburgh tax form. The date is 1857 or later.

N. W. Texas, Utah, New Mexico, the proposed Arizonia. There is room enough for all—so vast—so roomy[1]

To much[2] of[3] these vast regions belongs the mark "Unexplored Territory"—but enough is known to make certain a few general features.— There is[4] marked individuality about it.— It is the land of the Rocky mountains—and of the Wasatch.[5] It is the land of[6] gulches, pure air,[7] pastoral plains, and inexhaustible mineral treasures.— It is the land of mighty rivers—Among[8] its rivers, after the Mississippi, the Missouri, the Yellowstone, the Columbia, and the Kansas in the north[9]—are the Bravo del Norte, the Pecos, the Colorado, and the Gila.—[10] Then of mountains, it presents[11] the most tremendous specimens—it is their peculiar land.—there they range, in mighty echelons, the like of which no other part of the globe likens.—(canals[?]—in the north in the south[12] minerals—gold, silver and gold.

1. "N.W. Texas . . . Arizonia" crammed in at top of leaf; "there is . . . roomy" written on six lines in upper right corner following "regions"
2. Uncorrected capital on "Much" not printed.
3. Deleted: "this"
4. Deleted:"a"
5. Sentence inserted above "about it."
6. Deleted: "mountains"
7. Deleted: "and"
8. Preceding eight words inserted on two lines above and preceding "after" in the insert noted in *n9*. Uncorrected capital on "Its" not printed.
9. Preceding fifteen words inserted on two lines above "rivers, . . . del Norte"
10. Deleted: "It" ; inserted above: "Then" . Uncorrected capital on "Of" not printed.
11. Deleted: "gr"
12. Preceding six words inserted under "the globe" and following "likens.—(canals [?]"

Sierra Blanca.

Manuscript in LC (#76, sheet #590). Inscribed in black pencil on scrap of Williamsburgh tax form. Below "Sierra Blanca" is a sketch of a rock or some sort of polyhedron. The paper indicates this was written after 1857.

Sierra Blanca (part of Rocky Mountains—in New Mexico (toward east line) and Utah (on east line)[1] *Elk Mountains* (Utah, (East)/ *Sierra Nevada* (snow mountains)[2]

1. Hanging indentation.
2. Deleted line follows: "Large tracts Vast National" . (See "Vast national tracts.")

One Feature.

Manuscript in LC (#76, sheet #591). Inscribed in black ink on scrap of blue Williamsburgh election form. The date must be 1857 or later.

one feature of N.A. Geography
What is called the Basin system—lakes—immense ponds,[1]—many of them without any visible outlet to the ocean—/

1. Deleted: "surrounded" ; inserted: "many of them" above "without"

One of the.

Manuscript in LC (#76, sheet #592). Inscribed in black ink on blue Williamsburgh tax from. The date must be 1857 or later.

One of the[1] most extensive feature[2] in[3] the Western Continent, inland, is the plateau or table-land, traversing[4] it from the unexplored region of the North to[5] its southernmost[6] extremity, very broad[7] about the 38th deg.[8] north latitude, and with the depression at the 32d degree, forming "The Pass."

1. Preceding three words inserted above "[*del.*] the" and "most" . Preceded by fist pointing right and deleted: "A" "The"
2. Deleted:"s"
3. Deleted: "this" ; inserted: "the Western" above the deletion and "Conti" in "Continent"
4. Deleted: "[*ins.*] the North American States" ; inserted: "it" above "s" in "[*del.*] states"
5. Deleted: [*illeg.*]; inserted above: "its"
6. Deleted: "boundary,"
7. Deleted: "at"
8. Deleted: "of"

—A Cañon (Kanyon).

Manuscript in LC (#76, sheet #593). Inscribed in black ink on a scrap of Williamsburgh tax form. In *Report on the . . . Boundary Survey,* 40, Emory mentions Mt. Elias, at 17,000 feet, as the highest peak in North America. The date is 1857 or later.

—a cañon (kanyon) river hemmed in by[1] vertical walls[2]

This plateau is broken with[3] ranges of countless mountains the highest of which is Mt. [*illeg.*][4] 17,000 ft above the sea.—

1. Deleted: "verticle"
2. Deleted: "This plateau is toward"
3. Deleted: [*illeg.*]
4. Paper torn.

This Western Two-Thirds.

Manuscript in LC (#76, #594). Inscribed in black ink and black pencil on scrap of blue Williamsburgh election form. The date is after 1857.

This[1] western two-thirds portion of the continent,[2] untouched national tracts [*illeg.*] large [*illeg.*] state, with exhaustless resources and riches—is entirely different in its physical geography from the eastern portion.—

See MS. slip p. 132[3]

Every thing is on a grander[4] scale, with broader sweeps and contrasts[5]—paradises—deserts—fountains as of[6] the immortal waters of youth and love—[7]/

1. Deleted: "eastern" ; inserted :"western two-thirds" above the deletion and "portion"
2. Deleted: "with whi" ; inserted in pencil on arrow from upper left: "untouched national tracts . . . resources and riches" . Inserted: "is entirely different" above "[*del.*] with whi"
3. Not identified. In loop in right margin.
4. "er" inserted.
5. Two words inserted above "eeps in "sweeps" and "para" in "paradise"
6. Deleted: [*illeg.*]; inserted above: "the"
7. "Every thing . . . love" on lines of small script in lower right corner after "portion"

In Some Places.

Manuscript in LC (#76, sheet #595). Inscribed in black ink on a scrap of blue laid paper. Emory mentions rock inscriptions in both his reports. WW appears to be drawing on the *Report on the . . . Boundary Survey,* 143. This probably was written in 1857 or later.

in some places, as about the Pecos river, many[1] paintings of men and animals rudely[2] pourtrayed on[3] the sides of perpendicular rocks.—

1. Inserted and deleted: "rude" above "pa" in "paintings"
2. Inserted above "s" in "animals" and "po" in "portrayed"
3. Deleted: "the perpen"

Emory Valley.

Manuscript in Virginia. Inscribed in black ink on a scrap of blue Williamsburgh property tax form dated in print "185-". In this respect it differs from other tax forms. The passage is a quotation with slight verbal variations from W.H. Emory. *Report of the United States and Mexcian Boundary Survey* (Washington, 1857) (34th Congress, 1st Session, Senate Executive Documents No. 108) Vol. 1, p. 72. The date must be 1857 or after.

Emory

Valley of the lower Rio Bravo. "Here, in the valleys formed by these mountains, we find large tracts of country, within the influence of some irrigating stream, sheltered from the northers of winter, and at an elevation above the sea sufficient to overcome the excessive summer-heat due this parallel of latitude, producing all the fruits of the tropics, and the cereals of the more northern climates.—The climate is unsurpassed in salubrity, and nothing is requisite to make this spot the garden of the Rio Bravo, but a stable form of government."[1]
(The above is in Mexico)/ This region seems to be the place for the vine[2]

1. Quotation marks appear to have been eradicated.
2. Set in about a quarter of the way across the leaf. Fist at left pointing upward.

April '63. Washington.

Manuscript in LC (#76, sheet #597R). On verso "Senate, Vol. 12". Inscribed in black ink on a white wove scrap, approx. 3½" x 8½". Blue rules ⅜" apart on verso. Ms. Barbara Malan McLain, who has studied these MSS, reports that "the onion-like camas," "Rivers in Idaho," "Idaho means," and "Idaho Capt. Mullen's map" are shown by the tearing to be from the same packet of paper. Capt. John Mullan (1830–1909) had a distinguished career as a cartographer and road builder (Carl I. Wheat, *Mapping the American West,* V [1] [1963], 85 ff.). When WW met him in Washington (*Corr.,* I, 87, 90), he had just submitted his report on his Pacific Wagon Road Survey made between 1858 and 1863 and was lobbying for the admission of Idaho as a territory. WW misspells his name. The date is April, 1863.

April '63. Washington.[1]

Idaho[2] from Capt. Mullen and his map, etc. (California Sketch.)[3]

1. At upper right.
2. Centered in large script, following words to right in hanging indentation.
3. Scrawled in large script below.

Senate, Vol. 12.

Manuscript in LC (#76, sheet #597V). Inscribed in black ink on white wove scrap. On recto "April '63. Washington." Ms. Barbara Malan McLean suggests that "Reports of Exploration and Surveys" may be Senate Executive Document, 36th Congress, 18th Session, Washington 1860, which includes Isaac Stevens' reports on railway routes near the 47th and 49th parallels. The Coast Survey reports would concern topography and cartography. The date is 1863. See "April '63. Washington." for dating.

Senate, vol. 12. Reports of Explorations and Surveys on a route for Pacific Railroad from Mississippi to Pacific 1853–5, vol. 12.[1]/
Coast Survey reports./

1. Preceding in hanging indentation.

I Am Back Again.

Manuscript in LC (#76, #598). Inscribed on a white wove scrap, approx. 3½" x 8½". Blue rules ⅜" apart on verso. WW is evidently working towards a poem. The date is March 26, 1863.

I am back again in the mines[1]/ Significant California sight[2] in Stanislaus mining[3] region (southern) *I see*—I am in the mines—back in Southern California[4] between day-break & sunrise.—in some favorite cañyon, to see the blue smoke rising from a score or more of tents a beautiful soft morning,—I hear roulade of[5] the California nightengale, the sweet short notes—[6] they are in twos and threes—they/ then at evening the notes of the dove cooing—the beautiful gentle evening/ from F. [*illeg.*] McGrath, March 26, 1863)—he was three years in California/ (California Sketch)[7]

1. Inserted in small script across top of leaf.
2. Original heading.
3. Inserted.
4. Since the Stanislaus mining region was west of San Francisco it would not be in Southern California in modern opinion.
5. Preceding four words inserted.
6. Deleted: "there"
7. Scrawled in large script at bottom of leaf.

—Idaho Means.

Manuscript in LC (#76, sheet #599). Inscribed in black ink on a white wove scrap approx. 3½" x 8½". Blue rules on verso, ⅜" apart. See "April '63. Washington." This was written in 1863.

—Idaho *means* the gem of the Mountains (the original name suggested was Montano).—

the Missouri & the Columbia head waters have both their rise in this territory—the Snake & Spokane are also full of salmon, some of them three or four feet long.—

—The map is dotted with yellow streaks representing[1] gold mines—(here the Atlantic & Pacific meet

Names of places in Idaho—Rocky Mts/

Area about[2] 350,000 sq. miles.

1. Preceding three words inserted.
2. Inserted.

The Onion-Like Camas.

Manuscript in LC (#76, sheet #600). Inscribed in black ink on a white wove scrap, approx. 3½" x 8½". Blue rules ⅜" apart on verso. (See "April '63. Washington.) The information is probably from Mullan in person or from his *Report on the Construction of a Military Road from Walla Walla to Fort Benton* (1863). The date is 1863.

the onion-like camas, sweet (like jujube paste)[1] all through Idaho territory (another root more characteristic than the bitter-root)[2]—makes a good liquor, used for that purpose/ Metals first gold, then silver—also lead & copper,—other minerals will certainly follow, probably iron & coal among them.[3]/ it is the[4] new crown of the north, the mighty crown, the[5] broad and solid democratic crown, crowning the north, full of gold and silver,—a crown of mountains/ Idaho
Crown of the North, new crown—the mighty serrated crown of the North
the new crown of democracy, with gold and silver

1. Preceding at top left.
2. Preceding at top right.
3. Entry in hanging indentation.
4. Deleted: "northern mighty mo" ; inserted: "new crown of the north"
5. Deleted: "vast"

—Rivers In Idaho.

Manuscript in LC (#76, sheet #601). Inscribed on a white wove scrap, approx. 3½" x 8½". Blue rules 3½" apart on verso. See "April '63. Washington." The information is probably from Mullan or his reports.

—rivers in Idaho Yellow Stone, river Missouri, Milk river, north fork of the Platte—/ Rocky Mts run through the eastern portion of it with the Wind River Mountains, (a spur of the Rockys)[1]/

Bitter root, the root grows from two to five inches down in the ground, something[2] like a parsnip,[3] outside has only a single leaf flat on the ground, with pointed edges, with a little purplish[4] red[5] flower[6] growing right out of the center of the leaf. All the Indians eat it. it is a first rate anti-scorbutic.

1. Preceding entry in hanging indentation. Rule across leaf.
2. Inserted.
3. Deleted: "the" ; inserted: "outside has only a"
4. Suffix added.
5. Inserted: "red"
6. Deleted: "looking" ; inserted: "growing"

Idaho. Capt. Mullen's Map.

Manuscript in LC (#76, sheet #602). Inscribed in black ink on a white wove scrap, approx. 3½" x 8½". Blue rules ⅜" apart on verso. See "April '63. Washington." Mullan made many maps in the course of his surveys, some or all of which are in the National Archives. Wheat, *Mapping the American West,* V (1) (1963), 85, 92, 93, reprints some and gives biographical data. No map of this size is known to exist. Mr. A.P. Muntz, National Archives and Record Service, in a letter to Ms. McLean, dated March 16, 1962, suggests that such a map might be made by piecing together smaller maps. Mullan might have constructed such a map for his own use. The date is 1863.

Idaho. Capt. Mullen's map.

A great map 16 ft. by 12 giving all the U.S. territory[1] between the Pacific & 90 deg. west longitude, & from 40 to 54, thus including five degrees of the British possions

—(names of stations in Idaho—Hell Gate Pass—the[2] Salmon River Mts. and Salmon[3] River, innavigable, broken by rapids & falls, but swarming with salmon, (they came up here from the ocean) Idaho is the land of salmon

1. Deleted: "from" ; inserted: "between the Pacific &"
2. Inserted.
3. Deleted: [*illeg.*]

In Western Texas.

Manuscript in Texas. Inscribed in black ink with a very broad-nubbed pen on a white wove scrap. The material might well have come from Emory, but more probably from WW's memory or current reading. The pen point and writing are those of WW's last years.

In *Western Texas* the prairies & oak-openings —the mesquit bush[1] pecan tree & prickly pear, and the far-stretching[2] spread of the land carpeted with flowers

1. Deleted: "&"
2. Inserted above "and the" and "sp" in "spread"

XIII. World Geography.

Russian Serfs.

Manuscript in Duke (32, #32). Inscribed in black pencil on a small scrap of bright green wove paper. Bowers, xli *n*13, identifies this paper as being wrapper stock for the 1855 edition. The small neat writing confirms the early date. Printed in *N&F,* 155 (Pt. IV, #9; *CW,* IX, 216).

Russian serfs.— It seems that the Russian empire, with a population of from 50 to 60 millions has 40 million of serfs, (or slaves)

[4]*Climate.*—A large part of China has about the same climate as New York, with snow and ice in winter, and[6] some very hot days in summer.

Executions.—Criminals are executed in several ways.—A common mode is to set the victim in a sort of box which tightens around his neck and ankles, and compresses his body by degrees,[7] with a special[8] screw against his breast; thus squeezing him to death.—Sometimes may be seen twenty or thirty such victims, in rows, dead or dying, with their eyes protruded and their tongues hanging out of their mouths.

[5]*Pekin.*—Away in the interior is Pekin, the great city, the "Chinaman's heaven".—Here is the Emperor, and the imperial government.—

Lascars.—Once or twice a year, the Lascars have a characteristic spree.— They attire themselves fantastically, one has a chain around his neck, one around his waist, another around his ankles and the others lead them through the streets, with dances and music.—And such music!—There are perhaps fifty or sixty primitive instruments, reeds, gongs, shells, &c., all keeping in a wild sort of uniform rythm.—The Lascars in [6] this way[9] march to and fro all, eating, drinking, making merry, and collecting money in a vessel which the proffer to everybody.— But the strangest destiny awaits this money.—At night the Lascars all go together out upon the water, some very deep place, and pour this money into the sea! This is a gift to the Chinese Neptune, or to Pluto—that they may have grace at the hands of those deities in their voyages, or after all voyages are over.—

[7]*Dates referring to China.*—

Fo, a[10] divine being, ruler, lawgiver, and teacher—a god—2500 years before Christ.
Silk is plenty—they have a[11] white coarse stuff of grass, that makes, for foreigners[12] very good shirts, lasting much longer than cotton or linen.
The Americans are in very good repute in China—the English and French very bad.—

6. Deleted: "warm"
7. Deleted: dash.
8. Inserted above "a screw"
9. Deleted: "go"
10. Deleted: "god, or"
11. Deleted: "kind of"
12. Preceding two words inserted above "very good"

Brutish Human Beings.

Manuscript in Virginia. Inscribed in black ink on blue Williamsburgh tax form. Clippings on wild men of Borneo pasted near bottom, on which WW makes his asterisked comment. For Pierson see "[*illeg.*] Dick Hunt." Capt. Gibson is possibly Walter Murray Gibson, author of *Report, American Geographical and Statistical Society. Monthly Meeting, March, 1854. Capt. Walter M. Gibson on the East Indian Archipelago: a description of Its Wild Races of Men*. NY, 1854, and *The Prison of Weltevredin, and a Glance at the East Indian Archipelago*. NY, 1855. The Ladrone Islands are in the South China Sea off Canton. WW used "Koboo" in *S of M* (1855), sec. 43, 1129, and "Salut au Monde!" (1856), sec. 12, 1. 201. Bucke prints as part of this a detached marginal note now in Duke (73): "Remember Le Brun's illustrations of 'Comparative Anatomy' where he groups the physiognomy of the native races of animals of a country and the physiognomy of the native races of human beings of the same country.—" This was written between 1857 and 1859. First printed in *N&F,* 78 (Pt. III, #8; *CW,* IX, 54).

Brutish human beings—
Wild men—the "koboo".—
Elias Pierson (June '57) describes to me a very low kind of human beings he saw in one of the Ladrone islands—they were quite hairy, had a few rags for clothing, and lived in earthen shelters, something like ovens, into which they crawled.—/

Capt. Gibson affirms that all his statements in his book are true, and made in good faith. Then the "koboo", must be so

After all, are not the Rocky Mountain and California aborigines quite as bestial a type of humanity as any?—

*What difference does it make whether they were Borneans or not?—Their brutish nature was certain, and that is enough?

British in China.

Manuscript in Duke (38, #32). Inscribed in black ink on pink wove scrap, approx. 3½" x 5". For Pierson see "[*illeg.*] Dick Hunt" [*18*]. Despite the paper WW used, the date is almost certainly 1857. First printed in *N&F,* 80 (Pt. III; #15; *CW,* IX, 59).

British in China

Hong Kong

(Elias Pierson
tells me)

is an island, something like Staten Island in size—of this *the British* have exclusive possession, and have fortified it, and keep regiments of soldiers there

(Independent & Chinese) Tartary.

Manuscript in Duke (38, #32). Inscribed in black ink on a scrap of blue Williamsburgh tax form. The date is between 1857 and 1859. First printed *N&F,* 155 (Pt. IV, #9; *CW,* IX, 216).

(Independent & Chinese)[1]
Tartary—the belly of Asia, (one third of that continent) from the Caspian sea to the Pacific.—
Anciently called *Scythia* Souther part—*Parthia*
—From this region sprang Zinghis Khan, a Mongol chief, 1226 A.D. —and, ravaging, stretched his empire—
—*Tamerlane,* (1400 A.D.) in time.[2] his successor)/
He extended his rule to *Hindostan,* founding the Mongul rule there which terminated 1803[3]/
From Tartary[4] issued the[5] Celts, Goths, &c.[6]—The Turks also

1. Fist at left, pointing to *"Tartary"*
2. Preceding two words inserted above "his" and "succe" in "successor"
3. Fist at left, pointing left.
4. Deleted: "must have"
5. Deleted: "Goths"
6. Deleted:"The"

Europe Inland Lakes.

Manuscript in Duke (13, #33V). Inscribed in columns in black pencil on tan textured wove paper, approx. 5″ x 6¼″. Faint rules ⅜″ apart. On recto is "Remembrances I plant American ground with" (verse). WW is here educating himself in the manner described in "A New Way & The True Way." First printed *N&F,* 155 (Pt. IV, #11; *CW,* IX, 217). The date is probably 1857, but may be earlier. (See "*Europe* bounded".)

Europe

Rivers—Laplanders
— Thames = Trent = Severn
— B { Shannon
Tay
— Seine
— F { Loire
— Rhone
Douro
— S { Tagus
Guadalquiver
Rhine
— Elbe, Prussia, Hanover
Saxony, Austria
Danube Austria, runs into
Turkey
— Oder (Prussia)
Po (Sardinia & divides
Austria from Italy
Tiber, Papal states
Arno, Tuscany
— Dneiper
— Volga
— Ural[2]

Cracow

Berlin
42,000
Munich
115,000 Bavaria
Frankfort
Dresden
85,000 Saxony,
Hanover,
40,000

inland lakes[1]

Cities
Christiana, 27,000 Norway
Copenhagen, 125,000,000 Sweden
Bremen, 53,000,000 Neth
Hague, 66,000,000 [*Neth*]
Paris
F { Bordeaux
Marseilles
Brussels
124000 Belgium[3]
S { Madrid
Cadiz
P Lisbon
Edinburgh[4]
Dublin
London
Palermo, Sicily
Naples
Florence 105,000 Tuscany
Genoa 120,000 Sardinia
Venice, 120,000 — Austria
Rome, 184,000
Berne, 24,000 Switz
Turin, 135,000, Sardinia
{ Vienna, 425,000
on the Danube
Prague, 114,000 Elbe
North Germany
Milan, 205,000[5]

1. This is written above the second column, but there is no relationship.
2. End of column 1.
3. Preceding four French-speaking cities at right of brace.
4. Three cities of British Isles are in column at right of "Madrid . . ."
5. End of column 2. Column 3 begins "Berlin" and is inserted between 1 and 2 towards the bottom of the leaf.

Europe. Cape Clear.

Manuscript not found. Text from *N&F,* 157 (Pt. IV, #15; *CW,* IX, 220–221). This is probably part of one of WW's scrapbooks. See "Language." Like most MS relating to WW's self-education, this probably dates from the late 1850s.

Europe. Cape Clear, southern point of Ireland; Malin head, northern point; Lands End, south-west point England; Kinnard's head, a north-east point Scotland; Shetland islands, away north; Hebrides, west Scotland; "The Minch," the passage between the Hebrides and Scotland.

Europe Bounded.

Manuscript in Duke (35, #27). Inscribed in black pencil in two columns on scrap of pink wove paper, approx. 6¼" x 4⅞". The MS is related to *"Europe inland lakes"* and "A New Way & The True Way." The paper is probably wrapper stock from LG (1855), but WW used it as late as 1857 (see *"British in China"*), which is a more appropriate date for the present material. First printed in *N&F,* 156 (Pt. IV, #12; *CW,* IX, 218).

Europe bounded

Countries
—Iceland, 60,000
—Norway, 1,328,000
—Sweden, 3,440,000
—Denmark, 2,300,000
—Russia, in Europe, 54,000,000
(England, 18,000,000 (incl.
Wales)
Scotland, 2,889,000
Ireland, 6,516,000
—France, 36,000,000
—Spain, 14,000,000
—Portugal,
—Austria 36,575,000
—Prussia,
—Netherlands 3,363,000
—Belgium, 4,360,000
—Switzerland 2,390,000
—Sardinia, 5,000,000
Rome 3,000,000
Naples 9,000,000
—(Hungary 11,000,000
—(Venice & Lombardy 5,000,000
Germany, Bavaria,
Wurtemberg, Baden,
Saxony, 2,000,000[2] (Greece 1,100,000
Sicily

north Arctic ocean
east—Atlantic
west—Black sea,[1] Caucasus
mts.—Caspian sea
Ural river & mts (Asia)
South Mediterranean

Seas
White Sea north Russia
North sea
English Channel
Bay of Biscay
Mediterranean
Baltic, between Sweden & Russia
Gulf of Bothnia ditto
Gulf of venice, (Medit)
Black sea (south Russia)
Caspian (south west)
Zuyder zee a great bay
in the
Netherlands
The Schelt

1. Deleted: "Caspian" following "Black Sea"
2. Deleted: "Parma" ; inserted to right: "Greece . . ."

Asia.

Manuscript not found. Text from *N&F,* 155 (Pt. IV, #10; *CW,* IX, 216–217). This is probably part of one of WW's scrapbooks. See "Language." Like most manuscripts relating to WW's self-education, this probably dates from the late 1850s.

Asia. Peoples: —Caucasians, Georgians, Turks (Asiatic) 10,000,000, Arabs 12,000,000, Persians 8,000,000, Afghans 5,000,000, Beloochistans 500,000, Tartars 5,000,000, Muscovites or Russians 66,000,000, Kamskatkans, Thibetians, Clans of Nomadic Tartans, Hindoos 142,000,000, Chinese 367,000,000, Burmese 2,000,000, Japanese 25,000,000, Bornese 3,000,000, Ceylonese 1,500,000, Anamese 5,000,000, Siamese 3,000,000, Malays—all the lands, islands, peninsulas etc. in the S. E. Sumatrans 2,500,000. Ancient—Celts, Goths, Chaldees, Assyrians . . . .

The Teutonic Includes.

Manuscript in Duke (35, #27). Inscribed in black pencil on heavy, tan, wove paper, approx. 7¼" x 6¾". At bottom left, fastened with sealing wax, is a clipping about lectures on prehistoric settlement in the New World. All entries in hanging indentation. The date is probably in the late 1850s. First printed in *N&F,* 152 (Pt. IV, #2; *CW,* IX, 210).

The *Teutonic* includes the *Scandinavian*—the Sc. is a branch or or portion of the Teutonic/

Visigoth—a western Goth, one from the western shores of the Baltic, in distinction from an Ostrogoth, or eastern Goth.—/

Asia now contains and has from time immemorial contained more than[1] *half the population of the earth* and more than one third the land of the earth—China alone has (so estimated)[2] 360,000,000 inhabitants[3]/

Scythia (the name given to the Northern part of Asia, and Europe adjoining to Asia—) from the same root as Scot—from a word meaning woods, or shade —viz. Scot—a man of the woods—

ancient
Numidia, Getulia, &c—Northern
part of Africa, on the Mediterranean
now Algiers, Tripoli, &c[4]

1. Preceding two words inserted above *"half"*
2. Parentheses and "so estimated" inserted above "has" and "360,00" in "360,000,000"
3. Rule across leaf.
4. Pasted-on scrap of blue Williamsburgh tax blank to the right of the clipping.

There Is a River.

Manuscript not found. Text from *N&F,* 152 (Pt. IV, #3; *CW,* IX, 210). Date unknown.

There is a river in the ocean—*i.e.* the gulf stream.

Finland.

Manuscript not found. Text from *N&F,* 155 (Pt. IV, #9; *CW,* IX, 216). Printed by Bucke as part of "(Independent & Chinese) *Tartary,*" of which a separate MS exists. Bucke's text probably comprises a number of MS scraps. The date is probably in the late 1850s.

Finland—a large ancient country, an important part of Russia.
Palestine, David 1020 B. C.
Dido 800 B. C.
Æneas 800 B. C.
Mahommedanism rose 600 A. D. Mahomet born 569, died 632.

The English Masses.

Manuscript in Duke (32, #31). Inscribed in black ink on blue Williamsburgh tax forms. The date, from the paper, is 1857 or later.

The English Masses

(Talk with Frank Leonard, "Yank," &c—their travels through English towns with the American Circus)

The large mass (nine tenths) of the English people, the peasantry, laborers, factory-operatives, miners, workers in the docks, on shipping, the poor,[1] the old, the criminals, the numberless flunkies of one sort and another, have some of the bull-dog attributes[2] but are[3] generally minus the best attributes of humanity.[4] They are not a race of fine physique, or any spirituality, or manly[5] audacity,[6]—have no clarified faces, candor, freedom, agility, and quick wit.— They are short, have mean physiognomies, (such as[7] are in the caricatures in "Punch,")[8] —fine-shaped men [2] and women, city bred,[9] being[10] very seldom met with in the city, and becoming less and less[11] common in the country.— Bad blood, goitre,[12] consumption, and the diseases that branch out from venerealism, gin-drinking,[13] excessive toil, and poor diet, are to-day apparent, to[14] greater or less degree, in two-thirds of the[15] common-people of[16] England.— They are wretchedly poor, own neither houses nor lands for them-selves—have no homes—cannot look to[17] have

1. Deleted: "the diseased"
2. Preceding seven words inserted above "another . . . minus"
3. Deleted: "all"
4. Deleted: "; they have some of the bull-dog attributes"
5. Preceding two words inserted above "ty," in "spirituality" and "aud" in "audicity"
6. Deleted: "or with" ; inserted: "—have no" above "[*del.*] with" and "cl" in "clarified"
7. Deleted: "you"
8. Deleted: "and" ; inserted above: dash.
9. Preceding two words inserted above "men" in "women" and "be" in "being"
10. Deleted: "almost hardly [*ins.* above "most" in "almost" and "he" in "hardy"] rarely ever met" ; inserted: "very seldom" above "[*del.*] rarely"
11. Preceding two words inserted above "ss" in "less" and "com" in "common"
12. Deleted: "scro"
13. Deleted: "and"
14. Deleted: "a"
15. Deleted: "population of"
16. Deleted: "Great Bri"
17. Preceding two words inserted above "not" in "cannot" and "h" in "have"

any homes—and are acquiring[18] something fierce,[19] morose, threatening in their physiognomy.— In [3] their phrenology there is the most substantial basis of any race known,[20] —all that can make a solid nation, and has made it.—

Among the common classes, in towns,[21] chastity is[22] dwindling out.—[23] All drink—few are virtuous. In regard to intelligence, education, knowledge, the masses of the people,[24] in comparison with the masses of the U.S. are at least two hundred years behind[25] us.— With all these terrible things about the common people, what grand things must be said about England! Power, wealth, materials,[26] energy, individualism,[27] pride, command, are her's—and there is to-day but one nation greater than she is, and that[28] is her own daughter.—

18. Deleted: "a"
19. Deleted: "and"
20. Deleted: "but with"
21. Preceding two words inserted above "chastit"
22. Deleted: "not common" ; inserted above: "dwindling out"
23. Deleted: "It"
24. Deleted: "all belong to the" ; inserted: "in comparison with the masses of the U.S." on three lines above and into the left margin above "people" and "[*del.*] are"
25. Deleted: [*illeg.*]
26. Inserted above "lth" in "wealth" and "ener" in "energy"
27. Deleted: "a proud"
28. Deleted: "one nation"

Russia.

Manuscript in LC (#75, sheet #578). Inscribed in black pencil on a scrap of white wove paper, 2½" x 7¾". Blue lines ½" apart on the recto only. The note could not have been written before 1857, since the eighth edition of the *Encyclopedia Britannica* was not published until that year. See also 1856–1858 clippings in *CW,* X, 75, 78, and "Scythia," "Subjects for articles," *"Education,"* "Area—doubles," "Russia—*Toward the* NORTH," "—one of the glories." WW's interest in Russia may have been aroused in the first instance by the Crimean War (1853–1855). See "memorials."

Russia—see "Karamsin"[1] the greatest of Russian Historians p 52 vol. 13[2] born 1755 *get his History of Russia*

1. Nikolai Mikhailovich Karamzin (1765–1826), *History of the Russian Empire,* 11 vols., 1803–1826. WW could not have read it, for there is no English translation.

2. The reference is to *Encyclopedia Britannica* (8th ed., 1857) which says: "Karamsin is with justice styled the father of Russian history."

Area—Doubles.

Manuscript in LC (#75, sheet #579). Inscribed in black ink on white wove paper 10" x 7¾". Blue rules on recto, ½" apart. The information, presumably about Russia, is inscribed in three hanging paragraphs with further indentations as noted. The date is after 1850 and before 1873.

Area—doubles the superfices of
Europe—nearly 7½ million
square miles—more than
twice as large as the
Area United States—2,000,000 sq. miles
in Europe
the rest in Asia[1]

Population—80,000
(67½ million in 1850)
—Caucasian element
very large—Germans
Sclaves
Poles[2]
Tartars
Greeks
Jews. &c
Mongolian
i.e. Calmuck Tartars
in the s.e. steppes
in Asia.

Most of the sea-trade is with
England & the U.S.
but the inland trade is most
inportant & very extensive—

1. Preceding three lines at right with curved line around left and below following "States—"
2. Inserted on arrow.

Education.

Manuscript in LC (#75, sheet #577R). Inscribed in black ink on white wove paper, 10" x 7¾". Blue lines ½" apart on verso only. Hanging indentation. Since WW's writing and the paper are like that of "Area—doubles," "Russia—*Toward the* NORTH," and "—one of the glories," it probably also dates from the early 1870s. The last sentence was printed in Furness, 250 *n*228.

Education— Every effort is made for education—the whole country is divided off into University Districts, in each of which is a university

Society—manners— From the time of Peter the Great, the policy of the Emperorshas been to form a great *middle-class*—for [1] the fact is, or rather has been that there were only *two* extreme[2] classes,[3] in Russia, the haughty, wilful, cruel nobility, & the slavish masses, the people— The serfs have been freed, & now *trade trade, intercommunication with the* world[4] is all that is needed

1. Deleted: "there" ; inserted: "the fact" above "[*del.*] there" and "is"
2. Inserted above "o" in "two" and "clas" in "classes"
3. Deleted: [*illeg.*]
4. A hand in the left margin points to the underlined words.

Russia— Toward The north.

Manuscript in LC (#75, sheet #576R). Inscribed in black ink on four scraps of white wove paper, all 7¾" across, which have been pasted together. Blue rules ½" apart. Irregular hanging indentation. The handwriting is loose and sprawling, suggesting a date perhaps after 1873.

Russia—

Toward[1] *the* NORTH *the Arctic Ocean*—a bleak climate nine or ten months ice

Toward[2] the West[3]

Baltic, Yes but, Russia cannot[4] pass out of the Baltic without the good leave of Prussia Denmark & Sweden[5] Then the Baltic is impassable with ice, many months of the year

Black (Crimea)— Just the same as she cannot pass[6] out of the Black[7] Sea without the leave of Turkey[8]/

Toward the[9] East the a narrow strip of the north Pacific—the Sea of Okhotsk and to the *south* land-bound in western parts[10] by[11] Austria, Prussia[12] Turkey,
&c & her Asiatic territories by China, &c—[13]

1. Deleted: "On" ; inserted: *"Toward"* above the deletion and *"the"*
2. Deleted: "On" ; inserted above: "Toward"
3. Deleted: [*illeg.*] ; inserted above: "West" . There is considerable space vertically between "West" and "Baltic." After the former word there is a characteristic hand with the extended index finger pointing down toward the latter.
4. Deleted: "even"
5. Preceding three words in column under "Prussia"
6. Deleted: "of"
7. End of first scrap.
8. End of second scrap.
9. Deleted: [*illeg.*]
10. Preceding three words inserted above "by" and illegible deletion in *n* 11 noted below.
11. Deleted: "[*illeg.*]" and "Turkey" under.
12. Inserted above "a" in "Austria" and "Tur" in "Turkey"
13. Trimmed words not legible.

—One of the Glories.

Manuscript in LC (#74, sheet #559R). Inscribed in red and black ink on white wove notepaper, 10″ x 9″. Blue lines on verso ½″ apart. Written on Department of Justice letter head for "187—." Published in Furness, 250*n*.

—one of the glories of the modern age[1] church is its[2]—Missionaries— I would not speak a word against the devotion, self-sacrifice, good intentions—[3] but what would are all the missions ever built,— ? sent forth—in comparison with the benefits that would ensue to[4] nearly a hundred millions of people—by the[5] putting of the great Russian empire in rapport with the rest of the world, through ports, trade, travel,[6] science, literature

1. Preceding two words inserted above "the church"
2. Preceding two words inserted above "naries" in "Missionaries"
3. The first three words and "g" of "glories" are in red ink. "Missionaries . . . intentions" in red ink. The remainder in black.
4. Deleted: "the"
5. Deleted: "open"
6. Deleted: "l"

Indianeer.

Manuscript in Texas. Inscribed in black ink on irregular white laid paper, approx. 8″ x 6⅜″. Red-blue-red margin 1″ from left and blue rules ½″ apart. Lightly emended. On verso, p. 2 of an illegible letter in another hand which mentions the Internal Revenue Office. "This" in black ink in WW's hand precedes the first word. WW cancelled the insertion and text with his characteristic blue pencil. "Indianeer" is not in the *OED*; "Indiaman" was the usual term. The reference to J. Thomas and Thomas Baldwin, eds., *A Complete Pronouncing Gazetteer on Geographical Dictionary of the World . . . Revised Edition of 1866 . . .* (Philadelphia: Lippincott, 1875), I, 896, suggests a date later than 1875. The writing and paper support this hypothesis. See "Carlyle Vol. 1."

Indianeer—a ship used in the India trade an Indiaman—India—from the river Indus Ancient name frequently used by poets[1] Ind India not [*illeg.*][2] only *Hindustan* & India beyond the Ganges but the N.E. islands of the Indian (Malay)[3] archipelago Farther India—viz: Chin-India—Indo-China see Lip.[4] Gaz. p. 896. abounds in vast & exhaustless[5] reservoirs of valuable mineral, vegetable & animal products.

1. Inserted above "used"
2. Inserted above "not" and "o" in "only"
3. Inserted above "arc" in "archipelago"
4. I.e., Lippincott, Philadelphia publishers.
5. Preceding two words inserted above "vast reservoirs"

XIV. Natural History.

Rock-fish.

Manuscript not found. Text from *N&F,* 174 (Pt. IV, #94; *CW,* X, 26). In *N&F,* Bucke inserted "[in]" before "N. A." A long list of fish, similar to his geographical and historical lists, on green wrapper stock for LG (1855), is in LC (Feinberg). Since this was a Bucke MS, it probably was written in the 1850s.

Rock-fish—viz., striped bass—more abundant in Chesapeake Bay and its tributaries than any other N. A.—ascend in spring to deposit eggs.

Pekan Tree.

Manuscript not found. Text from *N&F,* 165 (Pt. IV, #38; *CW,* X, 10).

Pekan tree—honey locust—black walnut—persimmon—Cottonwood—Mulberry—Chickadee—large brown water-dog—black snake—garter snake—vinegar plums—white blossoming dog-wood—sweet potato—plum-trees—plum orchard—cedar—chestnut—locust—birch—cypress—buttonwood.

—As Now Are Given.

Manuscript in Virginia. Inscribed in pencil on white wove scrap, 1¼″ x 4″. WW sometimes used small slips for notes in the 1850s; none have been noted later. The date is thus possibly in the late 1850s. First printed in *N&F,* 98 (Pt. III, #55; *CW,* IX, 96–97).

—As now are given to science many names, Geology, Botany, Astronomy, Physiology, &c.— But the real science is omnient,[1] is nothing less than all sciences, comprehending all the known names, and many unknown.[2]—

1. Preceding two words inserted above "ience" in "science"
2. Inserted and deleted: [*illeg.*] above "nown" in "unknown"

The Whale.

Manuscript in [1] Duke (39, #34) and [2] Virginia. [1] is two scraps of blue Williamsburgh tax form pasted together; [2] is a single scrap. Both are inscribed in black ink; both appear to be laid rather than wove paper. John Maher, seaman, is listed in the Brooklyn directories for 1843–1844 and 1854–1855. The conversation, however, almost certainly took place between 1857 and 1860. Directories, at least of this period, are rarely complete; the paper indicates a date after 1857, and it was not until *LG* (1860) that WW corrected "S of M," sec. 33, l. 742 from "calves" to "calf" as Bucke noted. This was written between 1857 and 1860. First printed in *N&F,* 117–118 (Pt. III, #114; *CW,* IX, 136–137).

The Whale
(talk with Mr. Maher, an old whaleman)/

When the black-whale is[1] sculling itself along[2] feeding,[3] its head projected[4] two thirds out of water, (scooping up its food from the surface,)[5] its great[6] lips turned back, it is one of the most hideous looking objects that can be imagined[7] and would frighten badly a "green hand" who should see it for the first time.—[8]/

The sperm-whale, a good specimen, is one of the grandest looking creatures, for beauty and strength—when enraged, and swiftly moving it is splendid[9]/

When a cow-whale is struck, the others never desert her—but new ones continually arrive as if to assist her.— When a bull is struck, all the rest leave[10]/

1. Deleted: "moving" ; inserted: "sculling" above "[*del.*] moving" and "itself" above "along"
2. Deleted: "with"
3. Parenthetical passage transferred down according to WW's "tr" and asterisks. Deleted: "of the sea, with"
4. Inserted above "ad" in "head" and "two"
5. Deleted: "and"
6. Inserted above wordspace between "its" and "lips"
7. Remainder of sentence added in small script on two lines. WW's terminal punctuation here not printed.
8. End of first scrap. Rule across leaf.
9. Rule across leaf.
10. Rule across leaf.

Sometimes, the whales sport in the water, coming straight up, perpendicular, quite out—others turning with their[11] bodies[12] half out, vibrating their flukes playfully.—/—others again descending, after elevating their flukes a great distance straight up in the air, and waving them.—

The white spout of air and water—when dying the red[13] spout of blood.[14]

[2] the whale-boat,

— "The harpooneersman"[15]/

the blubber, the clear oil in the head,[16]

an old whale is probably a thousand years old.[17]/

the cow has but one calf at a birth.

She will sometimes, when alarmed,[18] enclose it,[19] as with her fins, and dive down into the deep sea—(just like a mother[20] protects her child,)/

(feeding on *squid*—large chunks, a foot square, or larger, are sometimes found in the belly of a whale—it is I believe,[21] like the white meat of the halibut, drum, &c

11. Deleted: "flukes [*illeg.*]"
12. Deleted: [*illeg.*]
13. Inserted above "s" in "spout"
14. End of second scrap.
15. Rule across leaf.
16. Line deleted: "the whale-boat" . Rule across leaf.
17. Rule across leaf.
18. Preceding two words inserted above "es" in "sometimes" and "enclose"
19. Deleted: "with"
20. Deleted: "with"
21. Preceding two words inserted above "like"

The Air.

Manuscript in NYPL (Berg). Inscribed in pencil and black ink on blue Williamsburgh tax form, approx. 4⅝" x 6¹³/16". From the use of the tax form, the date is 1857 or later. Printed in *N&F,* 75 (Pt. III, #1; *CW,* IX, 47).

The[1] Air[2] (Space)
considered with reference to the earth—as all[3] parts of the universe bear reference to each other, and all other things therefore bear down their influence more or less upon this earth.—[:][4] A Description of those things that may be said to be most closely[5] identified with the air,—(for movement, visibility, occupancy &c) as the orbs, Space, light, heat[6]—(as Silliman[7] says—Cosmical—not Terrestrial)/

The Sea [:][8] All the wonders of the Sea—the Sea covering three-fourths of the land/

The Land [:][9] *Physical* facts of the land—as first its nebulous beginning—then its geology all through to the present—then its *present beauty; reality, & diversity,* as the home of man.—

1. The "A" in "Air" is inscribed over a partially erased capital "S" . "The Air" is in a very large hand as are "The Sea" and "The Land" . "Space" inserted in smaller hand after "Air"
2. The following thirty-three words are in black ink to left of brace.
3. Inserted: "parts of" above "the"
4. A brace encloses this entry at the right.
5. Deleted: "related to" ; inserted above: "identified with"
6. Following six words in black ink.
7. Benjamin Silliman (1779–1864) was Professor of Chemistry and Natural History at Yale. He lectured and published extensively for popular audiences.
8. Brace.
9. Brace. Remainder of MS in black ink.

Animal Life.

Manuscript in Texas. Inscribed in black pencil on white wove leaf from a top-bound notebook, 6¾″ x 4″. Blue rules approx. 5/16″ apart. On verso in other hands are the addresses of two Bostonians: Dr. William Wesselhoeft and Judge Mellen Chamberlain, whom WW mentions in correspondence in 1887 and 1889 respectively (*Corr.,* IV, 114, 268). WW has copied this material with a care that was unusual, especially at the end of his life. He began using top-bound notebooks in the 1880s.

Animal life first appeared in the form of

Radiates—in construction resembling a flower or plant but having a mouth & stomach. Their bodies are nearly transparent & seem only to float or rest on the water—then

Mollusks—soft bodies without bone or skeletons—some naked, others in shells, like clams, snails, etc. then

Articulates—such as worms, spiders—of jointed articulated coverings consisting of a series of rings / then /

Vertebrates—all animals having a back bone—the first vertebrates fishes then reptiles birds and mammals— Mammals those which [*illeg.*] with [*illeg.*] suckle[?] their[?] young[?] & have warm blood

Hersschel's Theory.

Manuscript in Texas. Inscribed in black pencil on leaf from top-bound notebook, approx. 6″ x 4″. Blue rules approx. 5/16″ apart. The careful writing and clean copy are similar to that of "Animal life," and the paper seems to be the same. "Hersschel" is probably J. F. W. Herschel (1793–1871), the English astronomer. WW had two clippings on Herschel (Bucke #110 and #523), both of 1848. He was, of course, fascinated by stars. The present note probably comes from a later reading. The paper and writing suggest a date in the 1880s.

Hersschel's theory is that the[1] millions of orbs are not promiscuously scattered through space, but collected in a great line or highway, with two[2] branches, something like the letter Y—and that the position of[3] our sun system, earth, &c. is about[4] at the crotch or centre.

1. Deleted: "orbs"
2. Deleted: "arms or"
3. Three preceding words inserted above "that our"
4. Inserted above "is"